HISTORY OF BIBLICAL INTERPRETATION

VOLUME 1: FROM THE OLD TESTAMENT TO ORIGEN

Society of Biblical Literature

Resources for Biblical Study

Susan Ackerman, Old Testament/Hebrew Bible Editor
Tom Thatcher, New Testament Editor

Number 50

History of Biblical Interpretation
Volume 1: From the Old Testament to Origen

HISTORY OF BIBLICAL INTERPRETATION

VOLUME 1: FROM THE OLD TESTAMENT TO ORIGEN

By

Henning Graf Reventlow

Translated by

Leo G. Perdue

Society of Biblical Literature
Atlanta

HISTORY OF BIBLICAL INTERPRETATION
VOLUME 1: FROM THE OLD TESTAMENT TO ORIGEN

Original title: *Epochen der Bibelauslegung Band I: Vom Alten Testament bis Origenes*, by Henning Graf Reventlow, copyright © Verlag C.H. Beck oHG, Munich 1990. English translation produced under license from the publisher.

Library of Congress Cataloging-in-Publication Data

Reventlow, Henning Graf.
  [Epochen der Bibelauslegung. English]
  History of biblical interpretation / by Henning Graf Reventlow
      p. cm. — (Society of Biblical Literature resources for biblical study ; no. 50, 61–63)
  Includes bibliographical references and indexes.
  ISBN-13: 978-1-58983-202-2 (paper binding, vol. 1 : alk. paper) — ISBN 978-1-58983-455-2 (paper binding, vol. 2 : alk. paper) — ISBN 978-1-58983-459-0 (paper binding, vol. 3 : alk. paper) — ISBN 978-1-58983-460-6 (paper binding, vol. 4 : alk. paper)
  1. Bible—Criticism, interpretation, etc.—History. I. Title.
  BS500.R4813 2009b v.1
  220.609—dc22   2009045014

17 16 15 14 13 12 11 10 09   5 4 3 2 1
Printed in the United States of America on acid-free, recycled paper conforming to ANSI/NISO Z39.48-1992 (R1997) and ISO 9706:1994 standards for paper permanence.

CONTENTS

ABBREVIATIONS

PRIMARY SOURCES

Ant.	Josephus, *Antiquitates Judaicae* (*Jewish Antiquities*)
CD	Cairo Genizah copy of the Damascus Document
Cher.	Philo, *De cherubim* (*On the Cherubim*)
Comm. Cant.	Origen, *Commentarius in Canticum* (*Commentary on Canticles*)
Comm. Jo.	Origen, *Commentarii in evangelium Joannis* (*Commentary on the Gospel of John*)
Comm. Matt.	Origen, *Commentarium in evangelium Matthaei* (*Commentary on the Gospel of Matthew*)
Det.	Philo, *Quod deterius potiori insidari soleat* (*That the Worse Attacks the Better*)
Dial.	Justin Martyr, *Dialogus cum Tryphone* (*Dialoge with Trypho*)
Epid.	Irenaeus, *Epideixis tou apostolikou kērygmatos* (*Demonstration of the Apostolic Preaching*)
Haer.	Irenaeus, *Adversus haereses* (*Against Heresies*)
Hist. eccl.	Eusebius, *Historia ecclesiastica* (*Church History*)
Hom. Jer.	Origen, *Homiliae in Jeremiam* (*Homilies on Jeremiah*)
Hom. Luc.	Origen, *Homiliae in Lucam* (*Homilies on Luke*)
Hom. Num.	Origen, *Homiliae in Numeros* (*Homilies on Numbers*)
Il.	Homer, *Iliad*
Leg.	Philo, *Legum allegoriae* (*Allegorical Interpretation*)
Marc.	Tertullian, *Adversus Marcionem* (*Against Marcion*)
Metam.	Ovid, *Metamorphoses*
Mos.	Philo, *De vita Mosis* (*Life of Moses*)
Mot. an.	Aristotle, *De motu animalium* (*Movement of Animals*)
Mut.	Philo, *De mutatione nominum* (*On the Change of Names*)
Od.	Homer, *Odyssey*
Opif.	Philo, *De opificio mundi* (*On the Creation of the World*)

Pol.	Aristotle, *Politica* (*Politics*)
Princ.	Origen, *Peri archōn* = *De principiis* (*First Principles*)
Quaest. hom.	Heraclitus, *Quaestiones homericae* (*Homeric Problems*)
Somn.	Philo, *De somnis* (*On Dreams*)
Spec.	Philo, *De specialibus legibus* (*On the Special Laws*)
Theog.	Hesiod, *Theogony*

Secondary Sources

AKG	Arbeiten zur Kirchengeschichte
ALGHJ	Arbeiten zur Literatur und Geschichte des hellenistischen Judentums
BFCT	Beiträge zur Förderung christlicher Theologie
BHT	Beiträge zur historischen Theologie
BU	Biblische Untersuchungen
BWANT	Beiträge zur Wissenschaft vom Alten (und Neuen) Testament
BZAW	Beihefte zur Zeitschrift für die alttestamentliche Wissenschaft
BZNW	Beihefte zur Zeitschrift für die neutestamentliche Wissenschaft
CRINT	Compendia rerum iudaicarum ad Novum Testamentum
CThM	Calwer theologische Monographien
FC	Fathers of the Church
FRLANT	Forschungen zur Religion und Literatur des Alten und Neuen Testaments
FthSt	Freiburger theologische Studien
GCS	Die griechische christliche Schriftsteller der ersten drei Jahrhunderte
LCL	Loeb Classical Library
NovTSup	Supplements to Novum Testamentum
NTL	New Testament Library
OBO	Orbis biblicus et orientalis
QD	Quaestiones disputatae
SBB	Stuttgarter biblische Beiträge
SBLDS	Society of Biblical Literature Dissertation Series
SBS	Stuttgarter Bibelstudien
SC	Sources chrétiennes
SNTSMS	Society for New Testament Studies Monograph Series
SNTU	Studien zum Neuen Testament und seiner Umwelt

SUC	Schriften des Urchristentums
TUGAL	Texte und Untersuchungen zur Geschichte der altchristlichen Literatur
VTSup	Supplements to Vetus Testamentum
WdF	Wege der Forschung
WMANT	Wissenschaftliche Monographien zum Alten und Neuen Testament
WUNT	Wissenschaftliche Untersuchungen zum Neuen Testament
ZNW	*Zeitschrift für die neutestamentliche Wissenschaft und die Kunde der älteren Kirche*
ZTK	*Zeitschrift für Theologie und Kirche*

Introduction

This book is the first of a four-volume series that is designed to guide the reader who is interested in tracing more than two thousand years of biblical interpretation.

The significance of the Bible for the Western world should not be underestimated. It has influenced our culture in thousands of ways. Poets have cited it, and artists have depicted its best-known scenes in the styles of many periods. Above all, however, its intrinsic significance is that it is Holy Scripture. It is directed to both Jews and Christians, although the latter have attached the New Testament to the Hebrew Bible.

A sacred tradition stands at the beginning of every religion. This tradition may be transmitted orally, and, indeed, this is the case with many world religions. Others, however, have a written Scripture. This Scripture provides the means to grasp firmly the memory of a religious community, which is in danger of being lost. For Israel, this memory recalled experiences that its people had with their deity. The commandments, which were to regulate the everyday life of this people, were traced back to divine instruction and became a collection known as the Torah. These commandments were written down, incorporated into legal corpora, and formed the Torah, which became the kernel of Holy Scripture. The narratives, which were written in order to serve as the framework for the Torah, inserted into it the events of salvation history. Together, these laws and narratives formed the living traditions for the people and the priesthood. Later, other texts were added: descriptions about the later periods of Israel's history, the collections of cultic songs (i.e., the Psalter), the wisdom tradition, and the words of the prophets. These texts, which originated as the deposit of a tradition recognized as binding, became normative or canonical. Thus, the Bible is a collection of texts that became canonical.

What we shall see in the following chapters is a sacred text that, from its very beginning, was understood as Scripture. Each tradition continues to be effective only when it maintains its contemporary significance in the constantly changing circumstances of a people's life. However, this may occur only when the interpretation is constantly readjusted in order to adapt to a new period. This is no different even when a tradition has become Scripture. There are two paths that Scripture may take. First, the written composition of the tradition may continue to be fluid; it has not yet reached its final form. This allows it to be altered by means of making additions and modifications. Often, these change the content in a considerable manner. This is the first stage of the development of Scripture, and traces of this activity often may be found even in the Old Testament itself. Taken in this sense, sacred Scripture from its very inception continues to be interpreted Scripture. Second, however, there eventually comes a point in time when Scripture has obtained its final form. In this manner, it has become sacrosanct so that it may not be altered. When speaking of the Old Testament literature, the Torah (or the five books of Moses) was first understood in this way. It may have been the case that in the fifth century B.C.E. the Priestly redaction provided the Torah with its final structure, thus concluding this first group of texts. A little later, however, the Samaritans separated the Torah from the Jews and made it into their own sacred Scripture. As a whole, the Old Testament canon continued to develop through additional stages until, by the end of the first century of the Common Era, it came to be regarded as fixed in its final form.

As soon as a sacred Scripture or collection of writings reaches its final form, the second stage of interpretation begins to take place. Since the text was fixed and prohibited further additions, interpretations were required to concentrate on the meaning of this established form. However, an interpretation can successfully be related to a new context only when the statements of the text can first be related to the features of its original setting. This required a methodologically governed means of understanding, a hermeneutic, to be developed in order to carry out the art of interpretation. Above all others, the preacher is officially charged with the task of serving as the hermeneut. Relatively early, since the fourth century B.C.E., Judaism knew intimately the worship service of the synagogue, which served as the social center of the gathered community. Active in this service was the synagogue preacher. Initially, this preacher could have been anyone well-versed in Scripture. However, this role eventually was reserved for educated rabbis. In the Christian church, this preacher originally would have been the apostle, followed later by presbyters and bishops. Eventually, well-educated theologians filled the office of the preacher. Preaching is an activity that seeks to enable the community to understand what an interpreted text has to say to their own contemporary situation. This presupposes that the preacher and the audience come to a common understanding that governs the manner and means by which the text, originating in the distant past, can address the present. The building of this bridge between past and present must occur, if the text, which addressed its original setting, is also to speak to the present. This means that already inherent within the text as it moved from tradition to canon there resided the potential of meaning that transcended the original situation in order to speak to the present. This common agreement presupposes a mutual preunderstanding regarding the content that provides the basis for the interpretation of the text. For Jews, this preunderstanding or hermeneutical basis was essentially the Torah. For Christians, however, the hermeneutical basis was the view that all of the statements of the Scriptures (Old Testament) referred to Jesus Christ. The recognition of a fixed collection of writings as Holy Scripture, that is, as "the Book" (the Bible), which was believed to be the means through which God speaks to humans, requires that the reader and interpreter are ever prepared to learn anew and to follow the dictates of this word of God that encounters them. This understanding that I shall describe in the following history is a varied and ever-changing process.

The volume that follows treats the first period of the history of biblical interpretation. This period begins with the text itself and continues into the middle of the third century C.E. The ancient church reaches the end of this first period with Origen. With Origen, the early church had established the essential groundwork for its interpretation of Scripture. The major rules of hermeneutics were developed during this formative period.

Much that occurred in the various interpretations of the early church is foreign to modern understanding. Indeed, at times, they will appear rather arbitrary. In the twenty-first century, we have become adjusted both to the epistemology of the Enlightenment and to the concurrent development of historical consciousness. Subsequently, we are not able to relate to the earlier methods customarily used in interpretation as though they are self-explanatory. Indeed, our consciousness of history requires us to retain certain judgments that do not take into consideration the conditions of a bygone era. We are, ourselves, certainly dependent upon conceptual presuppositions that are conditioned to a large extent by the time in which we live, presuppositions that we consider to be self-evident. We should not separate the methods of the Christian interpretation of the Bible in the first centuries of the Common Era from their own environment. We shall also see that the early Christians borrowed widely from their Jewish and pagan environments. Therefore, our description shall be related to the Jewish interpretation of the Bible and also take a look at the sphere of the extrabiblical systems of hermeneutics that were operative at the time when these sacred texts were composed. These comparisons will allow us to extrapolate, as far as it is possible, the particular features of Jewish and Christian exegesis by contrasting them with the objectives of pagan philosophers.

The following description is, in the first instance, one that takes into consideration the original sources of the interpreters. Those who are more interested in addressing the meaning of texts to their own situation may find answers in the more recent interpretations of the text. Added to these are the modern translations. The appendix also contains some of the most important secondary literature that allows one to continue to explore in more depth the meaning of texts.

1

BIBLICAL INTERPRETATION WITHIN THE BIBLE

1.1. THE WORK OF REDACTORS

One may observe, in recent years, a distinct change of viewpoints in Old Testament study. Earlier in this discipline the scholar's major interest was to trace the earliest materials that could be encountered in the Old Testament: the narratives in the historical books or the original words of the prophets. Recently, the number of scholarly works that are chiefly concerned to interpret the final stage of the biblical books has increased significantly. In the course of the investigation of Old Testament texts, scholars have increasingly recognized that these do not represent a single stage of development but rather have behind them a lengthy history of evolution. The recognition and explication of this evolution has been the task of redaction history. This method's essential argument has been that the present form of Old Testament books is due to the activity of editors. While their work was carried out anonymously, meaning that their names are not known, traces of their activity can be demonstrated in many places in Old Testament writings.

The ancient Near East was a literary culture since approximately 3000 B.C.E. Texts continued to increase in number and were eventually reworked and recorded in writing by professional scribes. These scribes were associated in particular with the temples and royal courts. The Phoenicians invented the form of the alphabet from which both the writing system of Paleo-Hebrew as well as our own modern Western system derive. This required a broad spectrum of social classes within the population to develop the ability to read and to write. Likewise, in ancient Israel the profession of the scribes is witnessed in a comparable location, namely, in the royal courts (see 2 Sam 8:17; 20:25; 1 Kgs 4:3; 12:11; Ps 45:2; Isa 33:18). The priests in the temple also cultivated the recording of material. This fact is demonstrated by the existence of the

Priestly Document, one of the four sources of the books of Moses. In addition, the prophets obviously had students who collected their words and recorded them so that they would not be forgotten. In this task, the scribes did not limit themselves to the mere recording of the words of the master but rather sought to have them adapted to the different and later situation in which the scribes found themselves. By this means, these words remained relevant. They were expanded and transformed to meet new situations, often completely altering their message in the process. The result of this editing issued forth in the prophetic books as they exist today. At first glance, they do not appear to possess a demonstrable arrangement. In addition, many of the sections do not belong to the time of the prophet whose name is associated with the book but are, in part, several centuries later.

We are able to recognize in these redactional activities frequently recurring models that point to ways in which older prophetic words were transformed to speak to a later time and a situation that had changed.

1.2. THREATS AS WORDS OF SALVATION

An example of this may be found in the book of Isaiah. Not all of the chapters in this substantial book belong to Isaiah, who was active in the second half of the eighth century B.C.E. This has been recognized for more than two centuries (Johann C. Döderlein, 1775). Since that time, it has been recognized that the book contains the words of an unknown prophet from the second half of the sixth century B.C.E., the time of the Babylonian captivity. These words, which begin to appear in Isa 40, are those of an unknown prophet whom scholarship calls Second Isaiah (Deutero-Isaiah). Passages such as Isa 44:28 and 45:1 (see also 41:1–4; 45:13; 46:11; 48:14–15), which, for example, mention the Persian king Cyrus, indicate that this second group of chapters (Isa 40–55) could not have been written by First Isaiah in the eighth century B.C.E. As scholars have recognized since the work of Bernhard Duhm (1892), chapters 56–66 are even later. The title Trito-Isaiah (Third Isaiah) is reserved for this latter section of the book (Isa 56–66).

Recent analyses have also shown that one may identify presumably older and later passages within the third section of this prophetic book. Likewise, if we investigate First Isaiah more carefully, we are able to discover many sections that can have nothing to do with the prophet Isaiah. This is clearly so in the appendix of Isa 36–39, which contains for the most part narratives that have been appropriated from 2 Kgs 18–20. Themes that refer to the fall of the Babylonian Empire may be found in Isa 13; 14:3–21; and 21:1–10. This theme would have been current during the period of the Babylonian exile. These sections also may not be attributed to First Isaiah himself. It is not sufficient simply to state the secondary origin of these passages; much more is required. One needs to ask how it is that these materials were placed within the larger prophetic book, in particular in this very place. One may then observe that Isa 13 and 14:3–21 are placed before 14:24–27, which contains a threat against the Assyrians, the archenemy of Israel in the eighth and the greater part of the seventh centuries B.C.E.

The placement of this section leaves both the original intent of the earlier threat against Assyria unaltered, while making room for a new interpretation of this ancient prophetic word of doom. What once was true of the oppressive ruling superpower of Assyria, which had long since dissipated, continues to be valid analogously in the carrying out of a new political agenda against Israel (Judah). This new word, which has been inserted into the book of Isaiah, receives the authority of a well-known prophet. The modern ideas of an author holding a "copyright" to his or her material and of authorial originality as possessing value were unknown in the ancient world. Instead, there was the understanding that there were valid traditions in which one had to insert new materials in order for them to participate authentically in new situations. Examples for this may be seen in the New Testament and in the philosophical exegesis of Homer.

If this view of multiple interpreters holds true, Isa 13 offers, in addition, an example of a different kind of engagement with a subject than was offered by previous understandings. Thus, with the exception of the superscription in 13:1, one finds the name "Babylon" occurring only in 13:19. This implies that the earlier subject against whom the threat was directed in this section was Assyria. The passage has been only slightly retouched in order to redirect it to a new world empire.

Already in this example one is able to speak of interpretation, even if it is not certain whether we can understand the term in the sense of exegesis. A great deal of uncertainty obtains in attempting to determine the period of time and the circumstances of the development of a text that is in the process of becoming Scripture. A text such as Isa 8:16, which is probably to be read: "I desire to bind the testimony and seal the instruction for my disciples," is so unclear that it is impossible to be certain that Isaiah himself had already sought to have his words recorded. On the other hand, the culture of the ancient Near East was a thoroughly literary one, which presumably permeated Israelite culture by means of the simple alphabetic script of Hebrew. This cultural diffusion led to the development of the skill of reading and writing in Israel.

A further example of the reinterpretation of a text that had already achieved what was tantamount to a canonical status is found in the addition of the section Isa 24–27, the so-called Isaiah Apocalypse. This section is a collection of oracles and songs that belong to the latest parts of this prophetic book and indeed of the entire Old Testament. The Song of the Vineyard in Isa 27:2–5 evidently refers to Isaiah's well-known Vineyard Song in 5:1–7. In the latter text, Isaiah had rewritten a secular love song—the vineyard symbolizes the beloved one—in order to present a gruesome announcement of judgment against Judah and Jerusalem. Because the vineyard did not bear any fruit, its owner decided to deliver it to ruin. This intends to indicate that the same is true of God's possession, Judah and Jerusalem. The meaning of the new song in 27:2–5 is entirely different. Now Yahweh is the guardian of his vineyard who will defend it and fight against all of its enemies, depicted as thorns and thistles.

One can observe traces of later editing in almost all of the preexilic prophetic books. These ancient prophetic texts, the words of which continue to be regarded as binding and therefore cannot be altered, are adapted to meet new situations. The new situation had dramatically changed from the period of the prophets' activity. The judgment that they had announced had for the most part been accomplished in the decimation of Samaria and Jerusalem, which led to the dissolution of the independent status of the northern and southern kingdoms and to the destruction of the temple. In the works of Ezekiel, Second Isaiah, and all the nameless editors, the motto expressed in Isa 40:1–2 has been inserted: " 'Comfort, comfort my people,' says your God. 'Speak to the heart of Jerusalem and announce to her that her time of bondage has come to an end, her guilt has been absolved, and she has received a double portion for all of her sins from Yahweh's hand.' " One now lives in a new time in which Israel, especially the exiles, scattered among the nations and far away from their land, may now expect for the first time an unconditional salvation. In addition to Second Isaiah, this hope also exists, for instance, in the conclusion of the book of Amos (9:11–15), where an unknown editor expresses the hopeful anticipation that God will raise up again in its entirety the subjugated empire of David in a day that resides not too distantly in the future. The addition of Second Isaiah to First Isaiah expresses a similar purpose. In addition, there are smaller additions in numerous places, such as may be found in Isa 4:2–6 and in the concluding sentence in 6:13, that serve as a type of commentary on the prophetic pronouncements of judgment. These commentaries have the new purpose of turning to their own time in order to bring into view future salvation for the new generation.

It is clear that Isa 56–66 (Third Isaiah) frequently reached back to Isa 40–55 (Second Isaiah) in order expressly to cite the older tradition. Thus there is in Isa 58:8 the statement from 52:12 that God will go before his people in the wilderness during their return home from exile and follow behind them like a type of rearguard. However, the passage has now been changed to "your salvation goes before you, and the glory of the LORD will serve as your rear guard." Similarly, in Isa 62:11 the concrete image of the "mighty arm of the LORD" is taken from 40:10 and spiritualized. This same metaphor is used to speak of the general anticipation of coming assistance. Additional verbal citations are found in Isa 60:4 (from 49:18); 60:9 (from 55:5); and 60:16 (from 49:3). One may conclude from these and many other passages in Third Isaiah that this prophecy, which is treated like a prophetic word, did not originate with the prophet Second Isaiah. In regard to these words' relationship to an earlier prophetic text that had already achieved canonical status, one may conclude that they are themselves an interpretation for a new time.

1.3. THE TORAH AS A NORM FOR REDACTION AND INTERPRETATION

It is clear that the editing of the prophetic texts following the catastrophe of the Babylonian destruction of Judah in order to present a theology of the expectation of future salvation was not the only occasion for the editing of Old Testament books. In the final years of the preexilic period, one notes that already a literary strand of authentic words of Isaiah was reworked by a redactor active during the reign of King Josiah of Judah (639–609 B.C.E.) in order to direct these pronouncements of judgment against Assyria and to announce the impending destruction of this super power.

The time of Josiah also is shaped by the reform that stressed the centralization of the worship of God in the temple of Jerusalem and by the process of effectuating this claim of its being the only place for sacred worship. This king is to have carried out this assault on other sanctuaries and cults according to the demands set forth in the book of Deuteronomy. In Deuteronomy, the concept of the Torah as the summarizing of the will of God in codified form was set forth for the first time. Thus, an established standard was set up that could serve as the foundation of divine judgment concerning the past as well as the future.

Deuteronomy and its particular theology became the norm for an entire school of theological scribes who are given the intentionally vague and nondescript name the Deuteronomists. It is difficult to decide whether there was actually an organized movement of this type or whether an entire generation of theologians for a limited period shaped a common interpretation. In any case, it is striking that, extending from the final period of the Judean monarchy and continuing well into the time of the exile, one is able to note that there was a remarkably uniform terminology and worldview that was very close to the book of Deuteronomy.

In the Deuteronomistic History (Joshua–2 Kings), which underwent multiple redactions, the Deuteronomists shaped a common description of the history of Israel, from the conquest of the land reaching down to the period of the exile. Older sources were used. However, these previous materials were manipulated into a unique formulation based on selection, presentation, and structuring. Furthermore, a large number of older materials, apparently already written down in previous books, were modified through additions and comments based on a Deuteronomic understanding.

One case in point is the book of Hosea. Hosea was active as a prophet in the northern kingdom of Israel shortly before its destruction in the year 722 B.C.E. His words were directed originally to the inhabitants of the northern kingdom and had in view their particular situation. However, later on, the material, presumably already in a written form, was taken to the southern kingdom of Judah and there was collected and redacted in a manner that not only achieved a new actualization in an altered context but also gave validity to the theological views of the Deuteronomistic movement. One example is Hos 14:2–4, which calls on Israel to confess. The unconditioned announcement of salvation 14:5–8(9) is placed under the condition of a previous return. Other examples are 5:5 and 12:3, originally a threat against Israel (seen in the parallel name Jacob), later replaced by the name Judah. Thus, Hosea's word has been reshaped to take on new meaning. Similar to this is the instance in 4:15.

The book of Amos was, in its original formulation, the proclamation of a prophet active during the middle of the eighth century B.C.E. The Deuteronomistic redaction of this earlier book is easy to see. For example, the redactors insert a later oracle against Judah (2:4–5) into the list of oracles against the foreign nations and Israel in 1:3–2:3, 6–16, thus including Judah's condemnation. Judah is judged for having cast aside the teaching of Yahweh, formulated in the Torah, and for not observing its commandments. One encounters the characteristic terms "Torah" and "commandments" that are typically Deuteronomic in the expression that God has directed his announcement of judgment against his people, a judgment that is no longer limited to the destruction of the north but now includes the inhabitants of Judah and Jerusalem, since his own people have demeaned the Torah codified in the form of Deuteronomy.

This oldest form of biblical interpretation also includes the commentary that is incorporated into the text. A text that has been transmitted in an earlier form, which has already received an aura of authority, is not altered in terms of its substance. However, additions are made that allow the text to address a new situation that embodies new and different circumstances. Thus, another audience, this one those who dwell in Judah instead of northern Israel, encounters a text that has a transformed theological perspective. This presupposes, therefore, that the prophetic word continues to be valid in so far as it is demonstrated to be authentic according to the criterion of the "law of the prophet" articulated in Deut 18:22. This law requires that a prophetic word, to be authentic, must be a prediction that comes to pass (Jer 28:9). Thereby it achieves already a canonical validity.

Another form of engagement with the prophetic tradition, found in the book of Jeremiah, is more difficult to explain. The material in this text is so complex that scholarly interpretation has not been able to produce a basic consensus. In addition to texts that are presented in the poetic form common to the early classical prophets, that is, poetic oracles that likely originate with the prophet himself, there are narratives about the prophet and prosaic speeches. These narratives and prosaic speeches resemble Deuteronomistic texts. However, behind these speeches there appears to be a tradition that harkens back to the original words of the prophet himself. In the so-called temple sermon of Jeremiah, we have a double form of the tradition. The first occurs in Jer 7:1–15 and is presented in the form of a sermon edited in a Deuteronomistic style. The second is found in 26:1–19, ensconced in a narrative that relates the circumstances and the results of this speech. This second expression also has been edited in the same style. The relationship between chapters 27 and 28 is seen in the treatment of the same theme. In chapter 28 Jeremiah engages in a symbolic action in which he wears upon his neck a yoke signifying a threatened exile followed by an antagonistic encounter with a prophet of salvation, Hananiah, who announces just the opposite message. However, while this conflict of Jeremiah with the false prophet Hananiah occurs in the style of a sermon in chapter 28, it takes place in the form of a narrative in the preceding chapter.

1.4. Historicizing and Idealizing Interpretation

One is able in like fashion to compile other groups of Old Testament texts and make observations comparable to these prophetic passages that pertain to the interpretation of the Bible. Certainly, the phenomena are often filled with ambiguity so that in numerous texts there is considerable debate about what was an older existing tradition and what was a new interpretation. Cultic texts, as, for example, the Psalms, are characterized by a formal language and a significant measure of timelessness. The situation of one offering a lament that concerned illness and other needs presented to God was often quite similar to other lamentations. Therefore, it is extremely difficult to determine the time of a lament's origins. In any event, there are traces of editing that may be determined as occurring at a later time. A later origin is in each case indicated by the situation set forth in the superscription of thirteen psalms (Pss 3; 7; 18; 34; 51; 52; 54; 56; 57; 59; 60; 63; 142), which brings the particular psalm into an association with an event from the life of David. In these situations, one finds a late effort to historicize the Psalter that sees David himself as the poetic author of the psalms. However, this usually does not conform to the text itself. Nevertheless, the criticism of the redaction of the Psalter and the psalms is still in its infancy, so that one may not draw a conclusion that enjoys a great deal of certainty.

This contrasts with the relatively simple case of the Chronicler. In the Chronicles, which is divided secondarily into two parts, as is the case with Samuel–Kings, we have a historical work that originates in a considerably later period (fourth–fifth century B.C.E.). It is greatly dependent on the Deuteronomistic History as a source to which it reaches back, in so far as the period of the monarchy is in view. If one sets the two texts side by side in the form of a synopsis, one is able to recognize the convergences and the deviations at first glance. The author of the Chronicles (a group of writers could have composed this) works with his sources by omitting elements, adding others, and transforming still others. In tracing these occurring features, one is able to recognize the specific theological interests of the Chronicler.

The Chronicler begins with a succinctly expressed genealogy that begins with Adam and is followed by a registry of male descendants that continues to the period of Saul (1 Chr 1–9). It is obvious that the Chronicler already knew the common comprehensiveness of the genealogies of Genesis and the Deuteronomistic History. However, he quickly passes over most of these in the first nine chapters and introduces his narrative history for the first time with Saul. It is striking that only Saul's downfall in the battle against the Philistines is described (1 Chr 10), while the other narratives concerning this first king of Israel present in 1 Samuel are omitted. In compact form, the story relates two details: the entire house of Saul died in the battle; and all of the Israelites present in the valley fled (10:6–7). This narrative provides the end of Saul a theological basis (10:13–14), in which he serves as an example of an unfaithful ruler. It is also conspicuous that in the section concerning David (1 Chr 11–29) the Chronicler simply omits many parts: the narratives about David's ascendancy and his kingship over Judah in Hebron (1 Sam 16–2 Sam 4), as well as the entire Succession Narrative, which is rich in details (2 Sam 9; 11–20; 1 Kgs 1–2). This latter narrative describes the final succession to the throne of Solomon after many affairs, intrigues, and incidents, while David himself is not always presented in a favorable light. Instead, the Chronicler introduces David immediately as king over all Israel (1 Chr 11:1–3) who quickly takes Jerusalem (11:4–9). David's success as a military king is underscored by the placement of the modified list of his warriors at the initial part of the extensive narrative. The promise of Nathan to David (2 Sam 7:1–16), which concerns his perpetual dynasty, is changed by chronologically delaying it until the end of the narrative, and here it is an eternal covenant promised to Solomon and his descendants (1 Chr 17:11–14). Thus, the perpetual dynasty is not promised to David but rather to Solomon. For the Chronicler, this decisive promise of Solomon's eternal dynasty results from the fact that he is the one who should build a house (i.e., a temple) for God (17:12).

Even if reports of military campaigns are strewn throughout the wider course of the David narrative (14:8–17; 19:1–20:3; 20:4–8, taken from 2 Sam 5:17–25; 10:1–11:1; 12:26–32; 21:18–22) and continue to make their way through the description of the time of the reign of David, what is emphasized is his role in the preparation for the temple cult in Jerusalem. It was certainly well known from the tradition that it was not David but rather Solomon who had built the temple. The Chronicler sets forth his theological rationale for this: David could not come into consideration as the builder of the temple because he had spilled too much blood as a man of war (1 Chr 22:8; 28:3). Instead, the Chronicler describes how David had participated with all Israel in the bringing of the ark to Jerusalem (1 Chr 15; 16:1–6), purchased the place for the temple (1 Chr 21; cf. 2 Sam 24 and the characteristic alterations), and took in hand the planning of the building of the temple. Solomon, by contrast, only assumed the task of carrying out these details by actually overseeing the building of the temple (1 Chr 22). Indeed, David introduced to the dignitaries his son Solomon as his successor and transmitted to him the detailed blueprint for the temple and its outfitting (1 Chr 28). Finally, he set the example by making his own contribution to the temple (29:1–9) and concluded with a prayer of thanksgiving along with the associated community sacrifice (29:10–22). The Chronicler did not find these latter components in his preceding narrative (Samuel–Kings) but wrote them freely as his own composition because he wished to bring to bear the broad emphases of his own concerns.

Similar alterations and additions to the narrative source are discovered in the section concerning the period of Solomon's rule. The earlier narrative makes the transition to his reign with capricious murder occurring at the beginning (1 Kgs 2:13–46), followed by his marriage brokerage with the Pharaoh (3:1). Instead of these, the Chronicler introduces the story by a sacrificial festival in Gibeon in which all Israel participates (2 Chr 1:1–13; cf. 1 Kgs 3:1–15) and a commissioning of Hiram of Tyre, who here appears as a vassal, to deliver construction personnel and cedar for the building of the temple (2 Chr 1:18–2:15), an activity that immediately unfolds (2 Chr 3). The report of the building of the temple has changed its source (1 Kgs 6) by taking up elements from the Priestly narrative concerning the "tent of meeting" in Exod 25:23–31:11, while the grandeur of the temple far exceeds the actual furnishing of the Solomonic temple and the rather modest new temple building of the postexilic period. Therefore, the Solomonic period is presented as a golden age with a king of legendary wealth who embodies the perfect king and builds the temple. In the background is the expectation, which the Chronicler wishes to impress upon all of his readers, that the impoverished circumstances of the present time, especially the condition of the temple on which all eyes are cast, will be replaced in the salvific end time by a temple whose glory reflects that of the Solomonic sanctuary.

In the description of the history that occurs after the death of Solomon, it is noticeable that, following the report about the withdrawal of the northern kingdom, Israel, from the kingdom of Judah and the Solomonic dynasty, the kings of Israel are no longer mentioned, save when they play a role in the history of Judah. All of them obviously were regarded as apostates. The Chronicler tracks exclusively the history of the southern kingdom. He uses a good deal of license in the writing of his description of the Jewish kings when using his source. This is clearly due to his purpose to make the behavior of the rulers an example of admonishment or encouragement for his readers. The reigns of several kings, including

Rehoboam (2 Chr 10–12), Asa (2 Chr 14–16), Jehoshaphat (2 Chr 17–20), Joash (2 Chr 24), and Manasseh (2 Chr 31:1–20), are placed into the pattern of righteous behavior, apostasy, punishment, confession, and, finally, restitution in order to gauge the ruler's commitment to the Torah and to the cult of Yahweh in the Jerusalem temple as the standard for assessing his rule.

It has often been asked whether the additional information about various rulers that the Chronicler does not derive from his earlier source, the Deuteronomistic History, rests instead on other traditions that also were available to him. Recently it has been demonstrated that, with few exceptions, this could not have been the case. The reports over the measures undertaken for fortifications, military outfitting, and wars serve to depict the power of God and the kings who were obedient to his Torah. This obedience was especially underlined in the case of Jehoshaphat, who, through special measures, undertook to instruct his people in the Torah and to institute an order of law (2 Chr 17:7–9; 19:5–11). Reports like these are almost totally spun out of the whole cloth of the previous books of Kings, which possesses only a few insinuations of these. The same purpose is served by the description of an entire series of prophets whose materials are not found in the Deuteronomistic History (Shemaiah, 2 Chr 12:5–8; Azariah, 15:1–7; Hanani, 16:7–10; Jehu, 19:2–3; Jahaziel, 20:14–17; Eliezer, 20:37; Zechariah, the son of Jehoiada, 24:20–22; Oded, 28:9–11; and the anonymous prophets in 2 Chr 25). These collectively are fictional characters created to serve the historical theological significance of the kings. In the concluding remarks in 2 Chr 36:15–16 that bring to a conclusion this historical period, the Chronicler offers a common explanation of the destruction of Judah, Jerusalem, and the temple: these catastrophes occurred because the kings, notables, priests, and people ignored the messages of the prophets continually sent them by God.

1.5. REDACTION AS INTERPRETATION

In the Chronicler's work of history, we have the first example of a type of exegesis that we shall encounter frequently in early Judaism: a text's narrative expansion regarded as authoritative (haggadah). This style of interpretation sets forth an explication that is derived from the text and continued, abbreviated in parts and in other parts adapted, but above all developed in the direction of the author's commentary rather than the intention considered relevant for its own time. In past years, a much-discussed topic has been whether or not one can speak of Chronicles' own interpretation. In objection to this, it has been argued that in those places where Chronicles is incorrect, these are due to the fact that the Chronicler has no source outside of the books of Kings to draw upon. However, even this is a typical manner of proceeding for the midrash (Hebrew "investigation," "interpretation"). Furthermore, the same theological point of view is present in all of the material that is unique to Chronicles. This results from combining the modified sections with the newly arranged source material taken from Samuel–Kings. According to our modern standards, these modified narratives are freely invented, although this process has in no way been formed arbitrarily. In its fundamental conviction, Chronicles follows the previous example of the Deuteronomistic History. The Chronicler views the catastrophes that are introduced, the later effects of which are still felt by the community, as punishment for the disobedience of many kings, the leading representatives of Judah and the nation as a whole.

Especially of concern to Chronicles is the pure worship of Yahweh. The perception of these books is that this purity of worship may occur only in the temple of Jerusalem and according to the commandments of the Torah. The punishment exists in the troubles that continue to beset the Chronicler's community: the giving of praise to heathen powers; the exploitation of the land that occasions the economic need of its inhabitants; and the poor state of the sanctuary in Jerusalem. The expectation is that the rebuilding of the temple according to the ideal picture of the Solomonic sanctuary is imminent.

Corresponding to this, the lists in 1 Chr 23–27, as viewed by modern exegesis, are a later addition containing the understanding found either in Levitical circles or in the viewpoint of the author of Chronicles himself. The special concerns of this professional group, which may have come to expression in the postexilic period, are felt to be those of the protagonist of a strong faith in Yahweh, oriented to both the Torah and the temple.

A similar purpose already resides at the basis of the Deuteronomistic History, the previously existing text used by Chronicles. Also, in the former literary text, sources are utilized that express established theological standards and present the requirement of one legitimate theological cultic site. These are used in judging the different kings. Thus, the sections considered to be that of the redactors' own creation, nevertheless, are quite small (see the summaries in Judg 2:6–23; 2 Kgs 17:7–23, as well as the judgment of the kings occurring within the different narrative parts). Even so, the Deuteronomistic composition imposed on its sources tends to be dominant. On the other hand, the earlier existing sources of the Deuteronomistic History did not obtain the status of "Scripture" but rather bear the often official-sounding names such as "the annals of the kings," while others possess the character of folklore, like those of the prophetic narratives. In the case of Chronicles, however, the situation is different: Chronicles clearly presupposes knowledge of the Deuteronomistic History, something also familiar to its audience. The entirety of this history is considered to be normative, including even the individual excerpts appropriated by Chronicles. These books attach portions of the Deuteronomistic History to their own fundamental theological intention, even while taking into consideration the situation and the hopes of their own altered time period. In this sense, these books offer a creative, new interpretation of the older books without fundamentally rescinding their meaning.

We especially see rather clearly in the example of Chronicles how the interpretation of the Bible already was beginning. There is no fixed point of entry for the beginning of "interpretation," since interpretation grows out of the texts themselves. Part of this interpretation belongs to the books themselves in so far as they are a *post ex eventu* "history" of the earlier texts. Throughout the process of their finally becoming canonical books, they were redactionally altered and their contents changed in order to correspond to the needs of a later period. Thus, precanonical texts are commented upon, interpreted, and actualized. In regard to interpretation in the more narrow understanding of the term, one may speak above all of another construal when a normative text already has been brought to a conclusion. In this sense, the text is interpreted and reactualized. It is difficult in this regard to establish clear lines of separation in the different domains of the Old Testament. It is a different matter in regard to Chronicles, since we are in the unique position of having a text existing in its final form (the Deuteronomistic History) that stands over against the interpretation (Chronicles), which is itself a concluded work. However, it is considerably different in the prophetic texts discussed prior to Chronicles, since the final form of the actualized work has been brought together. Thus, both the original and the meaning are shaped into a completed book. We are forced to attempt to reconstruct through analysis the older stages of a work. If there were a preexilic book of Isaiah that existed beside a later, postexilic form and the two together had entered into the canon, we would have a further example of the type of process of formation and interpretation that we find in the two large historical works of the Old Testament (the Deuteronomistic History and Chronicles).

The considerations discussed here may be amplified by reviewing additional sections of the Old Testament, for example, Genesis. In the Primeval History, the literary sources defined by modern source analysis as the Yahwist and Priestly documents are transmitted, clearly developed, and newly interpreted when later redactors attach older traditions to meet altered circumstances. These sources and their ongoing development through redaction have entered into the interpretation process by offering new theological emphases. Similar to this, as regards the Torah, the book of Deuteronomy obviously has gone through several stages of development that continued to introduce new perspectives and that proceeded frequently from antithetical theological standpoints. Legal texts such as those present in the older collection known as the Book of the Covenant (Exod 20:22–23:33) experienced continuing change because of steadily altered social conditions. New situations arose that called for a rule not present in the previously existing legal precedents. Therefore, the text was constantly changed by the addition of new grounds as well as altered fundamental points of view. Thus, for example, in comparing the Sabbath commandment in Exod 20:5 with that found in Deut 5:5, one discovers that the first example is provided a cultic foundation, while the second is given a social basis.

In regard to this first look, one must be satisfied with the selection of examples offered. This is the case because redaction history is one of the latest fields of work in Old Testament criticism. Therefore, many questions are still contested that have kept a broad consensus from emerging. One cannot speak of the unanimity of views concerning the findings and their explanations. We may expect that, in the future, many illuminating understandings will be achieved.

2

BETWEEN THE TESTAMENTS

2.1. TRANSLATION AS INTERPRETATION: THE SEPTUAGINT

We possess a legendary narrative, the so-called Letter of Aristeas (ca. 150–100 B.C.E.), that tells of the origin of the older Greek translation of the Old Testament, the Septuagint. This text reports that, at the suggestion of the Egyptian king Ptolemy II (285–247 B.C.E.), the Torah (the Five Books of Moses), was translated by seventy-two scholars of Scripture, each of whom, after consultation among themselves, produced a translation that was in exact agreement with the others. Subsequently, this text was recognized by the Jewish community in Alexandria to be authoritative. In reality, this translation was made, not at the suggestion of the Ptolemaic king, but rather to meet the undeniable needs of the Greek-speaking colony, not only in this metropolis but also in the other regions of the Diaspora as well.

We now find ourselves in the period of Hellenism: the victorious march of Alexander the Great into the East had widened the expanse of the Macedonian administration, military, and, above all, the Greek language and culture throughout the eastern Mediterranean region. His successors, the Diadochoi, especially the Ptolemies in Egypt, who also ruled over Eretz Israel in the third century B.C.E., and the Seleucids in Syria undertook every effort to gather together their widely diverse subjects in the population under the one roof of Greek forms of life and to forge them into a unified people of the state. Greek became the language of the political, economic, and cultural upper class, especially in the cities.

In addition, many Jews, not only in Egypt but also in Israel itself, had learned perfect Greek, since only this ability opened the door to influential positions. Greek education especially was disseminated through the gymnasium. To be educated in this school was the pass to affiliation with the elite. Thus, Jews sent their children to the gymnasium in spite of the compromises that they were required to make. This did not mean, at least for the faithful, that they were prepared to become followers of polytheistic religions, which would lead to the integration of their own religion into the religious mix that served the Diadochoi in the form of a state ideology. The Jews held fast to their monotheistic faith, a position that would become even more decisive in the Roman Empire. Added to this was the synagogue, which first appeared as early as the Babylonian exile and became the place of assembly for worship among Jewish communities scattered over the entire world. The sacrificial cult in the Jerusalem temple played out its role with its final destruction in 70 C.E. The temple no longer enjoyed its exclusive position as the place of worship once the exile to Babylon occurred. Synagogues after the return were eventually established even in Jerusalem. In the middle point of synagogue worship, however, the reading of Scripture, and that meant primarily and almost exclusively the presentation and interpretation of the Torah.

The beginnings of the Torah are encountered already in the Old Testament. As early as Deuteronomy (31:9–13) there is a prescript: "this Torah" is to be read every seventh year in the central sanctuary in the presence of "all Israel." In addition, during the postexilic period, one finds the report that the Book of the Torah of Moses was read by Ezra during the time of the Festival of Tabernacles (Neh 8:1–8). Presumably, the translation of the books of Moses as the center of the Septuagint also originates from the use of the Torah in worship. One may presume that the mostly orally presented Greek translations of the sacred texts already composed and read in Hebrew developed eventually into a standard form that finally was recognized as official. As the canon was later expanded by the addition to the Torah of first the prophetic books and then the Writings, they were translated into Greek. This process was concluded toward the end of the second century C.E.

The Septuagint contains a number of additional books that are not in the Hebrew canon that rabbinic authorities and later the Reformers recognized as Scripture. In both the Greek Orthodox and the Roman Catholic churches, these additional texts, written before the translation of the Septuagint, were considered authoritative. In the Roman Catholic Church, these were translated into the Vulgate, the standard translation of Saint Jerome. These later books were written during the Hellenistic period. In addition to the Greek canon, which included these later books, a larger number of other writings were composed—the Pseudepigrapha—that remained outside of the canon. Many of these writings are known only by their titles, while others were preserved solely in

Christian translations. Parts of the Hebrew originals of many of these have been discovered.

The Septuagint translators of the Torah, that is, the Five Books of Moses (Greek: Pentateuch) were in large measure successful in their efforts to translate accurately the Holy Scriptures into Greek. A successful translation is not simply the mechanical transmittance of the words of a text into the expressions of another language; it also transforms the forms of thought and expression of one linguistic, living world into those of another. Forms of thought and expression belong together and build a horizon of language that reflects a specific sociocultural milieu. The Hebrew of the Old Testament, with its rich repertoire of literary forms of expression for the variety of activities, expresses the concrete things of the real world and personal encounters of the rural background of life in Israel. By contrast, the Koine Greek of the Septuagint reflects the Egyptian milieu in which it originated. The Jews of the Diaspora, in particular those of the upper class who enjoyed a Greek education, sought to integrate their received faith with this social environment.

The period of Hellenism was the time in which Judaism was most extensively open to its environment. To refrain from the understanding that Judaism lost its tradition of faith by merging entirely into this environment, we should, therefore, designate two fundamental ways that Hellenistic Judaism was distinguished from its context: through the uniqueness of a purely monotheistic faith imprinted by a strongly ethical tradition and the Torah piety of the synagogue; and through a missionary tendency that reached beyond the older boundaries of the nation and sought to win a large number of proselytes (the converted) and "God-fearers" (who did not adopt all of the Jewish prescriptions, e.g., circumcision). All of them possessed the capacity to understand the Holy Scripture in their own Greek language.

It is remarkable, on the one hand, to note how far the translators succeeded in preserving the Old Testament in its original character. The Septuagint is in its original form a typically Jewish translation. Scholars have recognized this in the more recent period. The oldest complete manuscripts of the Septuagint already had originated in the first Christian centuries and are edited christologically. In this period, rabbinic Judaism rejected the Septuagint and chose to make the Hebrew canon their Scripture and to interpret it alone. They rejected the Septuagint due to the fact that the Christians had made the Old Testament Septuagint their Scripture and interpreted it according to their own understanding. The manuscripts of the Old Testament from the Christian period introduced the term *kyrios* ("Lord") for the name of God. Older textual discoveries have shown that the Tetragrammaton YHWH in a square script was inserted into the earlier manuscripts of the Septuagint, due to the well-known fact that Judaism avoided saying the name of God. This may already have been orally read aloud as "the Lord," as some Jewish witnesses demonstrate.

On the other hand, one can clearly see that this translation originated in a Hellenistic milieu. This is apparent with respect to the designations for God. For example, in the account of the famous announcement of the name of God in Exod 3:14 one finds "I am who I am" or "I shall be who I shall be." The Septuagint translates this "I am the one who exists," in the language and thought of Greek ontology. Conversely, one frequently encounters for the word *God* in the Hebrew Old Testament the image of the "rock" (on which one is able to trust). However, this was not taken into the Septuagint, due to the fact that it would correspond to the Hellenistic religions that accepted rocks and stones as the dwelling place of the deities. In addition, anthropomorphic presentations of God are deleted. Thus Moses did not ascend to God but rather went up the mountain of God (Exod 19:3). In Isa 6:2 the borders of the garment of God do not fill the temple, but rather his glory (*doxa*). The Septuagint also altered texts that tell of "seeing" God (Exod 24:10–11; Isa 38:11). In addition, references to God's resting were not set forth without alteration (thus the corresponding statements in Gen 6:6–7 and Exod 32:12 were modified). The transcendence of God is emphasized. The translation *Pantocrator* ("Almighty") differs from the ancient title Sabaoth ("Lord of Hosts") or Shaddai (the "Almighty"), thus making these expressions attune to Greek ears. Frequently the term *demiurge* and the word *demiurgein* (which can designate the act of handiwork) are avoided in describing the work of divine creation; instead, *ktizein* is used, which designates, for example, either the initiative of a ruler in founding a city or an intellectual, deliberative process. On the whole, one can observe a development throughout the Old Testament of a spiritualization of the conceptions of God (e.g., in the comparison of the creation narratives in Gen 2:4b–25 [Yahwist] and Gen 1:1–2:4a [Priestly]). Even so, not all of the human images for God are removed.

Often the Greek text makes small alterations of the earlier Hebrew text that allowed Hellenistic readers to understand a statement more easily. Thus one encounters in the Septuagint's translation of the book of Isaiah Egyptian technical expressions emerging from a variety of spheres: the term *ibis*, which appears in Isa 34:11, is called an unclean animal in Lev 11:17 because it is sacred to the Egyptian god Thoth. In Hab 3:5 a mistaken reading is made. The Septuagint renders the term "pestilence" with "word," due to an Egyptian mythological image. In the Hebrew text one reads: "Pestilence goes before him [God]; an epidemic follows his steps." In the Septuagint the text reads: "Before him the word goes forth; winged shoes are on his feet" (like the sun god). The famous Egyptian water canals occur in their designations with technical terms (Exod 7:19; 8:5; Isa 19:6; 27:12; 33:21; 38:9), like the Nile marshes (Exod 2:3, 5; 7:19; 8:5; Isa 19:6; 33:9; 35:7; 41:18; 42:14). Even jewelry, clothing, and toiletries of noble women in Egypt have replaced the Hebrew expressions in Isa 3:8–24.

During the period of the origin of the Septuagint translations after that of the Pentateuch, one is able to see an increase in the expectation of the end time. Thus, Isa 62:11 promises to the city of Jerusalem that their savior is coming (the Hebrew original has "their salvation"). Deuteronomy 24:7 explains its Hebrew source by introducing the mythical opponent Gog from Magog (Ezek 38–39) in order to set forth the anticipation of a final kingdom. The translation of Isaiah, approximately in the middle of the second century, offers in different places explanatory references to address the period of the translator. Thus, for example, in Isa 10:5–6 the translator understands the word concerning the Assyrians in 14:4–21 to refer to the Syrians threatening Jerusalem during the time of the Seleucid ruler Antiochus IV. In contrast to the announcement of judgment against Jerusalem in 22:1–14, the passage is referred to the contemporary result of this ruler's conquest and plundering of the city in 167 B.C.E. This is the period in which the book of Daniel originated, with its apocalyptic interpretation of events.

The themes of the resurrection of the dead and eternal life, which stand only on the periphery of the Old Testament in late writings (only Dan 12:1–3; Isa 26:19), are introduced in various places by the Septuagint: Ps 1:5; Isa 38:16; and Job 19:26. In the Hebrew poetry of Job, the patient sufferer speaks out of the confidence that before his demise he will experience the divine justification that he has demanded. The statement of resurrection found in the Greek text relocates this compensation to the future life. This corresponds precisely to the expectation that is made about the seven martyred brothers in 2 Macc 7, when they are slaughtered and martyred one after the other on account of their refusal to obey the command to eat the flesh of swine.

One may also observe shifts being made in the portrayal of humanity by the Septuagint. It is frequently emphasized that humans are mortal (Job 30:23; Prov 3:13; 20:24; see also Wis 7:1; 9:14; 15:7; 2 Macc 9:12; 3 Macc

3:29). The oppression and distress of humans are often underscored. The Greek translation of the book of Ecclesiastes, in contrast to the Hebrew text, changes once more the fundamental tenor of the writing by translating the term *hebel* ("breath of wind") with the Greek term "vanity." *Hebel* in Ecclesiastes serves as its motto and presents an image for the transience of existence, robbing, as it were, in the view of Ecclesiastes, life of any meaning. The repetition of "vanity" in the Septuagint makes the term into the notion of a moral and religious concept: human arrogance is the root of all evil. The futility of all human efforts to maintain life under the encumbrance of existence is no longer the theme. Rather, now the term points to the restlessness of the human soul under the curse of sin and the unsolved mystery of the meaning of life. The lament over the inanity of all efforts becomes the accusation against the hubris of the human spirit. The Septuagint contrasts the poor and pious more strongly with the rich and carefree by characterizing the former as those who are sustained by their trust in God. Having said that, the Septuagint can move beyond the simple Greek idea of the "righteous" as those who comply with civil requirements in everyday life by delving into the fulfillment of moral obligations toward God and community. While the Septuagint's translation of all Hebrew concepts for "guilt" with the Greek word *hamartia* raises this understanding to a fundamentally new plateau, still the requirement to trust in the awe-inspiring amazement elicited by the leadership of God (especially in the Psalter) and the conception of the divine education of humanity are adjusted to be in conformity with the fundamentally positive piety of Hellenistic Judaism.

At one essential point, the Septuagint reflects an adjustment that built a bridge between the synagogue and the faith of preexilic Israel: the translation of the word *torah* (Hebrew: instruction, teaching) with the Greek term *nomos*, "law," clearly points to an understanding of the interpretation of the Torah in the context of the synagogue, which was then understood as a book of the law that comprises a collection of prescriptions that are to regulate the entire life of a Jew. This understanding was offered as an analogy to the Hellenistic understanding of juridical law and also was partially influenced by it. The interpretation of the Torah as law signifies, then, the halakah: the use of a legal corpus for the guidance of everyday life and a casuistry that added new prescriptions to the old legal clauses for cases that they had not previously regulated. This led to the development of a tradition that linked life ever more exactly to a comprehensive body of legislation.

One recognizes that the Septuagint translation functions at the same time as an interpretation of the Hebrew Bible. This is indicated especially by the not infrequent additions to its source. In a closer examination, such additions are not infrequently meant to serve as interpretations of a biblical text by means of another principle known in later Jewish interpretation: the principle of analogy. Accordingly, a proximate meaning of a statement in the text is able to help to explain a verse that is difficult to understand. In this regard, associations with catchwords play a special role. Behind the rule that related biblical passages are appropriated to explain a scriptural text stands the fundamental theological point of view that Scripture is a unity in that it is understood as the Word of God. Its passages, therefore, are related to each other and are mutually informative.

An example of this process is found in Isa 48:21. Verses 20–21 announce a new exodus of Israel, only this time from Babylonian exile, and a new journey through the wilderness, during which the people will not thirst: "He [Yahweh] will cause water to flow from the rock for them. He will split open the rocks, and water will stream forth." The Septuagint adds: "and my people will drink." It is clear that this addition originates in Exod 17:6, where Moses is instructed: "Strike the rock so that water will come from it, and the people will drink." The original prophecy of Second Isaiah already contains the controlling theme that the new exodus will correspond to the exodus from Egypt. Thus, the Septuagint offers an even clearer allusion to this theme by referring to an episode of the text that already has become Holy Scripture. In this case, the Greek text underlines a previous incident from the wilderness wandering in Exodus.

Another example is found in Isa 29:24. At the end of this brief speech (29:22–24), which announces a transformed character of Jacob (Israel) at the end time, the Septuagint adds, "and the tongues of those who stammer will learn to speak of peace." It is apparent that the translator has in view Isa 32:4. He develops out of both texts a view of the time of salvation during which the muddled speech of the people, caused by their stubbornness, likewise will become lucid (6:10). In addition, the concept of "peace," which the Septuagint independently inserts into 29:24, is probably to be understood in the fuller sense: even the mouths of those who previously were speechless shall speak then of the quintessential salvation (Hebrew: *shalom*).

An example where the translator stood the meaning of the original text on its head is found in Isa 42:13. Here the intervention of God for the good of his nation is compared to that of a brave, victorious warrior: "Yahweh moves forth like a hero; like a man of war he unleashes his fury." The Septuagint has completely altered the meaning: "The Lord ... shall destroy war." This same alteration occurs in Exod 15:3. Instead of "Yahweh is a man of war," the Septuagint reads: "The Lord is he who destroys war." The text in Isaiah obviously alludes to the Song of Miriam in Exod 15, since the Torah is the first part of the Bible to be translated. Behind both of these alterations stand references to the passages, Pss 76:4 and 2:20, in which already in the original text of the Hebrew Bible the "destruction" of war is mentioned as an important salvific act of God. Hosea 2:20–23 especially makes clear the concept that perfect peace will reign during a future time of salvation. The combination of all of these passages is expressly dependent on the linkage of the key word "destroy" that encompasses the substantive "war." However, this external association permits the translator to articulate what is for him the important anticipation of an eschatological condition of peace. The needs of the present time of the translator cause him to alter the meaning of the text itself in order that it may speak anew to the current situation.

An actual interpretation of a well-known biblical passage is present in the Septuagint's version of Isa 9:9. In the original Hebrew text, one finds a threat of Isaiah that is issued because of the arrogant pride of the northern kingdom of Israel and the inhabitants of Samaria. This prophecy is announced before their destruction by the Assyrians in 722 B.C.E. In the course of this event, the prophet cites an arrogant word of the Samaritans concerning the invasion of the enemy: "Brick walls have been torn down; we shall erect dressed stones. Beams of sycamore are fallen; we shall replace them with cedar wood." The Septuagint adds: "and build ourselves a tower." Without doubt this refers to the well-known story of the building of the tower of Babel (Gen 11). The same key words (dressed stones, build; Gen. 11:3–4) brought this narrative into view, and, at the same time, for the translator it became an appropriate description that pertains to the consequences of human hubris. During the translator's period, the Samaritans were sectarians bitterly opposed by the Jews. Subsequently, this obvious reflection of the story of the building of the tower of Babel allows the translator to brand the prophetic speech in Isa 9 as an expression of the hubris of opposing God.

Deviations of the Septuagint's understanding of the wording from that of the Masoretic Text do not necessarily or generally signify the wording of a different Hebrew textual tradition but rather may more simply be understood as a conscious interpretation that proceeds from a biblical text that had not yet achieved the status of a binding and therefore unalterable form.

Other problems of the translation of the Septuagint may only be mentioned here. First, the Septuagint offers a different arrangement of the main sections of the book of Jeremiah: announcements of destruction against Jeremiah's own people; speeches against the foreign nations; and prophecies of salvation. Then there is the case of the shorter form of the Greek text of Ezekiel, which is perhaps based on a Hebrew tradition different from the one that we know. Also, the sequencing of the books in the canon signifies different theological principles of arrangement. Thus, Daniel is regarded as one of the great prophets and the prophetic canon comes at the end of the entire Bible.

On the whole, one may say that the translators succeeded in maintaining in a foreign language the essential content of the Hebrew Old Testament. They also made it accessible to an expanded circle of hearers and readers who either were adherents of Judaism or were former devotees of Hellenistic religions. Hellenistic Judaism held strongly to specific cultic proscriptions, in particular circumcision and the sanctification of the Sabbath, which they required of proselytes, and it cultivated Torah piety in the sense of halakah. This expression of Judaism opened up its own world that, in later periods, especially under the pressure of external persecutions, only seldom was to be reached.

The Septuagint was also the form of the Old Testament read and cited by early Christianity. As we shall soon see, this had many consequences for understanding its contents. Many emendations reflecting Christian views were introduced into the text of the Septuagint. At the same time, Jews continued to work on the problem posed by translation. There appeared in the early Christian period the translations of Aquila, Symmachus, and Theodotion. In addition, translations in Aramaic, known as the Targumim, originated for the Jewish communities, which spoke Aramaic. One is able to observe in these texts similarities to the Septuagint.

2.2. Early Jewish Interpretation: The Qumran Scrolls

As we have seen, Ezra, a fifth-century b.c.e. Persian official with the Aramaic title of scribe (saphar, perhaps secretary of state or governor), after coming to Jerusalem, publicly read for the first time the book of the law of Moses (the Torah) and declared it to be binding for the postexilic community. Within Judaism, his title was transformed into a "scholar of Scripture, learned in the commandments of Yahweh and his statutes concerning Israel" (Ezra 7:11). The tradition of the origin of the Great Synagogue is associated with Ezra. His purpose was to interpret the Torah as the basic law of the community, to provide provisions for its fulfillment, to effectuate modifications due to its fragmentary nature, and to actualize its teachings. The oral tradition was added to the written Torah and was to become just as binding as the composed text itself. This form of interpretation, which referred to the Torah and the character of the law, is called the halakah in Hebrew. Although the Great Synagogue, known in Greek as the Sanhedrin, is legendary, it was the official body of priests and elders in Jerusalem and the governing organ responsible for the development of the law, beginning with the period of Seleucid sovereignty. Scholars of Scripture (scribes) eventually assumed this task. The Sanhedrin continued until the Roman destruction of Jerusalem in 70 C.E. The profession of the scholars of Scripture (*sopherim*), by contrast, was occupied with the transmission and interpretation of the canon (see Sir 39:1–3). The members of this group eventually received titles of respect, "Rabbi" or "Master," and later developed into specific schools of educated rabbis.

Before the Second Temple was destroyed in 70 C.E., there were different parties and groups in Judaism that may be detected as early as the second century B.C.E. The party of the orthodox, which consisted chiefly of members of the priestly line, was made up of the Sadducees. In opposition to them stood the Pharisees, who were committed especially to careful observance of the prescriptions of the Torah and yet were also open to new ideas, including, for example, belief in resurrection. A third group was the Essenes (Hebrew: the Hasidim or the Pious). Earlier, little more than their name was known, and they are not even mentioned in the New Testament. Now, however, their literature is accessible in the form of original manuscripts discovered at Qumran in 1947. They lived in a community located on the northwestern shore of the Dead Sea from the end of the second century B.C.E.; the Romans destroyed it in 68 C.E. The community was similar to a cloistered settlement. The Essenes had moved from Jerusalem due to the strongly Hellenized and worldly high priesthood that had developed in Jerusalem during the reign of the Hasmoneans. They represented an especially rigorous application of the Torah. Some of them led an ascetic, unmarried existence, but others lived there as members of the sect who were married.

Although the people of Qumran represented an extreme sect, their writings still serve as a unique witness for the methods and content of biblical interpretation in early Judaism. Before the discovery of this community and its texts, one was familiar only with the interpretations of the Torah of the rabbis. Their interpretations were known for the first time in the Mishnah (Hebrew: "teaching") when they were codified toward the end of the second century C.E. These, in turn, were modified by the Gemara (Aramaic *gemar*: "to learn") and edited in the third to the sixth centuries in Eretz Israel and Babylonia in the Talmud (Hebrew: "study"). However, with the Qumran scrolls we have at our disposal documents from as early as the second century B.C.E. In addition to biblical manuscripts, which are significant for understanding the textual history of the Old Testament, there are many fragments of other writings, including especially the commentaries from which we may obtain a direct impression of the rules and methods of early Jewish biblical interpretation. Much is learned from comparing these to the principles of interpretation that go back in rabbinic writings to older traditions, in particular during the turning point of history those associated with the leading schools of Hillel and Shammai. Yet comparisons may also be made with Philo and Josephus, whose history (*Jewish Antiquities*) of the Jewish people, told in a midrashic style, narrates the period from creation to Josephus's day. These comparisons demonstrate that the community of Qumran undertook its exegesis by using views and concepts that were common in early Judaism. However, these presumably were not actually of a Jewish origin but rather went back to the Hellenistic science of interpretation (see below pages 33–40).

In addition to these writers, we find the two essential spheres of rabbinic biblical interpretation also represented in the community of Qumran. One is research in the Torah, the other its actualization, the halakah. We learn about the organization and life of the community of Qumran in the so-called Community Rule (1QS) and the Damascus Document (CD) for the married members of the community. It is debated whether the name of the location Damascus that emerges here means an actual place of residence of this group in Syria or is rather a code name. The entire life of the monastic community on the Dead Sea is oriented to cultic purity and a rigorous fulfillment of all of the commandments of the Torah. To seek God and to do his commandments belong directly together (1QS 1:1–3). The new convert is obligated by the oath of entrance to "return to the law of Moses in accordance with what he has commanded" (1QS 5:3). The community of Qumran is the community of those who "hold fast to the covenant" (1QS 5:3). Membership in the community meant the renunciation of the wicked and the "men of evil," an expression by which the Hasmonean priestly king in Jerusalem and his followers are to be understood, including especially all Jews who did not practice the same severity of rigor (see, e.g., CD 1:1–21). The War Scroll (1QM) in its available form from the Roman period describes in military images, which are to be interpreted metaphorically, the war between the "Sons of Light," that is, the people of Qumran, and the "Sons of Darkness." This fight has already begun as the final event. The awareness prevails in Qumran of living in the end of time. Responsible for the study of the Torah are the priests (1QS 5:9). In each group of ten, there is not to lack at least one who is occupied with this study day and night (1QS 5:9). The last authority for the interpretation of the Torah, however, is the "Teacher of Righteousness" (CD 1:11; 6:7, 11). He is to be seen as the founder of the community, although he was already dead (CD 19:35–20:1). The law is indeed given through Moses (1QS 8:15); however, the teacher, "the instructor," must teach ever anew what is commanded and revealed in the law for the present time to the members of the community (1QS 9:12–26).

Examples of halakah as actual Torah are found in the Damascus Document. Its rigorous character is clear, for example, in the precepts for the Sabbath (CD 10:14–11:18). Thus it is forbidden on the Sabbath to help when a cow is giving birth or to haul it out of a stream or a ditch. If humans fall into a water hole, one is not allowed to come to their aid with a ladder or a stick. An especially interesting example for the halakic interpretation of the Torah concerns the exclusion of a potential spouse. In an argument by analogy to the interdiction mentioned in Lev 18:13 that forbids taking as a wife a sister of the mother, the same is also true for disallowing a man's marrying the daughter of his brother or sister. This is something that is not forbidden in the rabbinic halakah: "While the laws prohibiting incest are written for men, they are also (valid) for women" (CD 5:7–11). In opposing polygamy, allowed in Judaism, Gen 1:28 is cited: "man and woman he has created them," thus appropriately as a pair (CD 4:21). The arguments may be more rigorous than elsewhere in Judaism. However, the method of the argument by analogy is the same, because the entire halakah insists that the gaps in the Torah are to be filled with the occurrence of new cases of analogies to those that are already known.

Besides the interpretation of the Torah, the exegesis of the Prophets plays a special role in Qumran. This is found above all in the more or less fragmentary commentaries that are preserved. According to a fundamental presupposition, the interpretation of the Torah and prophetic exegesis conform to each other: the community of Qumran sees itself existing in the end time. What the Old Testament prophets had revealed and can be read in their writing pertains to the end time and must be interpreted in order to obtain what is meaningful for those now living. In the Habakkuk Commentary (1QpHab) we find proclaimed the essential statement: "And God spoke to Habakkuk that he should write down what will come over the last generation. However, the consummation of this time he has not made known to him" (7:1–2). The prophet himself therefore still did not know what his proclamations should signify. Now in the present they can be interpreted and understood in their true sense. For this purpose has come the "priest, the Teacher of Righteousness, in (whose heart) God has given (insight) in order to explain all the words of his servants the prophets, (through) whom God has proclaimed all things that shall come over his people and his land" (1QpHab 2:8–10). Therefore, the interpreter himself draws on a divinely conferred charisma for interpretation (see Dan 9:2, 22–23).

This kind of interpretation, as one finds it especially in the Habakkuk commentary of Qumran, has been regularly named by the recurring keyword "pesher." The commentary is a verse-for-verse exegesis of the first two chapters of the book of Habakkuk. To begin with, one notes that one section of Scripture is cited at a time. Then follows the remark: "The interpretation (pesher) of the word (or its interpretation) is…." There follows an interpretation relating the word to the present situation of the community of Qumran. For example, "see, then, I am allowing the Chaldeans to arise, that fierce and impetuous nation" (Hab 1:6) is understood to mean the Neo-Babylonians who under King Nebuchadnezzar were the great world power during the climatic period of the sixth century B.C.E. Now follows the interpretation: "Its meaning [pishro] relates to the Kittim, before whom all nations lie in fear and terror" (1QpHab 3:4–5). "Kittim" is again a key word that in the Old Testament means the inhabitants of Cyprus. Presumably in the Qumran Pesher of Habakkuk these are the Romans, for this equation is found also elsewhere. The Romans during this period have begun to reach with their legions into the ancient Near East. However, this document is concerned in its interpretation not as much with global politics as it is with the dispute between the Teacher of Righteousness and his opponents in Jerusalem. Thus, to the well-known assertion of Hab 2:4, "The righteous shall live by his faith," is added: "This interpretation is concerned with all those who practice the law in the house of Judah, whom God will redeem from the house of judgment due to their hardship and their loyalty to the Teacher of Righteousness" (1QpHab 7:17–8:3).

The text of the Bible and interpretation thus continue to stand in combination with each other, for they are tied together in certain key terms in the text (righteous, faith, life). However, the original situation in which the word of the prophet was spoken is consciously passed over. The innerbiblical and religious debate with the people of Jerusalem adjusts the plains of understanding, such as in 1QpHab 9:3–7, where the statement of Hab 2:8 is directed against the Babylonians: "You have plundered many nations, and those that survive of the remaining nations shall plunder you." This is understood in the following way: "This concerns the last priests of Jerusalem, who shall collect wealth and assets from the booty of the peoples." This means, presumably, the raids of the Hasmoneans against small populations of neighboring peoples, with the Romans (Kittim) named as the executors of the punishment. To make a more precise observation, the text and interpretation appear to be related to each other in an often complicated connection according to which a series of techniques known to rabbinic interpretation are used, including the use of other readings of the text, reinterpretation through the altering of vowels, wordplay, and so on.

Examples for exegesis practiced in Qumran are found also outside the usual commentaries, as, for example, the interpretation of the "song of the well" (Num 21:18) in the Damascus Document (CD 6:3–11). Here we find the comparison of the well with the Torah. Those who have dug the well, that is, the nobles and the princes, are equated with the members of the community of the converted, the members of the sect. The "staff" is identified in CD with the lawgiver, the Teacher of Righteousness. Thus, the Hebrew word for *staff* is used with a double meaning. One cannot, however, really call this an allegory, for while in allegory two materially and completely separate levels are placed in parallel to each other, there exists for the exegetes of Qumran a depth of relationships between the key words of the text and interpretation that our own logic certainly cannot comprehend.

The library of Qumran offers also other kinds of evidence for the history of exegesis. A scriptural work of a special form is, for example, the Genesis Apocryphon from Cave 1 (1QapGen). We have in this text partly a literal Aramaic translation of Genesis, thus a targum (Aramaic translation). But for the most part, it is a paraphrase with considerable expansions in the form of a midrash, as we are able to observe in the biblical books of Chronicles (see pp. 15–17 XXXX). Thus, the Genesis Apocryphon contains a partially destroyed but elaborate account of the birth of Noah (Gen 5:28–31), an explanation of the lie Abraham told about Sarai in Egypt (Gen 12:10–20), and the narrative of a dream in which the picture of a cedar and a date palm is imparted to Abraham as he is entering into Egypt, together with a fortunate outcome. A full description of the beauty of Sarai makes it understandable as to why the delegates of Pharaoh and then he were so impressed that he brought her into his harem. However, he (in contrast to the biblical narrative) was not able to touch her because he had fallen ill and knew that only Abraham could heal him with a prayer. Obviously, this text possesses an edifying, legendary character that serves the purposes of both amusement and instruction. Another midrash of Genesis to Exod 12 is the book of Jubilees, which is also called "The Little Genesis," a title by which it is known principally in the Ethiopic and Latin manuscripts. However, more recently fragments of the Hebrew original have been discovered at Qumran. This text covers the period between creation and the exodus in order to identify the precise observance of the Sabbath and festival regulations according to a solar calendar, which also was considered valid in Qumran. The patriarchs appear as ethical exemplars and careful observers of the cultic regulations in the manner of the Priestly document. Different interests of the redactor were able therefore to develop very different adaptations (midrashim) of biblical materials.

For the history of interpretation, it is, after all, remarkable that there has been discovered in Qumran also a small collection of Old Testament instances (testimonies) of the messianic expectations of the community. One reckons with the appearance of the prophet of the end time and the two "anointed" ones: Aaron, the priest; and Israel. In this collection (4QTest), the biblical passages of Deut 5:28–29; 18:18–19; Num 24:24:15–18; Deut 33:8–11; and Josh 6:26 are strung together. This type of testimonies obviously later has been used more frequently in Christian interpretation of the Old Testament. While they facilitate quotations, the verses, however, are torn from their original contexts.

2.3. The Philosophers' Interpretation of Homer and Hesiod

In order adequately to understand the interpretation of Scripture in the first centuries c.e., it is important that the contemporary reader not view the means of understanding and the methods that emerged in an isolated manner. By no means were these limited to the exegesis of the Bible; they were found in other spheres as well. The methods applied by Jews and Christians to their Holy Scriptures had already been highly regarded for a considerable time in the Hellenistic philosophical schools. Someone looking for the first time at an example of Jewish or Christian biblical exegesis of this period may form the impression that this was a completely tendentious practice that approached the text with absurd methods and that the interpreters were reading their own meanings out of it. However, this is not the case. The biblical interpreters only put to use the methods that were generally practiced in their own time. These methods were used to interpret the subject matter of their literary tradition. They did not appear tendentious at all to people at the time of their use. Even if the rules of interpretation in antiquity appear to us foreign and often strange, they still formed a consistent system that had issued out of a long exegetical tradition and were seen by most of their contemporaries as authoritative.

The methodology had already originated several centuries prior to its use by biblical interpreters in the difficulties that the oldest of the Greek philosophers, the pre-Socratics, had with the great works of mythic and epic literature: the poetic writings of Homer (eighth century B.C.E.), the *Iliad* and *Odyssey*; and the *Theogony* of Hesiod (seventh century B.C.E.). Homer belonged to the fundamental treasure used in classical education: children learned to recite his writings, took pleasure in the suspenseful adventures of Odysseus, and marveled at the deeds of the heroes of Troy. In the gymnasium, where citizens sent their sons to reside and study, the *Iliad* and the *Odyssey* were the basic books of instruction. However, on the other hand, the stories in the Homeric epics were highly objectionable to the philosophers, due in part to the fact that Homer presented the gods of Olympus as humans. Already Xenophanes (second half of the sixth century B.C.E.) had made sport in a satire: "If the cattle or horses had hands, if they could paint with these hands…, then the gods would be given the form of horses." Homer and Hesiod were guilty of "having ascribed to the gods those very things that humans condemn: robbery, adultery, and deceit." The philosophers took umbrage at the behavior of the gods in Homer's epics, who not only continued to engage in continuing conflict but also were tendentious in assisting their favorites at the time. Hesiod transmitted what was presumably a pre-Greek myth that related the story of Kronos, who had emasculated his own father (*Theog.* 180–185) and devoured his own children (453–491), and continued then to tell of Zeus obtaining sovereignty and placing his aged father in chains. Hesiod's composition of this and other similarly atrocious events was considered blasphemy. Thus, Pythagoras (active in the middle of the sixth century B.C.E.) narrated that he had seen the soul of Hesiod, chained to a brass pillar, go weeping into the underworld and the soul of Homer hanging from a tree surrounded by snakes. A little later Heraclitus was similarly critical of Homer and Hesiod.

Beside the critics of Homer and Hesiod, there were other philosophers who shared with most other Greeks an ardor for Greek poetry and held in honor classical poetry. They were convinced that there was only an *apparent* antagonism between the epic tradition and their own knowledge. If the readers' own understanding of the truth did not conform to the literal statements in the *Iliad* and the *Odyssey*, then they must discover a meaning to assign them. They provided them a purpose different from that which Homer previously had had in mind. While these writers had wished to entertain their readers, the philosophers sought to discover in their writings rational and moral knowledge. Therefore, we find ourselves standing at the beginning of a pervasive, broadly conceived method called allegory. The presupposition of allegorical interpretation is that the word "signifies something other" than what is said, for it transmits a concealed meaning that possesses a deeper sense. The art of the interpreter consists in correctly bringing to expression that which is actually meant. It would be wrong to accuse the allegorical interpreter of knowingly seeking to read into the text something else than was meant. These interpreters were convinced much more that they were obtaining the well-recognized truths that a text so honored as that of the *Iliad* or the *Odyssey* must have contained. Homer was for them indeed a philosopher. One only needed to know how to read his writings!

The different kinds of allegory with which we are familiar originated out of the most important areas of instruction that were a part of early Greek *paideia*. To these belonged, above all, physics, which dealt with the structure and elements of the world and also included theology, and ethics, which had to do with the rules of human behavior and the moral order.

One of the first persons mentioned to concern himself with the allegorical meaning of Homer was Theagenes of Rhegium (end of the sixth century B.C.E.). Porphyry (third century C.E.) says that Theagenes sought to dispel the charges brought against Homer for having narrated unseemly things about the gods. For Porphyry, this interpreter of Homer made assumptions as to what was intended by the poet's manner of speech. Porphyry argues that there are interpreters like Theagenes, who

> believe that things are spoken allegorically in order to describe the nature of elements, as, for example, those that are expressed in the conflicts between the gods. So, according to their view, moisture wars against drought, warmth against cold, and what is light against what is heavy. Water extinguishes fire; however, fire makes dry the air. Thus, it goes with all elements that comprise the world. A fundamental opposition reigns between them. ... From battles like the ones Homer has described, he gave to fire the names of Apollo, Helios, and Hephaestus, to water the names Poseidon and Scamander, to the moon Artemis, and to the air Hera. (Porphyry, *Quaest. Hom.*, Schrader 240,14–241,7)

Here the physical form of allegory is described, which, read from the depiction of Homer, is a description of the elements of the world and their opposites, corresponding to the model of the explanation of the world in the Ionic philosophy of nature.

This same Theagenes was also credited with the discovery of the psychological form of allegory: "In the same manner, he [Homer] engaged in giving names of deities to the attitudes of the soul: to contemplation he gave the name of Athena, to unreasonableness the name of Ares, to desire that of Aphrodite, to eloquence the name Hermes, all of which were faculties associated with these various deities" (Porphyry, *Quaest. Hom.*, Schrader 241,7–10).

An additional methodological means of assistance that led to these equations was etymology, which was widespread in antiquity. Thus, on this basis, Homer named Zeus, the father of the gods, Zena in the accusative (in a poetic form), since Homer understood by this term the origin of life (*zen* = "life"). He named him Dia (the usual form of the accusative) because through (*dia*) him all things originated. Also, Artemis is called the moon because this body cuts through the air during its journey (*aero-temis*). This type of etymological derivation, which we today assume is a gimmick, was considered to be an art in antiquity and continued to develop in the later philosophical school.

Anaxagoras, who lived in Athens during the fifth century B.C.E. as a contemporary of Pericles, is considered to have presented the first ethical explanation of Homer. He posited the view that virtue and righteousness were Homer's actual themes. The Cynics, among others, who propagated the ideal of a life without need, preferred this manner of reading Homer. The most popular Cynic was Diogenes of Sinope, who lived in a tub (fourth century B.C.E.). The founder of the school, Antisthenes, a student of Socrates and the teacher of Diogenes, considered Heracles and Odysseus to be moral paradigms. By means of an allegorical interpretation, the various adventures of Odysseus were examples demonstrating his moral and intellectual integrity in the sense of Cynic morality. Thus, according to Antisthenes, the hero of the *Odyssey* resisted the seductions of Circe (*Od.* 10.135–574) due to his temperance, while his companions surrendered to their lustful appetites (Circe transformed them into swine; *Od.* 10.237–243). The *wise* Odysseus rejected the treacherous joy of corporeal love offered him by Calypso and chose over the beautiful Nymph his less beautiful but wise wife, Penelope.

Diogenes justified the deed of Medea by means of allegorical explanation. According to the legend (transmitted by Ovid, *Metam.* 7.297–349, among others), Medea, the sorceress who possessed the power to restore the youth of every creature, tricked the daughters of Pelias into bringing their father to a kettle that was supposed to contain a magic brew to render eternal youth, dismembering him, and throwing him into the brew by promising that he would be restored to his youth. For Diogenes,

Medea signified a wise Cynic counselor of health, and the kettle referred to a steam bath and gymnastic exercises that could revive the languishing body and restore its original power.

The physical, psychological, and ethical forms of allegory also had other representatives beginning as early as the sixth century B.C.E. The high esteem in which Homer and Hesiod were held made certain that they were to be mentioned in the teachings of the philosophers. Few opposed this. The most noted was the protest of Plato, who decisively rejected the stories of the gods in Homer as immoral, especially when it came to the instruction of youth. He also considered allegorical interpretation of them to be impossible. Without question, he himself made use of allegory (e.g., in the well-known parable of the cave) when it was necessary to express a deep truth in an indirect manner. In contrast to Plato, his student Aristotle (384–322 B.C.E.) returned to the allegorical interpretation of Homeric exegesis. One example of his allegory from the realm of physics is the explanation of the famous scene of *Il.* 8.18–27, in which Zeus demanded that the other gods engage in a tug of war. He boasted that he could suspend a golden rope from heaven and that, even if all the gods together would pull from the lower end, they could still never succeed in pulling him down to them. Instead, he would pull up to himself all of them, including the entire earth and sea. Then he would fasten so tightly the chain at Olympus that the entire universe would be suspended in space. Aristotle (*Mot. an.* 4.699b32–700a6) found in this episode the allegorical expression of a teaching concerning the first mover, who is found to be immovable beyond the universe that he holds in its movement. Aristotle also was familiar with psychological allegory and interpreted the legend that spoke of Athena, after she had invented the flute and would no longer use it, thus: it is said that the practice of the flute no longer contributes to meditation, "for we credit Athena with science and art" (Aristotle, *Pol.* 6.1341b2–8).

In the Hellenistic period, the allegorical method of interpretation was maintained by the leading philosophical schools and blossomed even more significantly than it had before. It was especially favored in the Stoa. Already in the older Stoa it was widespread, but it became even more developed in the late phase (ca. 20–250 C.E.), as we may determine from our possession of extensive sources relating to it. In this period the philosophy of the Stoa became during the reigns of the Roman caesars a leading worldview. As we are yet to see, Philo in Alexandria became familiar with it by means of his Hellenistic education, and it provided a significant influence on his interpretation of the Bible. The Stoics raised the etymological explanation of names to a higher level. In their school, the realistic (or historical) allegory was developed. The one who originated this type of allegory was Euhemeros (ca. 340–260 B.C.E.), a Sicilian who developed the theory in a fable taking the form of a travel report. All of the gods of Olympus together were deified humans who signified kings and other doers of good deeds from among humanity. These people, following their death, were worshiped as gods. From this point of view, the epics of Homer and Hesiod were the manuals of instruction for the prehistory of humanity that antedates the time of writing and chronicles.

A variant of this view is the interpretation of the well-known geographer Strabo (ca. 63 B.C.E.–20 C.E.). According to his perspective, Plato wanted to provide instruction in his poetry about ancient geography: the myths and the adventures contained in them were only a means by which to shape this instruction in an entertaining fashion. Elsewhere it was in the Stoa that the traditional forms of Homeric allegory continued to be cultivated. An example is the writing of a certain Heraclitus from the first century C.E.: *Homeric Problems Concerning the Form in Which Homer Wrote Allegories Concerning the Gods* (*Quaestiones homericae*). An example of allegory concerning physics is the explanation of the episode where Zeus remembered to punish Hera, an action he soon thereafter carried out against her. When he suspended her in the air between the clouds, two anvils attached to her ankles weighed her down, and her hands were tied with a golden chain (*Il.* 15.18–21).

Heraclitus defended Homer against the charge of impiety with the allegorical explanation (which had already become traditional) that one may see in this legend in reality the four elements that make up the universe: the air at the beginning comes from Zeus above, from which ether as the second element is suspended; the two anvils are water and the earth below, the golden chain is the thin skin that separates ether from the air and resembles gold (*Quaest. hom.* 40). Even more than the physical, Heraclitus is concerned with psychological and moral allegory. One example is the explanation of the two episodes in the *Iliad* (5.330–340, 855–863) in which Diomedes, a hero of Troy, was inflicted with severe wounds by the gods Aphrodite and Heraclitus. Also here, the Stoic defends his idol against the charge of blasphemy. Using the allegorical tradition of the Stoa, he explained that Aphrodite, who was wounded by Diomedes with the support of Athena, describes the unreasonableness of the barbaric warriors who were slain by the Greek fighters in part by means of their intelligence. Ares is the destruction (*aren*) that war brings, while Diomedes represents the war that the barbarians conduct (*Quaest. hom.* 30–31).

The Homeric allegory was also favored by the Neo-Pythagoreans and above all by the Neo-Platonists. The Neo-Platonists used the allegorical method in a particular manner in order to discover their specific teachings in Homer. A writing of the last important Neo-Platonic philosopher, Porphyry (232/233–305), called *The Grotto of the Nymphs* (*De antro nympharum*), provides an example. In this text Porphyry interprets a short section of the *Odyssey* (13.102–112) in which Homer describes a cave on the Island of Ithaca, the homeland of Odysseus. The passage deals with the grotto of the nymphs (Naiads). In the grotto are found tankards, stone amphorae in which bees are housed, and stone weavers' looms with strings of purple material.

For Porphyry, the grotto represents the world, which is filled with darkness. The nymphs (water goddesses) are the souls, which come into the world and receive a body, because they seek moisture. The nymphs, with their purple materials on their stone weaving looms, are therefore the souls, because they weave around their bodies' flesh and bones. Also the bees, which are housed in the amphora, are the souls. The work of the bees is the making of honey, the metaphor of sweetness and pleasures.

The delight of the souls that come into the world is the incarnation (receiving flesh), which leads to fleshly associations whereby new incarnations originate. However, the bees can also symbolize the good souls with their flesh, which possess the desire to try to return to their true home, heaven. According to the exegesis of Porphyry, Homer is a Neo-Platonist. The world-denying teaching of Neo-Platonism, its dualistic interpretation that sees the world as the prison of the soul, and its true purpose to return to its original home are all a result of allegorical interpretation and its essential features that are found in these few verses of Homer.

Thus, the philosophical schools were different united by means of their allegorical interpretations and by making Homer into one of the most prominent witnesses of their concerns. He was a recognized authority by all sides. If one could successfully find one's own worldview in Homer's works, one was especially fortunate in having a decisive demonstration of its truth. Common to all was the presupposition that Homer had meant something different from what the simple wording of his writings indicated. Ever again the interpreters explain that Homer must be defended against his detractors. The wording of his writings was only a covering that transmitted what the true meaning of Homer sought to convey.

Certainly there were also opponents of the allegorical method. In addition to the Epicureans, above all the grammarians of Alexandria should be mentioned: Eratosthenes and Aristarch, who in the third and second centuries, B.C.E., one after the other, headed the famous library in Alexandria and founded the philological-grammatical approach to exegesis. They could not support the process of the allegorical method.

If one is acquainted with the methodological presuppositions of exegesis practiced in antiquity, one will evaluate differently the interpretation of Jews and Christians in this period, even though they contradict the results of valid standards that are present today. The features of biblical exegesis are clearer when seen in the light of this background. Certainly, most important is the realization that Christian interpretation of the Bible proceeded from a historical truth and not from a timeless understanding of reality, as was the original approach of natural philosophy that strongly shaped the system of Greco-Roman philosophy. As we soon shall see, it is above all the method of Christian biblical interpretation that characteristically separates it from pagan, philosophical understanding.

2.4. ALLEGORICAL INTERPRETATION OF SCRIPTURE: PHILO OF ALEXANDRIA

A member of a rich and influential Jewish family, Philo was born around 20 B.C.E. in Alexandria and lived there until his death in the first half of the first century C.E. At an advanced age, he entered public life as the leader of a delegation of Jews from Alexandria who journeyed to Rome to meet the emperor Gaius (Caligula) in the winter of 39/40 C.E. For a long period of time, as a member of the upper class he obviously possessed the luxury of dedicating himself entirely to leisure and study. As may be seen from his writings, he had enjoyed a comprehensive Greek education and was instructed in a most detailed way in the Hellenistic philosophy of his time. By the same token, he was well versed in the Holy Scripture of his community of faith. Some even assume that his commentaries on the Bible originated from presentations in the synagogue, although there is no evidence for this. However, he certainly participated regularly each Sabbath in the interpretations of the Torah.

The interpretation of Genesis received the most space in his commentary on the Pentateuch. A separate commentary treated the stories of the creation and fall in Gen 1–3: *De opificio mundi* (*On the Creation of the World*). This "allegorical commentary" comprises twenty treatises of selected sections of Genesis. Much is obviously lost. Additional writings with biblical themes include the *Life of Moses* (*De vita Mosis*), an interpretation of the Decalogue, as well as four books *On the Special Laws* (*De specialibus legibus*).

There has been a great deal of discussion about the origin of the Philo's interpretive method and whether he understood Hebrew or not. That obviously most likely was not the case. In Hellenistic Judaism, the Septuagint was the text that Philo used; it was also regarded as inspired as the Hebrew original. Some of the methods of interpretation that were practiced in the synagogue are also found in his commentaries. Identified even more strongly, however, are the exegetical principles of Greek philosophy.

During the time of Philo, an impoverished Athens was no longer the center of the philosophical schools. Alexandria, now under Roman dominion, had surpassed it in ranking as the main intellectual city of the Mediterranean region. There Philo could learn to know Platonism first-hand, which, in addition to elements of the system of the Stoa, came to have the strongest influence on him. His dualistic thought, noted in his division between a kingdom of ideas and one of the visible world, which according to the well-known parable of the cave by Plato indicated that things that could be known by the senses were but shadows of the actual nature of things that took up residence in ideas, corresponded to the ethical orientation and philosophical "monotheism" of Philo's fundamental outlook. For Plato, the all-powerful agent who was also the one and the good stands over all ideas. Aristotle speaks, then, of "god." Philo certainly follows no individual school but rather mixes eclectic thoughts of different origins, as was characteristic overall in Hellenistic popular philosophy.

The most penetrating motif for the allegorical interpretation of the Bible is Philo's conviction that the writings of Moses are to be viewed as the witness of the truth. He views Moses as one who corresponds to the Hellenistic outlook, in opposition to the perspective of the rabbis, that Moses was the "lawgiver and writer of the Pentateuch." Philo's view that the Torah is binding corresponds to the conviction of his Jewish contemporaries in the faith. There is not a page in his writings where he does not place value on the literal validity of the commandments in the Pentateuch. However, truth in the actual meaning of the word, which Philo frequently uses, is for Greek thought to be discovered only in a sphere that transcends what may be observed. According to the Platonic system, it is the sphere of ideas that encompasses the actual nature of things, and the highest idea of the good is at the same time the ethical aspect. If the writings of Moses, therefore, contain the truth, they must be interpreted according to that which resides behind the wording of the text in order for the actual meaning of the text to come forth. The wording of the text resides far from the conceptuality of Greek philosophy and appears to address entirely different matters belonging to the world of things that are seen. To bring this true meaning to light, one must make use of allegorical interpretation. In so doing, it is Philo's conviction that Moses is far superior to all philosophers, since God had granted him in his prayer the exhibition of the universe through an impression of the powers of his unobservable being (*Spec.* 1.108). The thesis that the Greeks appropriated their philosophy from Moses found its inception in Philo (see *Mut.* 225).

At first glance, the allegorical interpretation of Scripture as undertaken by Philo appears both arbitrary and strange to the modern reader. Nonetheless, in the context of the traditions of interpretation in which Philo stood, it operates according to clear and recognizable rules. It is a fundamental supposition that expressions such as names and ideas are not explained literally but rather are assigned symbolic meanings. In the sense that is assigned to them, they designate the spiritual world.

One example is the meaning of the snake in paradise, found in Gen 1:1 in the allegorical commentary (*Leg.* 2.71–76). The snake is the incorporation of ruinous sensual pleasure. In essence, Philo asserts: "Sensual pleasure is compared with the snake, for lust is as twisted and variously shaped as the movement of the snake." He then explains how sensual pleasure winds its way through the five senses. The basis of the comparison is therefore a common element that is accorded in equal measure to the symbol (the snake) and the meaning. However, the snake can also still be accorded an entirely different set of other features. When Philo speak subsequently in further biblical passages in which the snake likewise is mentioned, he follows another rule of interpretation known from rabbinic rules: different passages of the Bible may be brought into connection with each other and may interpret one another, if the same key word occurs in them (the rabbinic designation *gezera shawa*). He names, among others, the bronze snake that Moses fashioned in the wilderness (Num 21:8), remarking: "How may healing now result from suffering? By the shaping of another snake that is entirely different from that of Eve, namely, the concept of prudence." The point of comparison is here something different: "With the strong and sturdy bronze, however, the idea of prudence is compared. This is due to the fact that it is resilient and incapable of being cut, because it exists in the beloved of God, and it is valuable and comparable to gold" (*Leg.* 2.79, 81). The same symbol, therefore, is capable of a variety of different types of explanation; however, this is not tendentious. Rather, this occurs according to the association of cited passages. Common to both explanations is the fact that what is symbolically described is a moral attitude.

In addition, explanation of a term, which the Greeks considered the earliest form of exegesis, was a favorite method of Philo's. An example is the explanation of the name *Abram*, which Philo (not at all deviously) thought was transmitted with the meaning "exalted father," while he interpreted *Abraham* as the "elected father of the soul." In the latter case, the name is divided into groups of letters that produced in Hebrew the beginning of a new word. This technique is well known from rabbinic exegesis. In all likelihood, this manner of explanation preceded Philo, since he could hardly have known Hebrew.

In the disputation with the Hellenistic cultural world, it was important to prove that the Bible contained a cosmological knowledge equivalent to that of the Greeks. The symbolic interpretation of the robe of the high priest (Exod 28) provided this meaning in Philo's *Life of Moses* (*Mos.* 2.117–130): "its entirety is a true image, even as its parts are the image of the individual parts of the cosmos" (2.117). Philo begins with the undergarment (*chiton*) of the high priest: it has the colors of hyacinth and is thus a symbol of air. The undergarment reaches unto the feet: this is true also of air, which reaches to the earth. It flows around the entire body, even as air flows around all that is. In the lower border are pomegranates, blossoms, and little bells that are connected to it. "The blossoms are a symbol of the earth, from which everything blooms and sprouts." For the meaning of the pomegranate as a symbol of water, Philo tries an etymology: the Greek word *roiskoi* ("pomegranate") is connected with *rysis* ("to flow"). The little bells are a symbol of the harmony of the elements earth and water. In this case, no special rationale is necessary, for "harmony" is a musical idea. Another sphere of the cosmos is its arrangement, according to ancient perception, into hemispheres (upper- and underworld). For this there is already a model that originated in the Greek interpretation of myth in which the two Dioscurs, Castor and Polydeukes, were interpreted as the description of the hemispheres. Philo knew of this but rejected it. In its place, he searched for a biblical symbol, primarily in the two mythological figures, the cherubim of the holy of holies in the temple (*Cher.* 25–26; *Mos.* 2.98). In the holy of holies, the cherubim stood on both sides of the ark of the covenant as an unmovable center, which described, according to the view common in antiquity, the stationary earth. By contrast, the cherubim have moving wings. The fact that there are two of them points to the number of the hemispheres, while the flapping of their wings indicates the movement of the clouds around the earth. The cherubim also are the sentinels at the entrance to paradise (Gen 3:24), once again the association of a keyword, whose circling, flaming swords describe at the same time this cosmic movement. Another allegory of the hemispheres is the meaning of the two jewels on the shoulder of the garment of the high priest (*Mos.* 2.122–123). This explanation of the two halves of the world contrasts with the other type of meaning, rationally based (see Josephus, *Ant.* 3.1850), that Philo gives to the sun and the moon: "Like the stones that, to wit, consist of two kindred parts: those that are part of the earth and those that are under the earth, and neither of the two possesses the capacity to rise or set as does the moon."

Upon close examination, the methodology standing behind the allegorical explanation is absolutely coherent. Philo takes pains each time to set forth very carefully the evidence that there exists a factual commonality between the symbol, the keyword in the biblical text, and the meaning that comes from the sphere of the ideas, ethics, or cosmology. The methodology of Philo and Aristotle follows the developed model of the so-called *diarese*: the classification of the world of phenomena according to the dialectical principle of the separation from one another of things that are similar and yet still different. The purpose of Plato in following this procedure was to penetrate to the supreme ideas. Through the determination of what is common to two ideas (including, e.g., the world of plants and of animals), one reaches the highest concept under which one may subordinate all related things. In this way, one may respectively ascertain all things that are currently different and determine a separation that allows the recognition of subgroups. There was for Philo the preexistence of the biblical text and the world of ideas. He methodologically arrived at the position that every specific feature possesses a keyword in the text that connects to a preassigned meaning. By recognizing this connection, one may establish the feature's classification. Thus, Philo is able to give a multifaceted, symbolic interpretation to Jacob's dream of the heavenly ladder (Gen 28:12). One is the ladder on which the angels as God's messengers ascend and descend. This describes the air, because its basis is the earth and its top reaches into heaven. However, the ladder is also the symbol of the human soul, "whose foot is virtually earthly and fleshly, while its head is at the same time the heavenly and the purest spirit. The entire ladder, unbroken from top to bottom, represents the words of God" (*Somn.* 1.147).

The image of humanity in Philo corresponds to his dualism that speaks of two parts: the carnal as the lower sphere; and the spiritual sphere of the *nous* (reason), which is the seat of knowledge. This reflects Greek anthropology. However, in distinction to Greek philosophy, humanity is assigned the Word of God as the source of knowledge. For Philo, God is transcendent, as taught in Greek philosophy. On the other hand, Philo's God is the Creator, as is specifically treated in his *On Creation of the World*. While this corresponds to the biblical narrative, it is a strange conception in Greek thought.

In his ethical concepts, Philo conforms closely to the Stoa. The Stoic ethic possesses both a dualistic contrast between good and evil and a catalogue of virtues that are to be acquired. Reason has the ability to allow one to recognize virtues, and the one who recognizes them is also able to do them. Philo closely agrees with these views. For the Stoa, reason is the Logos, and this is identical to God. As such, he rules over the entire cosmos. Philo is also aware of the concept of the Logos; however, for him it is not equated with God but rather is in subjection to him. Certainly the Logos possesses the power of the mediator who is active in the world, radiates within the human soul, and draws one to God. While it is not identified with God, it is also not separate from him. However, the Logos still remains an impersonal entity.

One can see that Philo exerted an enormous influence on early Christianity. Methodologically, he prepared the instrument by which the first Christians could interpret the Old Testament in the sense of salvific events occurring in Jesus Christ. He also considerably shaped the purpose and contents of their interpretation. As a mediator of the Greek spirit in the world of the Bible, he was also able to exert considerable influence on the content of Christian understanding of the Bible in the ancient church.

By contrast, in Judaism Philo is a unique individual. If his writings had not been received and continued to be handed down by Christian admirers, he would have been lost in history, as was the case with many other witnesses to the spirit of antiquity whose names no longer exist. Some are even continued in Armenian Christian translation. Rabbinic Judaism's exegetical method did not remain untouched by the Hellenistic spirit, although its thought was consequently eliminated. Today there are Jewish interpreters who are occupied with the interpretation of Hellenistic Judaism, and we owe to them a great deal. However, this system, on account of its ineffectual effort at unifying Jewish and pagan (Greek) thought, may lead to a dead end. In the history of interpretation, this system stands at the junction of development. The fundamental conundrum is this: How does the transmission of the integration of Western thought and biblical interpretation in altered forms infuse the entire, expansive history of biblical understanding?

3

THE OLD TESTAMENT IN THE NEW

Our portrait of Judaism in the first century B.C.E. has acquired many facets through the results of recent scholarship. Some Jews lived in Palestine under the direct rule of Rome, while others were scattered throughout the entire empire. In either case, Judaism received its unique form as the officially "authorized religion" by means of faith in the God of Israel. This contrast of the Jews with all other peoples and religions preserved their identity. Nevertheless, Judaism still comprised many groups and sects, of which primitive Christianity was only one. Jesus himself was a Jew, something that one notes more strongly today than previously, and his first disciples and the members of the early community were also Jewish. This community took its earliest form after Easter in Jerusalem. For these Jewish Christians, the canonical books of the Old Testament were quite obviously sacred Scripture to which they looked in their early proclamation, the gospel, and gave their new interpretation. It is certainly anachronistic to speak of these books as the Old Testament during this early period, for this expression achieves its meaning only as a corpus that contrasts with the New Testament. It is the New Testament, that is, the collection of the writings of the apostles, that later became the second part of the Christian canon. Thus, the primitive community in Jerusalem remained primarily still bound to the temple and enlisted followers among Jews and proselytes who were non-Jews and thus had linked themselves to Judaism.

When Paul undertook the mission to the Gentiles, Christianity began to move beyond the land of its birth. However, it still did not abandon the validity of the Old Testament. One ought not to posit the view of opposition between Jewish Christians and pagan Christians as absolute. As we have already seen, the Hellenistic culture did not fail to take root in Palestine, although there were various efforts devoted to repelling its religious, cultural, and political influence. In addition to the Aramaic dialects of the population and the Hebrew used by the rabbis above all in the synagogue, the Greek language was also widely used among the Jewish population. Thus, the Bible was used in several different languages: Hebrew for liturgical readings in the synagogue, followed by an Aramaic translation (Targum), as well as a Greek rendition based on the Septuagint or one of the related texts that was considered not to have the authority of the original. The primitive Christian mission among the Jews was able to proceed with an uncontested authority of the Bible. This mission sought to show that the proclamation of Jesus as the Christ, who was the Messiah expected by the Jews, took place according to the Scriptures. This message corresponded to the witness of the Bible (John 5:39). This demonstration in no way was limited to serve apologetic purposes, as was recognized in the adoption of the Old Testament as sacred Scripture by the pagan Christian communities. The Old Testament was unknown outside of Judaism or at most was not considered to be sacred Scripture. The conversion of the non-Jews to the Christian faith signified at the same time the appropriation of the Old Testament as authoritative. This was not, however, always uncontested, as one sees, for example, in the gnostics and above all Marcion. Finally, the Old Testament still came to be regarded as sacred Scripture in the entire Christian church.

If one wishes to understand the association of the New Testament with the witness of the Old Testament in regard to its theological association, one must take into consideration the principles of interpretation that generally were current in Hellenistic Judaism. The writers of primitive Christianity who produced the texts that were collected to form the New Testament cited the Bible according to methodological rules common to their environment. It is not astonishing that we discover these in the New Testament. The question of the legitimacy of understanding Scripture according to historical criticism for contemporary theology must continue to be debated, but this does not mean that we are to recognize the methodology and its consequent meanings that were articulated as the only valid interpretation. Indeed, even conservative interpreters do not do this. Rather, the question is whether the claim made by Christian faith, that it is based on the Old Testament as sacred Scripture, was and is true for today.

Now one must certainly add that the manner of the Old Testament's appropriation by the New is by no means uniform, for the New Testament comprises a rather broad spectrum. In addition to the multiple traditions held in common by the Synoptic Gospels of Matthew, Mark, and Luke, which build upon and order them in different ways, there is also the uniqueness of the Gospel of John, shaped by both its own traditions and its heavily theological interpretation. In addition, the corpus of letters comprises the authentic correspondence of Paul, the epistles or letters of teaching produced by his followers, and additional letters. To these is added the Apocalypse of John as a New Testament example of a text that appropriates an early Jewish literary form. Thus, the diversity of the New Testament writings presupposes a similar variety in the Old Testament. There is only one thing on which all the New Testament writings concur: they interpret the Old Testament to point to the act of God occurring in Jesus of Nazareth. Unstated, likely because it was never questioned until Marcion, was the presupposition that the same Christian God speaks in the Old Testament. This God is the one whom Christians worship and the one who is believed by them to be the father of Jesus Christ.

3.1. The Kingdom of God Has Drawn Near: Jesus Christ

There is no doubt that the earthly Jesus, due to his belonging to the Jewish people and to the education he enjoyed in the home of his Jewish parents, regarded the Old Testament as his Bible. However, it is more difficult to answer the question about the manner in which he resorted to this text in his proclamation and how he cited and explained it. It is due to the difficulty inherent in methodology that this question, in the approximately two hundred years since it was raised, has not become less complex. We know of the words and deeds of Jesus only by means of the tradition that is contained in the Gospels. The Gospel of John is already far removed chronologically and transformed theologically in its own particular way from the original life situation of Jesus. That leaves only the Synoptic Gospels as the bearers of this tradition. The complicated process of the course of this tradition is never made clear in these texts. Even so, these three Gospels have in common so much material that it is possible to compare the different formulations and recognize very clearly the alterations that each has made in the previously existing pieces of tradition. This is true even for Mark, whose work preceded the other two Gospels and was used by them. This view of Markan priority is accepted by most scholars. If one assumes that this first Gospel was shaped shortly before 70 c.e. (the destruction of the Second Temple), then there would be an entire generation that separated the activity of Jesus prior to the time its author wrote. The other two Gospels, Matthew and Luke, used, in addition to Mark, at least a comprehensive collection of the sayings of Jesus (Sayings Source = Q). One is able to deduce from these two Gospels the sayings they hold in common. Even if this collection were found in written form, we would not have the words of Jesus himself but rather a tradition often modified and to which many things would have been added. This tradition would already have been shaped to correspond to the needs of the post-Easter community. To what extent this tradition would maintain Jesus' original words varies widely in scholarly perspectives. In any case, these words could not have been Jesus' original ones, for he obviously would have spoken Aramaic in conformity with his social environment.

For a long time scholars have held to the principle of dissimilarity. That is, to determine the expressions of Jesus, they must be so distinctive and unique that one is not able to find any previously existing exemplar in either the Jewish or the Hellenistic environment. This would lead, then, to the original basis of the Jesus sayings. Even this premise, however, has its limits. One must also accept the position that Jesus, due to his origins and education, thought in Jewish concepts and uttered expressions that the masses of the Jewish population as well as his Jewish disciples could have understood. It is understandable that scholars of Jesus, including those who are themselves Jewish, stress especially Jesus' Jewish identity. Even so, Jesus would have to have set forth a new, incomparable message that would have placed in question all previous attestations. His demeanor thus would have led to conflict with the Jewish authorities, which finally ended in his condemnation by the highest Jewish court (the Sanhedrin) due to blasphemy and in his execution by the Romans. He occasioned this demand through his acts and preaching from the background of the Old Testament and Jewish tradition.

It should be noted that Jesus did not stand in direct confrontation with the Old Testament. In the decisive points, we also see that he did not oppose the early Jewish understanding, especially that of the Pharisees in terms of their attitude toward the Torah. However, the priestly party in Jerusalem, the Sadducees, presumably did become his main opponents in the last phase of his ministry. His message unfolded in dialogue with his conversation partners who shared a common tradition. What he had to say that was new, however, was an innovative interpretation of a tradition that derived from the Old Testament and was legitimated by the Bible.

Modern criticism largely agrees that the announcement of the approaching kingdom of God, which was directly related to Jesus' appearance, formed the center of his preaching. In respect to this, the summary in Mark 1:15 indicates that the Evangelist already interpreted this expression in Jesus' proclamation as the message of the good news (*euangelion*) that was the appropriate rendition in which all of Jesus' works could be concentrated. God's sovereignty was to be fully realized in the immediate future. Indeed, this rule already had broken into reality. To stress this, Jesus presented to his hearers the parables of the kingdom (we find two beautiful examples in Mark 4:26–29 and 30–32) and represented this in his miraculous healings and forgiveness of sins by means of his all-powerful word (Matt 9:2 par.). The poor would participate in this forgiveness (Luke 6:20), and he required all who would follow him to act as though they belonged to this social group. We can imagine him as a wandering preacher moving from place to place in order to disseminate the message of the reign of God and to gather a band of disciples who would represent a revitalized people of God.

With the word of the reign of God, Jesus took an already widespread concept in the Old Testament that originally stemmed from the Zion theology of Jerusalem. In succeeding the Canaanite El, Yahweh was declared to be the one sitting enthroned on Zion as Lord of the entire world and King over Israel (see above all the so-called enthronement psalms of Yahweh: Pss 47; 86–99; among these, Ps 93 appears to be especially ancient). However, in the postexilic period this concept had already been changed. On the one hand, Yahweh's sphere of power was extended to become worldwide in the message of Second Isaiah; on the other, it spoke of the lordship of God as King of Israel (Isa 44:6; see also 41:21; 43:15), in particular in his care for his people (see Isa 43:14–15; 44:6, 52:7–12). In the later prophetic writings, the disappointment of many unfulfilled expectations led to a movement in the direction of a future hope in which the unlimited rule of God would be realized during the end time, which was fervently expected to break soon into reality. We see this in Isa 33, the Isaiah Apocalypse in Isa 24–27, the late section of Zech 14:6–11, and the book of Daniel (2:44; 7:14, 18, 27). The in-breaking of this reign would be introduced by a final judgment (Dan 7:9–14) in which the foreign powers would be destroyed and the reign of the world passed over to Israel. These ideas are similar in the apocalypses not taken up into the Old Testament canon. However, John the Baptist was at home with the idea of a final judgment, as may be seen in his call for repentance due to the final judgment being at hand. This is true even if he did not use the concept of the "reign of heaven," comparable to the "rule of God" (the Evangelist speaks in Matt 3:2).

On the one hand, Jesus addressed the expectations that were broadly shared among his people: he proclaimed the imminent in-breaking of God's sovereignty. The second request in the Lord's Prayer is directed to the kingdom's imminent coming. The statement in Mark 9:1 and its parallels, which possibly goes back to Jesus himself, deals with the in-breaking taking place in the lifetime of those who were present. The image of the leaven (Luke 9:13, 20–21/Matt 13:33) shows that the reign of God is still concealed but is active already in the present in the word of Jesus. As Jesus shows in the parable of the wicked servant (original form in Matt 18:23–30), the expectation of the final judgment is connected to the reign of God. Here the hearer confronts the unimaginable grace of God that leads to the forgiveness of sin. Accordingly, humans are then to act in a similar fashion (18:28–30). Jesus associates the coming of God's reign with his omnipotence, which is an aspect of his character. Whoever wishes to enter into the reign of God must decide for himself or herself, unconditionally and with all its consequences (Mark 10:15; Luke 12:31/ Matt 6:33). In the acts of Jesus and in the encounter with him, the reign of God is already present (Matt 12:28/Luke 11:20; 17:20–21).

Jesus primarily and principally presupposed the authority of the Torah, although the declarations in Matt 5:17–20 that serve as an introduction to the antitheses of the Sermon on the Mount were first formulated by Matthew and describe a Jewish-Christian program. Jesus never developed a theory about the Torah, as did Paul. Jesus contrasted the unconditional claim of his authority over against the Torah (Matt 5:21–22, 27–28). He placed himself in opposition to the commandments of the Decalogue (the fifth and sixth commandments), for his authority surpassed them. Here he opposes the implementation of the act of murder and adultery with an act that was considered to be harmless, that is, anger against the brother or covetous desire in the look at a woman. These acts expose an inner disposition that reveals a fundamental contradiction between the commandment and the actual intent of the commandment. Used in a positive way, the commandment expands universally into unconditional love of one's enemy, something the Torah had limited to Israel (Luke 6:27–28). The intention of God's will is fulfilled fully in the love of neighbor, which now is expanded to include all those who wish to become the citizens of the in-breaking kingdom of God. This is, however, not a demand that comes externally but rather is connected with the reception of the sovereignty of God as a gift of salvation. This is shown in the beatitude maintained in its original form in Luke 6:20–21: those who at present are poor and oppressed receive the promise of the rule of God. Those who are so blessed with this gift will be able to do the will of God. Jesus radicalizes the commandment of divorce, which Paul already knew as a "word of the Lord" (1 Cor 7:10), that is present in the Old Testament precursor in Deut 24:1 (Luke 16:18/Matt 5:32; see also the instruction of the community in Mark 10:2–12).

This authority is made clear in two places in which Jesus has the right to override the prescriptions of the Torah. The first one occurs when he calls followers to become his disciples. In opposition to the Torah's emphasis on maintaining strong natural bonds, Jesus requires his disciples under the current circumstances to break with their own families (Luke 4:26), something that he himself was willing to do (Mark 3:31–35; see also 3:21). Especially striking is the commandment to one who wants to be a disciple but wishes first to comply with the commandment of piety toward his dead father (Matt 8:21–22). The second one is transmitted particularly in the many conflicts with the opponents in connection to the Sabbath prescriptions. The Sabbath had achieved an especially high level of significance in the postexilic and intertestamental periods, even if the rabbis had attenuated the commandments that were authoritative in Qumran (CD 10:14–11:17) to help animals and humans in situations of emergency when their lives were in danger. All the same, the Sabbath has its prescriptions for Judaism even today, especially within Orthodox circles, because it is grounded in creation, according to Gen 2:1–4a, thus providing it with an especially important order. Indeed, according to the book of Jubilees (2:17–33), even God observed the Sabbath. In the Gospels, there is by contrast much more discussion about healings that Jesus knowingly performed on the Sabbath (see Mark 3:1–5 par.; Luke 13:10–17; 14:1–6; John 5:1–18; 9:1–41).

Here as well as in an action such as the plucking of heads of sheaves on the Sabbath (Mark 2:23–28), considered to be a violation of the prohibition against harvesting, Jesus expressed his messianic authority, which placed him outside of the regulations that were mandatory for others. The justification offered in this situation, in which Jesus invokes in a very deliberate explanation the Old Testament narrative of 1 Sam 21:2–10, appeals to David, who, in fleeing from Saul, together with his people ate the sacred showbread in the temple of Nob. This makes clear that Jesus regarded himself as a David *redivivus* and raises anew his messianic claims.

The question concerning Jesus' self-understanding of his role and mission is very difficult to answer, due to the fact that the theology of the community, on the basis of the resurrected Christ, later accumulated many titles for him. In any case, it appears rather certain that Jesus himself attributed to his identity key statements in the Old Testament in order to gain legitimacy. Of the places in the book of Isaiah, several appear in Isa 61:1–2 in a discussion concerning the announcement of joy. The joyous news is sent to the poor, and the proclamation of the freeing of the prisoners is made. This text also plays a role in Qumran, where often it is combined with Isa 52:7, which belonged to the recognized prooftexts in Judaism of that period. In the Jesus tradition, the passage often stands in the background. Thus, in the first beatitude beginning in Luke 6:20 (Matt 5:13), in the blessing of the poor, to whom are promised the kingdom of God, and in the message to John the Baptist (Matt 11:2–6 par.), when Jesus points to the phenomena accompanying his coming, he is identified as the one who has come (the Messiah). In the case of Luke, in the scene in Nazareth where Luke places Jesus' inaugural sermon (Luke 4:16–30), Jesus is presented as taking in his hand the scroll of Isaiah. Luke has added this to the parallel pericope in Mark 6:1–6, which does not mention a biblical text by name. However, it is obvious that Luke has reached back to an authentic word of Jesus. If the present form of the citation does go back to Jesus, one would be able to observe in it the contemporary manner of citation. The Lukan version eliminates the conclusion that contains the "day of wrath" of God announced against the enemies of Israel and instead inserts a passage from Isa 58:6. We find scriptural adaptations like this already at Qumran. This indicates that this belongs to the customary methods of the use of Scripture at that time. In the continuation of the Lukan pericope into verses 25–27, there is an indication of the insertion of the narratives in 1 Kgs 17 and 2 Kgs 5 about Elijah and Elisha and their gifts of salvation to two foreigners: the widow of Zarephath and the Syrian Naaman. These references by Jesus were intended to provide him the basis for proclaiming the gospel to the pagan world after his rebuff. This is likely already spoken by Luke from his situation, for Jesus himself limited his works with few exceptions to Israel. Nevertheless, it is possible that the combination of the citation, if it does go back to Jesus himself, is to be understood as the announcement of judgment from the mouth of Jesus against his own people, according to the manner of the Old Testament prophets. If Israel casts aside the salvation offered, it will pass over to the pagans. Jesus demonstrates already in his own behavior his opposition to the exclusivity of the Pharisaic expectation concerning salvation, which was limited to Torah piety. His socializing and above all his sharing of meals with tax collectors and sinners reflect the action of a God who places no moral preconditions upon his granting of salvation.

It has been debated for a long time whether Jesus designated himself as the coming "Son of Man," an apocalyptic expectation contained in Dan 7:13. Many problems plague this issue. There is neither an earlier Old Testament example nor any parallels for the heavenly form of the one who "is like unto a Son of Man" mentioned in Dan 7:13. The phrase does occur in the figurative speeches of the book of Enoch that is preserved completely only in Ethiopic. The dating of this book is not certain, since the Aramaic fragments of the part preserved in Qumran do not contain these speeches. It is not clear whether a presumed Aramaic original would have been the text that stands behind the Greek translation of "the Son of Man." Finally, there is the interpretation that the phrase simply signifies "man" and therefore would have no special title in view. Perhaps this would simply have been a circumlocution of "self."

There are words of Jesus that, at least at first glance, distinguish between Jesus himself and a "Son of Man" whose coming is first to occur at the end of time. Is such a distinction conceivable in the mouth of Jesus, and how are we to identify this form? With the proviso of offering a personal opinion not shared generally by others, one is able to say that it is possible that even the last-mentioned words could have gone back to Jesus. It is obvious that during his earthly life Jesus spoke of himself and his mission only in a veiled manner. To this end, his manner of speech would have left open any identification of himself with the "Son of Man" of Dan 7:13, who was expected to appear on the occasion of the final judgment. Thus, in this way he would allow his audience to confess through the expression of their faith that he is the "Son of Man." These types of statements are present in Luke 12:8–9 (see Mark 8:38), probably from the mouth of Jesus in Matt 19:28, and above all in Jesus' answer in his interrogation by the high priest Caiaphas in Mark 14:62. Even in the dramatic depiction of this interrogation, it becomes clear that Jesus made a judgment impossible as long as he could. This did not occur until Caiaphas asked him directly if he was the Christ (Messiah). This forced him to confess: "I am he." To that Jesus added an unmistakable citation from Dan 7:13 by which he explained the judgment of condemnation that is to come. In the imminent final judgment, the "Son of Man" will appear in the clouds seated on the right hand of God ("the power"; see Matt 25:31–46) and by implication will condemn Jesus' earthly judge. Thus, there is no one but Jesus to whom this text in Daniel may apply, indicating that he is the "Son of Man."

At this point the high priest tore his official robe and found it necessary to find Jesus guilty without even bringing witnesses against him. According to recent study, even this description corresponds to historical reality. It corresponds to the legal and political conditions prevailing at the time of the Roman rule in Palestine before 70 C.E. and to the limited degree of authority of priestly jurisdiction that forbade the high priest to address matters other than religious cases. The actual occasion leading to

Jesus' arrest was presumably his purification of the temple (Mark 11:15–16), which had made known his messianic claim over the temple. At the basis of this action, Jesus began by citing a question from Isa 56:7 and concluded with the word of Jeremiah in Jer 7:11 (which follows a prophetic threat against the temple). Here we see Jesus decisively grouped with the Old Testament prophets.

Finally, it must be mentioned that Jesus obviously understood his journey as a passion, according to the example of the Old Testament's righteous sufferers. My view is contrary to the widespread opinion that attributes this perception to the post-Easter community, who incorporated it into their theological themes. The saying about the "Son of Man" from Dan 7, which is bound to the concept of the substitution of a single person "for the many" and the reality of the effect of his life for them that is found in Isa 43:3–4 and 53:10–12, is found in the probably authentic saying of Jesus in Mark 10:45. In close proximity to this is the pericope of the evening meal of the Passover in the same Gospel (Mark 14:22–25, a text recently regarded to a greater extent as historical). This is especially the case with Jesus' explanatory word regarding the wine as the "blood of the covenant," which obviously reflects Exod 24:8. The blood that Moses sprinkled on the people for the removal of sins corresponded to the removal of the sins of the new people of God, for which his substitutionary death served. In this way, Jesus gained for sinners a new meaning: even to those cast out of the community of their people, a way was offered for their return and reincorporation into the status of the righteous.

On the basis of the Aramaic transmission of the words, it is as good as certain that Jesus himself uttered the prayer of the beginning of Ps 23 (Mark 15:34 par.); there is recognizable in this instance an appropriation of the Old Testament example of righteous sufferers. However, later the references to Ps 22 were added by the Evangelists to expand their versions of the passion story.

On the whole, we are able to say about Jesus' message that he understood himself to be the messenger who announced God's eschatological rule and sought to bring it about through his authoritative actions. Even if it is granted that he himself confessed that he was the Messiah, he did not interpret himself as this figure in the normally expected ways. If he himself explained what the "kingdom of God" meant, then he interpreted it differently than the usual expectation of the eschatological judgment. Indeed, he did not set aside conceptions about the coming judgment of God, but he did, however, think this expectation encompassed the certainty that God's goodness is far greater than his wrath and that he is prepared to absolve even the greatest sinner of his or her guilt (Matt 18:23–24). He understood his own way of the cross at the end of his life as a substitutionary suffering for sins that would open the gate to God's reign for both the righteous and the sinners who repented. With his self-understanding and in his preaching of the kingdom of God, Jesus acted on the assumption of the expectation shared with his contemporaries that the announcements of the Old Testament prophets concerning the end time would have been fulfilled. Like the people of Qumran, he also saw that the end time had drawn near; however, he related the prophetic message to himself.

3.2. Primitive Christian Explanations of the Christ-Event

The primitive community began early on to explain the Jesus-event by reference to the Scriptures. We find traces of the oldest post-Easter tradition in the authentic letters of Paul, which describe the oldest literary witnesses that have survived from the early church (these originated 50–60 C.E.). Here we mention only a few examples. In 1 Cor 15:3–5 Paul cites an early Christian confession that he expressly designates as having been received by him: "that Christ died for our sins according to the Scriptures, that he was buried, that he was resurrected on the third day according to the Scriptures, and that he appeared to Cephas [Peter] and then to the twelve." It is striking that the confession consists of two parts: the death of Christ for sins and his resurrection are the actual themes of the confession, which now is supported by additional witnesses to the burial and the appearances of the resurrected one; above all, however, these events are designated as "according to the Scriptures." That this statement is presented in such an all-inclusive manner has caused interpreters many problems. Direct scriptural citations cannot be demonstrated. In the first case, one thinks of Isa 53. As noted in the previous section, this text could probably be connected to Jesus' own understanding. The second remark primarily reflects Hos 6:2, for additional cases are lacking. Also, the negative evaluation of the statement contained in its original context is not considered. It is the case that Isa 53 definitely has spoken of God's exaltation of the "servant of the Lord," which is connected to his suffering. The resurrection of Jesus signifies a fulfillment that surpasses his promise. If the reference of the scriptural text should be directed not to the period "on the third day" but rather to the resurrection itself, then there are a series of texts that may be cited. Still, it is obvious in both cases that the Scriptures are mentioned in the plural. Thus no individual passage is intended; rather, the entire Old Testament canon is called on to serve as a witness for the death and resurrection of Jesus. Accordingly, a decisive gate has been opened: the young church is determined not to leave behind to Judaism the sacred Scriptures that they have adopted; rather, Christians are to interpret them according to their own understanding to be a witness to the Christ-event.

This is confirmed by the introduction to Romans, in which Paul introduces himself as set apart to be an apostle and the proclaimer of the gospel of God, which God had announced beforehand through his prophets in the sacred Scriptures (Rom 1:2). Here shines through the original reference of the word *gospel*, the early message, that is, the joyous message of Isa 61:1–2. It is probable that Paul reached back to Jesus' own message. Accordingly, once more he appears to have directed the use of the entirety of Old Testament prophecy to Jesus Christ. The plural form "sacred Scriptures" is intended to be understood as a single form in Paul. Presumably he readily cites for this reason a primitive Christian formulation that he has acquired. The one found in Rom 1:3–4 appears to be completely incorporated. It is worth noting that the formula for the resurrected one applied to the powerful position of the Son of God stresses the sonship of David. It is for this reason that the grandeur of the earthly Jesus as the Messiah is accentuated so frequently.

An additional piece of primitive Christian tradition is found in Rom 3:25–26a. As most recent interpretation has recognized, the central saying of this confession, which is conveyed in the translation of Luther with the expression "sin offering" (Greek *hilasterion*), probably is to be taken according to the usual Septuagint translation as the "cover of the ark of the covenant" (in the temple). For this reason, the statement is related concretely to the "great Day of Atonement" in Lev 16. This text, well known by all Jews (including proselytes), says in 16:2 that the cover of the ark of the covenant was the place where God would appear on the Day of Atonement. It is there that the high priest (Aaron) was to sprinkle the blood of the sacrificed bull (16:14). If Jesus Christ is compared to the cover of the ark of the covenant, then it should be said that he is the one whose death (blood) leads to the removal of sin. This is an action that earlier had been performed by the high priest in the temple's holy of holies and that took place along with the forgiveness of sins that is grounded in the patience of God. The significance of the conception of sin emerges once again in the primitive Christian community's understanding of Jesus' death. The relationship to the priesthood and the temple is removed, something that we encounter later and more expressly in the Letter to the Hebrews. The removal of sin through Jesus' death on the cross once and for all is in contrast to the annual ritual of the sprinkling of blood repeated on the Day of Atonement. That the primitive community saw some traditionally understood messianic passages fulfilled in Jesus may be concluded from the manner of their acceptance by Paul. Thus, Paul cites in Rom 15:12 what was generally confessed in the announcement of Isa 11:10, which was obviously already used before him. It is similarly the case in Rom 11:26–27 and Isa 59:20–21a, as well as Rom 9:33 (1 Pet 2:6) and Isa 28:16. The first Christians considered it self-evident that these texts could refer only to Jesus.

Paul cited in its entirety an early Christian hymn found in Phil 2:6–11, a text filled with Old Testament reminiscences. In the major cadence of 2:6–8 is reflected, if not in words at least in the process and many other features, the song of the Servant of God in Isa 53. Jesus is the Servant who by his own will humbled himself and followed obediently the way to death on the cross. The affirmation that God therefore exalted him and gave him a unique place of honor (2:9) also connects the hymn to Isa 53. In the concluding statements in 2:10–11, by contrast, the tradition of the kingship of God comes into consideration. Especially Isa 45:23 is cited from the passage in Isa 45:22–24a, which in Second Isaiah often is combined with the kingship of God. This indicates that the acknowledgement of the kingship of the God of Israel is made by all the nations who will have a part in salvation (see also, e.g., Isa 40:5; 52:10; Pss 22:28–29; 86:9). Although this concept is not directly cited, Old Testament scholars infer its existence from the context of the citation. It is a revolutionary idea to transfer the motif of the kingship of God to Jesus Christ, who here appears as the ruler of the world (*kyrios*, i.e., Lord, is the rendering of the name Yahweh in the Septuagint).

As a matter of fact, the use of Ps 22 in this text is paralleled in the passion story in the Synoptic Gospels. At the same time, the question must remain open as to whether there already existed a written version of the passion history before the production of the Gospel of Mark or whether it was composed first by the oldest of the Evangelists. Matthew and Luke continued to develop the composition in Mark, while John in part was based on a different tradition.

Psalm 22 is cited three times in Mark. The most important of these is the statement that is rendered in Aramaic (together with a Greek translation) that Jesus makes on the cross: "My God, my God, why have you forsaken me?" Not only does the tradition preserve the wording in the native language of Jesus (in the parallel text in Matt 27:46, the statement already has been Hebraicized), so also is the mistake in hearing made by the bystanders, recounted in Mark 15:35–36, which authenticates the reliability of the tradition. Further, the prayer of Jesus conforms to one that is offered by a righteous sufferer, a point that we can accept as authentic. The fact that the later Evangelists, Luke and John, replace these words on the cross with others demonstrates that they no longer understood their original significance. Psalm 22 is an individual lament that concludes with an individual thanksgiving (22:23–24). Like all other prayer formulas in the Psalter, this psalm is fundamentally defined by its ability to be used time and again by all those who pray, after they have fallen into a situation of need (lament) and are rescued (thanksgiving). From the point of view of the Old Testament, this expression on the lips of Jesus would be falsely understood, if it were interpreted as an expression of hopeless despondency. Rather, this statement expresses much more Jesus as the righteous sufferer who in his hour of death expressed the beginning of this psalm, which led into what follows. Thus, Jesus is likened to every righteous sufferer who in every kind of need, including the most trying circumstance of the threat of death, clings to God and trusts in his propinquity.

In the passion story in Mark, elements of Ps 22 occur two additional times. On both occasions the psalm is changed into narrative in order that details in the course of events may be described by analogy to the full measure of the psalm. In Mark 15:24, when the Roman soldiers divide Jesus' clothing, they do so according to the statement of the casting of lots in Ps 22:19. The mocking of those who walk past the cross in Mark 15:36 takes up a motif from Ps 69:21. This psalm also belongs to the psalms of the righteous sufferer. The purpose of their actions is not to produce a good result with the ending of the suffering but rather represents an attempt to extend the life of Jesus in order to see if the prophet Elijah might still come to his aid. This, of course, is due to the misunderstanding of Jesus' cry for help. Reflections of Ps 41:10 in Mark 14:18 and the refrain of the twofold psalm of 42/43 in Mark 14:34 likewise point to psalms that belong to the circle of those that have the topos of the righteous sufferer. This, the oldest form of the passion story, which we have in Mark, is saturated with echoes of the Old Testament Psalter. In the manner of biblical narrative art, a central theological statement is made: in Jesus Christ, the way of the pious one who prays obtains its goal. His questioning of God finds an answer, and his hope in the help of God is fulfilled, for Jesus exemplifies the way of perfect, patient obedience to the end that reaches its finality in death (see Phil 2:8). He is the example for all humans. By means of his resurrection, God has opened the door to life for all.

3.3. The Scripture Is Written "for Our Sake": Paul

Approximately ninety citations from the Old Testament are found in the authentic letters of Paul (Romans, 1 and 2 Corinthians, Galatians, Philippians, 1 Thessalonians, and Philemon). One can discern from this number of citations what a significant role the Tanak (Old Testament) played for Paul in substantiating and supporting his arguments. The citations are certainly distributed unevenly among these texts: 1 Thessalonians, Philippians, and Philemon contain no citation whatsoever; by contrast, some two-thirds of all the citations are found only in the Letter to the Romans. In addition to the possibility that a variety of different scrolls with biblical texts were used (since all texts had to be written by hand and all manuscripts of the Bible were placed on costly material), one should also consider the role that the development in Paul's thinking played. The Letter to the Romans, his most mature work, which originated not long before his martyrdom in Rome, can be considered to be his "testament." It summarizes many of the themes of his earlier letters. As a student of the famous Gamaliel (Acts 22:3), Paul enjoyed the education of the interpreter of Scripture. According to the witness of his letters, one may observe that, step by step, he developed in Romans the high-water mark of his knowledge of the Bible. It is also noticeable that Paul preferred some Old Testament books (Isaiah, Psalms, Genesis, Deuteronomy, the Minor Prophets) to others and gave no attention to Jeremiah, Ezekiel, and Daniel. He followed the practice of citation customary for the Judaism of his day. However, Paul passed over historical books that were important in Judaism. The tradition of Israel's history played, quite obviously, no role in Paul's thinking.

In addition, one is able to observe that Paul avoided Scripture in ways that are rather discrete. The early Christian confession transmitted to him affirmed that Jesus is the Christ: the Messiah expected by Israel. This confession was indeed presupposed by him (see especially Rom 1:2–4), and he notes that the death and resurrection of Jesus was according to the Scriptures. However, he did not attempt to demonstrate the truth of this confession simply by means of his own argumentation supported with citations from the Bible. Since he had entirely discrete theological concerns in view of the background of the tradition entrusted to all Christians, his reaching back to the Scriptures served him above all in basing the reception of his letters upon the indisputable authority of the Bible. This was especially important in his disputations with his opponents. Paul held in common with those with whom he communicated, from both contemporary Judaism and the early Christian communities, the position that the Scriptures were undeniably directed to the present period. Twice (1 Cor 9:10; Rom 4:23–24) Paul expressly remarked that a word of Scripture was written "for our sake" and established thereby his own interpretation. Or he could say that the Scriptures were written for present "instruction" (Rom 15:4) or "exhortation" (1 Cor10:11). The word of the Scriptures was addressed, not to the past, but rather to the contemporary hearer.

Elements of the interpretive methods that Paul held in common with his contemporaries as well as his differences with them point to some especially distinctive features of Paul's understanding of Scripture. The fundamental view already mentioned, that each word of the Bible was to be understood as directed to the present, has the consequence that citations from the Old Testament, independent of their original context, were handled in part as though they were building blocks of interpretation. For example, several citations could be combined, a technique also in evidence at Qumran. Many times Paul dealt with two closely related statements. This is the case, for example, in Rom 9:25–26 where he combines Hos 2:25bc and 2:1b to explain that the expression "not my people" refers to the calling of the Gentiles to become the people of God. Another example is found in Rom 11:26–27, where Paul combines Isa 59:20–21 with Isa 27:9. He interprets both passages as indicating that "Jacob's" godlessness was to be set aside. Paul expected, therefore, that all Israel would be saved. In Rom 3:10–18, Paul arranged together six different texts and parts of texts (Pss 14:1c, 2b, 3; 5:10cd; 140:4b; 10:7a, Isa 59:7, 8a; Ps 36:2b).

The contents of all these statements are related to each other and serve Paul's desire to demonstrate that all humans, both Jews and pagans, exist in a state of fallenness under the power of sin. He has abbreviated the citations so much that he has removed all the sayings in the related texts that do not conform to his point. Another manner of dealing with citations consists of explaining some of their parts with formulations from other scriptural passages. We encounter this type of mixed citation in Rom 9:33, where Paul (over against the text that already has been altered by means of a Christian interpretation) modified the wording of a saying concerning the "cornerstone," which 1 Peter appears to have used in a positive way about Christ. Paul's change comes from his addition of a proverb in Isa 8:14b that refers to the "stone of stumbling." The modified proverb is now able to show how Israel, in spite of its zeal for righteousness, has still fallen short, because the Lord has become for it a stumbling stone. Paul is able, however, entirely independently and willfully, to insert this text into his comment. Another example occurs in Rom 10:6–8. Here Paul cites the passage from Deut 30:12–14, where the discussion in the original concerns the law, that is, that the word of God is not removed to the ends of the earth but rather exists in the mouth and heart of the Israelites. Paul removes 30:11b, which speaks of the "commandment" by which all the following declarations are connected. In addition, he eliminates all the phrases that speak of the doing of the law and discontinues the passage at 30:14. Finally, t the beginning of his citation he adds a phrase from Deut 8:17a (9:4a): "You shall not say in your heart." This abbreviated and altered citation serves Paul's process of thought, when he offers his commentary step by step: justice, which comes from faith, makes it unnecessary to repeat Christ's ascent and his descent to the dead; his salvific act has occurred once and for all.

In other cases Paul is confident enough to reach into the wording of Scripture citations in order to make them useful for his particular process of thought. According to the principles of interpretation of the time period in which Paul lived, this procedure is not without an analogue. One encounters this type of approach in the Qumran literature. However, Paul's reshaping of the wording of passages is not found to such a wide extent elsewhere. The professional interpretation of Scripture that one finds, for example, in the writings of Philo or in the pesharim (commentaries) of Qumran do not demonstrate the same extent to which Paul goes in citing and changing his sources. It is striking that Paul feels most unfettered in his handling of Scripture when he wishes to establish his new theological interpretation of justification by faith that contrasts with the law and election. The strongly altered citation of Deut 5:30 in Rom 10:6–8 is a vivid example. The newly obtained understandings of faith are fundamental to Paul and determine what are the most decisive factors as well as the beginning point for his interpretation of the Bible. The Scriptures are consulted solely as evidence for this essential affirmation.

One also encounters in Paul other contemporary methods of interpretation, even if they are rather sporadic in their occurrences. Allegory, which was fundamental to Philo's method, is found only three times in Paul. In 1 Cor 9:9 the apostle mentions the commandment found in Deut 25:4, "You shall not muzzle an ox when it is treading out the grain." He cites this in order to establish his exhortation to provide sustenance through the community. The Old Testament text is directed originally to the Israelite farmer working his oxen on the threshing floor to grind the ears of corn with their hooves. The fundamental point, related to the present context, prompts Paul to come to the question (which is addressed similarly by Philo): "Does God care only for oxen but say nothing for our sake?" Another citation (which, however, cannot be identified) makes certain through its addition the meaning that the "oxen treading out the grain" are in reality humans so that the apostle is able to relate the word analogously to his personal maintenance. Additional cases of allegory occur in Gal 4:21–31 and 1 Cor 10:4. In a complicated process of thought, Sarah and her children according to the promise are free (and thus are the new covenant made up of both Jews and Gentiles). She and her offspring are contrasted to Hagar and her children, who are slaves. Sarah and her children represent the Jerusalem above, while the slave woman and her children represent the covenant of Mount Sinai and correspond to the present Jerusalem. In the second example, the rock that the ancestors followed in the wilderness, Paul identifies as Christ.

In 1 Cor 10:1–13, Paul puts forward the behavior of the "fathers" (the Israelites in the wilderness) in order to raise an example of warning that the Corinthians might see, since they are of the opinion that they may be protected from all temptations due to their possession of the sacraments. According to Paul, the ancestors also possessed things analogous to the sacraments. Baptism corresponds to their being under the protection of the cloud and passing through the sea: they were "baptized into Moses" (10:1–2). The Lord's Supper corresponds to the miracle of food and drink found in Exod 16 and 17 (see 1 Cor 10:3–4). In this context Paul repeats the customary idea that the rock from which the Israelites drank water followed them through the wilderness. An allegorical interpretation of the rock in Exod 17 is found in Philo (*Leg.* 2.86; *Det.* 118) and is commonly used in the Hellenistic Jewish interpretation. It is understandable that Paul would take an additional step and identify the rock as Christ. However, for Paul the events in the wilderness are not explained as timeless but rather are left in their historical setting. In this way, Paul is significantly different from Philo. Between the behavior of the ancestors in the wilderness and that of the Corinthians Paul sees rather an analogy, which he sets forth before this Christian community as a warning. In spite of these sacraments, the ancestors were not immune to the temptation of apostasy.

This form of the comparison of an episode from the salvation history of the past with the present comes close to a method that one designates "typology." Typology involves the comparison of events or persons in an earlier time to those in later periods. Those in the later periods are either placed in opposition to earlier events and persons or represent their repetition. Paul uses this type of scheme very rarely. The best known is the typology between Adam, the first man, and Christ, the Adam at the end of time (Rom 5:12–21; 1 Cor 15:21–22; 15:45–47). One may understand this contrast as a polemic against the Hellenistic Jewish typology, like the one found in Philo. According to Philo (*Opif.* 134–135; *Leg.* 1.31–32) the human created "after the image of God" in Gen 1:26 is a heavenly being, while the human in Gen 2:7 is an earthly person to whom a *pseuche* is given. The heavenly human does not have any earthly material. Every individual person, by means of reason, possesses a portion of the heavenly immortal being and thus, with virtue, can bring this into effect in life and can overcome the earthly person ensnared by the mortal passions. According to Paul, Adam is the first human being. Corresponding to a similar Jewish speculation (Sir 25:24; Wis 2:24; 4 Ezra 3:26; 7:118), every concrete human participates in a general state of sinfulness that, according to Gen 3, has entered into the world. On this basis, Paul builds his argument: if it is true that all humans have degenerated in following after the sin of Adam (which is ever and again always manifested in concrete deeds), then it is now even more the case that the grace of God has been revealed in Jesus Christ, a grace that is there for "the many." Therefore, Adam and Christ stand in a highly developed opposition. Paul brings together these elements in order to show that the guilt of all human beings, which he has addressed in the first chapter of Romans, no longer has the final word. By means of the event of justification effectuated through Christ, a manner of deliverance is made available to all those who believe.

Once again it is clear that Paul is intimately familiar with the characteristic interpretations of his Hellenistic Jewish environment and that he goes along with their methodological approaches, at least to a point. The message that he has delivered, however, is distinguished in essential features from the variety of ways of thinking common to Judaism. Corresponding to the uniqueness of the gospel, the traditional methods of interpretation are modified and made serviceable in the freedom the apostle takes in expressing his own point of view.

A previously existing opposition between the Old and New Testaments, found in the earlier Christian tradition, is taken up by Paul in 2 Cor 3:7–11 and transformed into an antithesis between the "service of death" and the "service of the spirit." "Spirit" is placed in opposition to the "letter," which is recognized under the law of Moses. Here Paul cites from Exod 34:30 the statement about the brightness that came upon the face of Moses as he descended from Mount Sinai and argues that if the "service of death" (because the law does not lead to life), which is carved into the letters of tablets of stone, has had such a brilliance, how much more so is this true for the "service of the spirit" (which Paul considers to be the source of his apostolic commission). As the following section then shows, the entire community also participates in this brilliance (3:18).

In the passage found in 2 Cor 3:12–18, Paul digresses with a rambling interpretation that expands the Old Testament text by the addition of the larger passage of Exod 34:29–35. He moves from the preceding theme of the defense of his apostolic office to deal with the reading of the Torah in the contemporary synagogue. Paul interprets proverbially the covering of Moses' face when he spoke with the Israelites but dispensed with when he spoke with God (Exod 34:33–35). While Paul places the original meaning of this statement on its head, he speaks of a similar covering that is now on the hearts of the Jews whenever someone reads from the books of Moses in the synagogue. The key word "Lord" (*kyrios*), which is used for God in the Septuagint, leads beyond the association "Lord—Spirit of the Lord—freedom" to the statement that "we" Christians now have access to Christ the Lord with a face that is not veiled. Further, we shall be conformed to the grandeur (brilliance) of his form. Paul obviously says with this statement that an actual understanding of the Scriptures is possible only in the Spirit of Christ. Therefore, we may have before us in this text a fundamental statement about his general understanding of the Scriptures.

Paul takes, therefore, the Scriptures into service for the proclamation of his gospel. Their authentic meaning is revealed only by the Spirit that operates in the way that he stresses. Whoever wishes to read the Old Testament without Christ cannot understand its true meaning. A Torah read in this manner is a "service of death"; the synagogue, which rejected Christ, is no longer successful in finding life through the law. In addition to these expressions, one must also take into consideration the fundamental statements of Paul about covenant, law, and promise in Gal 3 and Romans. With regard to Gen 15:6, he moves away from the promise concerning the law of Moses to the case of Abraham, who was justified by faith. Through the death of Jesus on the cross, who took upon himself the curse of the law, the Old Testament comes to the fulfillment of its original intention. In Rom 4 Paul brings to expression also a fundamental Jewish principle of interpretation: a biblical passage must be explained by taking it out of its context into a larger association. Thus, the statement about the circumcision of Abraham occurs only in Gen 17; he was uncircumcised in Gen 15!

On the other hand, the Torah is for Paul a valid expression of God's will, even though Christian existence is lived ethically under the sign of the freedom conferred by Christ (Gal 5:1, 13) through the Spirit that is freely given (5:25) in the renewing of the mind. Paul sees the Decalogue (Deut 5:17–21) fulfilled in the commandment concerning the neighbor according to Lev 19:18b (Rom 13:9; see Gal 5:14 and the attitude of Jesus in Mark 10:19 par.). Materially speaking, Paul does not wish to create a new ethic. On one occasion (1 Cor 15:33) he is able even to cite a saying from the philosopher Menander as an ethical principle. Therefore, there are statements in the Scriptures concerning the sphere of ethics that, unaltered, continue to be true.

3.4. The Promise Is Fulfilled: Matthew

For readers of the Bible, Matthew's use of the Old Testament is especially conspicuous when it comes to citations, for they are introduced by the formula "This was to fulfill what had been spoken by the Lord through the prophet...." This so-called "fulfillment citation," less felicitously called "citation of reflection," is found throughout the entire Gospel, although somewhat disproportionately. This formula occurs most frequently in the prologue, Matt 1–2 (1:22–23; 2:15, 17–18, 23), and afterward only rather seldom (4:14–16; 8:17; 11:18–21; 13:35; 21:4–5; 27:9). In spite of their conspicuous form, one may not isolate these fulfillment citations from Matthew's other citations from the Old Testament. There are a few that are rather close in form to that occurring in the introduction (2:5–6; 3:3; 13:14; see also 24:15), and even when this is not the case, the Old Testament is still drawn on in a similar manner. The fulfillment citations certainly are characteristic for the type of interaction with the Old Testament that goes back to Matthew himself (I mean not the Evangelist himself but rather the author who remains unknown). Other Old Testament citations occur in the passages that Matthew has taken from either Mark or the so-called Sayings Source (Q), something that also is true of Luke. These citations do not use the typically Matthean style and also are put forward in another literary form. It is also striking that the Old Testament is cited in a form in the fulfillment citations that is not encountered elsewhere, either in the primary Hebrew text or in the Septuagint. We find this fulfillment citation, for example, in the well-known narrative of the wise men (magi) from the East (2:1–12) in 2:6.

The prologue of the Gospel of Matthew has provided scholars with numerous riddles pertaining to the stories of the childhood of Jesus. Since there are narratives that are neither historical nor bear the character of the style of legend, one must determine the theological purpose that Matthew had in mind. It also may be that he took over stories that were a part of oral tradition, which assumes the role of the community. It is noteworthy that the citation in 2:6 is based on Jesus' origins in Bethlehem, thus in contradiction to the tradition that he initially came from Nazareth of Galilee (another form of the legendary explanation that points to Bethlehem as the place of Jesus' birth is found in the Christmas story of Luke 2:1–7). Thus two passages from the Old Testament are fashioned together: the beginning originates with Mic 5:1, 3; the concluding sentence comes from 2 Kgs 5:2. Now this is not an unusual practice for that period of time, as we have already seen. Even still more remarkable are the alterations in the passage cited from Micah: Bethlehem is designated as located in the tribe given the name Judah instead of the old tribal name, Ephrathah, which exists in the primary text. This change may be understood as a result of modernization. The use of "rulers" in place of the "thousands" rests presumably on another vocalization of the original recension of the text. The statement that "*by no means* are you the least" (Matt 2:6) alters the meaning in Micah, which originally made the notable point that the future ruler would come from Bethlehem, *even though* it was the smallest district.

Another example of changes in the original meaning with regard to our considerations of citations is the use of Hos 11:1 in Matt 2:15: "Out of Egypt I have called my son." Hosea is referring to all of Israel coming out of Egypt in the exodus, while Matthew uses the text to refer to the command given to Joseph to flee to Egypt with the child Jesus. The saying in Jer 31:15 concerning Rachel, the tribal mother of the northern tribes, who is described as weeping in Ramah for her children, is taken to refer to the murder of infants by Herod.

Exegetes are stumped, for Ramah is located a significant distance from Bethlehem. However, perhaps Matthew is following a contemporary method of interpretation when he picks up only the key word "children," which then provides an association with this citation. At the end of the prologue, in 2:23, a fulfillment citation appears, the origin of which is not transmitted: "He shall be called a Nazarene." Apparently Matthew himself was unaware from where the saying derived, for he speaks here in the plural: "which is said through the prophets." One may compare this to 21:4–5 and 27:9, which contain two citations, one of which does not mention the name of its source and the other of which is wrongly attributed to the book of Zechariah when, indeed, it originates with Jeremiah. These errors are understandable if one recalls that this Gospel originated at the time when the Jewish Christian community had been driven out of the synagogue. The opposition of the Jews who did not recognize Jesus is reflected clearly in Matthew's Gospel, and he thus no longer enjoys access to the scrolls of texts that were stored in the synagogue.

The fulfillment citations describe Matthew's commentary, which attaches important sayings concerning the way of Jesus. Most of these are connected to a short narrative or a saying. Thematically, many of them stem from the sphere of the messianic texts of the Old Testament, which were understood in the postexilic period as prophetic announcements of the Messiah expected in the end time. Thus the narrative runs from the proclamation of the virgin birth in Matt 1:8–25 to the prophecy of Immanuel in Isa 7:14 (which obviously is interpreted in a way that conflicts with its original meaning by making it into a prophecy of the Messiah). In addition, 2:6 picks up the messianic passage of Mic 5:1, 3. In Matt 8:17 (Isa 53:4), the miraculous healings of the Son of Man/Messiah occur, while in 12:18–21, the longest of the fulfillment citations, the entire first Servant Song (Isa 42:1–4) is taken up in order to point to Jesus and his silence as the hope of the pagans. The narrative of the entrance into Jerusalem contains, along with its introduction taken from Isa 62:11, the saying about the meek king of salvation of Zech 9:9. This type of messianic reference is recognizable once more in the reference to the narrative concerning the end of Judas (Matt 27:1–10) that refers to the thirty pieces of silver (found only in Mathew). This passage contains two references to Zech 11:13.

The main wording of Matthew's insertions into these citations, "to fulfill," expresses the theological purpose that motivated the Evangelists in their appropriation of these Old Testament texts: Matthew believed along with contemporary Judaism that the message of the prophets was directed to the present and announced the events of the end time. However, since for him the Christ-event was the central act of the end time, its meaning could be realized only in these ideas. However, in his view, it was only Jesus, the son of David (1:1; 9:27; 12:23; 15:22; 20:30–31; 21:9; 22:42–45), and no one else whom the prophets had in mind. This is true only in regard to the prophetic proclamation of salvation (especially the postexilic prophets). Classical prophecy that announced punishment is seldom mentioned. Wherever it does emerge, as above all in the parable of the wicked tenants in 21:33–45 (which Matthew adopted from Mark; see also Luke 20:9–19), it is related to their mission only to Old Testament Israel as the ancestors of Judaism of the synagogue, from which the community at the time of Matthew had already separated.

In the view of Old Testament prophecy as promise and the Christ-event as fulfillment, there appears in Matthew for the first time a model for the relationship of the Testaments that proved to be very influential in the continuing history of interpretation. Matthew was the most frequently read Gospel of the early church. His view was therefore especially significant for the understanding of the Old Testament in the time that followed.

Also, this Evangelist gave Old Testament law a place of prominence. In his introduction to the main section of the Sermon of the Mount, that is, the antitheses (see above), he placed an expression in the mouth of Jesus that according to its wording was probably largely from Jesus himself: "think not that I have come to abolish the Law or the Prophets; I have come not to abolish but to fulfill" (5:17). He here uses the same word as in the introduction to the fulfillment citations! As the two following sentences, taken over from the Evangelists, show, this has to do only with the Torah. Verses 18 and 19 essentially stem from Jewish Christian circles out of which the Matthean community had grown. This community, as was the case in the Pharisaic sect of Judaism, engaged in a very strong measure of piety based on the Torah. Not a single *yod* (the smallest letter of the alphabet of the usual Aramaic square script at the time) nor a stroke of a letter of the Torah should be disregarded. Not the smallest commandment is viewed as unimportant. We need not accept the view that Matthew himself deviated from this attitude.

In his Gospel, he described clearly enough the position of Jesus concerning the Torah. When Jesus required one to love one's neighbor, it always overrode the restraints imposed by the law. In the pericope mentioned above, the question about the greatest of the commandments (22:34–40 par.) is raised. Jesus responded by combining Deut 6:5, concerning love for God, which is the fundamental regulation for every Jew, with Lev 19:18, the command to love one's neighbor, and fashioned them into a twofold commandment (22:40, occurring only in Matthew). The text in 5:43–44 allows this commandment even to extend to the love of one's enemy. When one takes into consideration the structure of the entire Sermon on the Mount, as a previously transmitted tradition that has been shaped by the Evangelist to include modifications he himself composed and the arrangement of the beatitudes, which he has freely reworked, Jesus' Torah preaching is placed under the early signs of the kingdom of God breaking into history and with it the gift of the gospel. Jesus has laid down a new foundation for the law of God. It is now the in-breaking of the kingdom of God that has become the valid order, which stems from the gospel and the salvation that accompanies it. Thus, this is likely the meaning of "fulfill" in Matt 5:17. Certainly doing the will of God is important also for Matthew, and he is not as far from Paul on this point as appears at first glance, for he does not hold the view of salvation by means of works. Rather, doing the will of God is the free act of those who have been the recipients of God's gift by means of the gospel. With this Matthew turns back to the Old Testament valuation of the Torah. The "golden rule," placed by Matthew at the end of the major part of the Sermon on the Mount (7:12), makes clear once again a fundamental principle of this act according to a rational principle that is discernable for all. The content of this act is determined by the two citations of Hos 6:6 (Matt 9:13; 12:7): "I desire compassion and not sacrifice." The fundamental principle of compassion is decisive for the disciples (5:7; 9:13; 12:7; 18:33; see also 25:31–46). The most important features that are brought together, according to 22:23, are "justice, compassion, and faith." The feature of compassion requires of the disciples a "superior righteousness" (5:20; 6:33), in contrast to the scribes and the Pharisees, whose teaching is certainly correct but whose actions, because they are hypocrites, deviate from righteousness (6:1–6; 23:4–36). Agreement with but also separation from Judaism thus becomes apparent in this Gospel.

3.5. The Old Testament Is Prophecy about Christ: The Sermons of the Book of Acts

The use of citations from the Old Testament in the speeches of the Acts of the Apostles presents a practice distinct from other New Testament writings. We have a two-volume work from Luke: the Gospel of Luke and the book of Acts. In distinction from the authors of the two older Gospels, those of Mark and Matthew, Luke is introduced at the beginning of his Gospel (1:1–4) as a writer with literary aspirations. In the introduction to the book of Acts (1:19), this second volume is identified as the continuation of the first work and traces the spread of the gospel from Jerusalem throughout the entire world of the Roman Empire. Nevertheless, Luke has employed his abilities in an essentially more independent manner than in the Gospel tradition with which he began. He proceeded to shape a common outline for the materials that, to a large extent, were transmitted to him in small units.

As for the character of the work, which begins with the ascension of Christ and the events of Pentecost and ends with the imprisonment of Paul in Rome, the similarities in the composition's technique and style with those of the Greek and Roman historians (Herodotus, Thucydides, Xenophon, then later Dionysius of Halicarnassus and Livy) have already been demonstrated. Comparable elements of style are found, however, also in the Old Testament itself and in Hellenistic Jewish works of history, including the books of Maccabees and the descriptions of Flavius Josephus, in which a theological baseline like the one in Luke is capable of being determined. Belonging to the matter of style are the known insertion of speeches into the formation of scenes and the emphases of the climactic points in the course of the history.

The eclectic character of the Acts of the Apostles attracts one's attention. Even the name of the volume is essentially incorrect, since it in no way attempts to describe the history of all the disciples. The figure of Peter stands out in the first section, while in the second section (from Acts 13 on) Paul is the major character (his name before this was Saul; in contrast to his epistles, he is never called an apostle). After Acts 15, we no longer read of the apostles in Jerusalem and the fate of the Jewish community. The end of the book breaks off with the imprisonment of Paul in Rome, although Luke certainly was aware of his martyrdom. Although Luke builds his volume on his description of some significant personalities, such as Peter, Paul, John, Stephen, Philip, and Barnabas, he was not interested in their fortunes. The way of the gospel that he traces goes from Jerusalem to Rome, the last of which followed the spread of the message by means of the missionary journeys of Paul into the different parts of Asia as well as Europe. Indirectly, the book of Acts is therefore itself proclamation, even if the concerns and methods are explicitly those of a work of history related to some of the early Jewish ones.

The character of Acts as proclamation is demonstrated by the speeches contained in the book. Some of these speeches, which are concentrated in the first part of the book in chapters 2–13, are singled out because of their length and the common design of their carefully constructed configuration. Since they are formed as addresses of the early Christian apostles and missionaries either to a pagan or a Jewish audience, one designates them as missionary speeches. A lengthy discussion has been underway in biblical research to determine whether these speeches originate in an ancient tradition or are the creations of Luke himself. This debate has led to the result that the second of the two alternatives is more likely. Support for this second position is their well-planned insertion into the common structure of the book of Acts, where they serve frequently to characterize prominent results and turning points and contain particularly Lukan figures of speech along with his characteristic theology. No less important is the regular use of the Septuagint, which represents the Bible of this Greek-speaking author. At the same time, these factors do not exclude the possibility that Luke also placed into the common structure of his volume tradition statements he appropriated from the primitive Christian proclamation. This is strikingly indicated by all of the speeches of Peter in Acts 2, 3, 4, 5, and 10 and the speech of Paul in Acts 13 and by the occurrences of many individual phrases and formal statements that belong to this ancient tradition. A particular case in point is the speech of Stephen in Acts 7, which many interpreters have seen as having an earlier form that Luke has later reworked.

Striking is the introduction of the Old Testament citations that form a primary structural element. This contrasts with the other speeches that occur in the second half of the book. This feature can be demonstrated in the first speech of this type, which occurs in the sermon of Peter on Pentecost in Acts 2:14–40. Those addressed are the people of Jerusalem and the Jews from all the different parts of the world, who are streaming there to celebrate this annual festival week. The speech falls clearly into two sections. The first, found in 2:14–21, inserts the address of Peter in the context in which the Pentecost miracle occurred: the pouring out of the Holy Spirit on the early community, which had been described in the preceding chapter. In this speech he is at pains to explain what took place on this occasion. In verse 13 Luke narrates that some eyewitnesses had observed the ecstatic behavior of the gathered primitive community, presumably the miracle of speaking in foreign tongues. The people had thought that the disciples must have been drunk. Peter objected to this in verse 15, since it was not possible to be drunk so early in the morning (that is, in three hours, which is the ninth hour of the day). Rather, the event is explained as the pouring out of the Holy Spirit as corresponding to what the prophet Joel said in Joel 3:1–5. In the introduction to this citation, Luke characteristically intrudes: in one instance he expressly designates the proclamation of Joel as the word of God and thus bestows on him a special authority. In another instance he alters the vocabulary of the citation itself. Joel uses the vague formula "after this shall occur," but the next specification, "when the event shall occur," is left open. Luke adds to Joel's prophecy the phrase "in the last day." He considers this word of Joel to be a prophecy that points to the end of time. Even though it is not expressly stated, there stands in the background of this reference a model of thought with which we are already familiar: promise and fulfillment. Luke separates himself from the early Christian interpretation that broaches the topic of the coming of Jesus at the end of time, in that he no longer appropriates the initial expectation that the end is near. Still, he refers the events of Pentecost to the broader statement of the text of Joel, according to which the pouring out of the Spirit especially occurs in a prophetic speech. This explains, therefore, Luke's repetition of the key word "prophesy" at the end of verse 18.

In verses 19–21, Luke continues with the remaining section of the citation of Joel concerning the apocalyptic future. He includes the words "above" and "below," along with the parallel expression of "portents" and "signs," from Joel 3:3 in order to underline the point that the miracle preceding the "Day of the Lord" shall assume cosmic proportions. The concept of the final judgment is bound up with the apocalyptic concept of the "Day of the Lord." Here, in verses 20b–21, is found the second difficult point of the word of Joel for Luke. This involves making the main part of the speech actually refer to Jesus Christ. The miraculous activity of Jesus, which Peter mentions, is brought into view in verse 22 and highlighted. Verses 22–24 contain the typical statements of missionary speeches: God has disclosed the identity of Jesus through acts of power, signs, and wonders among the Israelites, who are addressed as the people of God. These acts, which Jesus performed in their midst, along with his crucifixion on the cross by the hand of the non-Israelites to whom Jesus was handed over by the Jews, took place according to divine plan and foreknowledge. (It is noteworthy that the designation of Jesus as the instrument of God brings into view an ancient Christology.) God, however, raised Jesus from the dead. This customary argumentation is found only in Luke, who emphasizes the guilt of the Jews for the death of Jesus on the cross. While this stresses the motive for their repentance, missing is any awareness of the impact of sin. Although some scholars contest the point, it is still possible, nonetheless, that Luke is dependent on an early Christian missionary sermon to the Jews for this model. Certainly, evidence is lacking outside the book of Acts. Also characteristic for this schema is the fact that the remembrance of the death of Jesus on the cross is followed immediately by the sentence about his resurrection through God. The expression the "pain" of death goes back to a passage of the Septuagint that involves a mistake in translation. In the original Hebrew text of 2 Sam 22:6 (par. Ps 18:6), which is echoed here, the "snares" of death, not "pain," is read.

The statement about the resurrection concludes in verses 25–28 with a prooftext made up of a citation of Ps 16:8–11 combined with the prophecy of Nathan (2 Sam 7:12–13). Luke, following the ancient tradition of David as the composer of the Psalter, designates this text as the word of David (see also Acts 1:16; 2:34; 4:25). Luke has already mentioned the prophet Joel as the source of the citation that begins in verse 17. These references to authors of Old Testament texts are used to bolster his claim of scriptural reference, even though he uses an often imprecise manner of quotation. This same lack of precision may be observed in other New Testament writings. Even so, this imprecision closely parallels the customary early Hellenistic Jewish method of interpretation. This allows Luke to refer to the verse in the psalm as a scriptural testimony to Jesus. This line of argument follows in verses 29–32. The ancestor David (only Luke uses this title) corresponds to a prophet in this psalm (once more a designation appearing only in Luke). Even so, this prophet, that is, David, speaks of one who will not experience the decay of corruption. Luke argues that David could not be speaking of himself, for everyone knows that he has long since been dead. Indeed, his grave may be seen in Jerusalem. Thus he can only be speaking as a prophet about Christ and his resurrection, for Jesus has not experienced corruption due to God raising him from the dead. Thus, this text may apply only to Christ. Therefore, all those Christians present are witnesses, an important factor for Luke as an historian (see Acts 1:8, 22; 3:15; 10:39; 13:31).

Directly following this is a second scriptural proof in Acts 2:33–35. Luke's separation of the resurrection and ascension of Christ (see Luke 24:50–53; Acts 1:9–11) likewise draws on a verse from the Psalms (110:1) in setting forth the second topos, the exaltation of Christ to the right hand of God. This psalm, understood messianically in the late period of the Old Testament, is used frequently in other places in the New Testament as evidence for the exaltation of Christ. The Septuagint translation, which uses the Greek word *kyrios* for God and the "Lord" mentioned in Ps 110:1, makes possible the use of this psalm to refer to Jesus Christ. Just as he identified David as the author of Ps 16, Luke indicates that, since Christ had not ascended into heaven at the time of this psalm's composition, "his [David's] Lord" can mean no one other than Christ, for this reference to his having taken his place at the right hand of God can refer only to him. From this twofold demonstration, the exhortation to the "entire house of Israel," referring to those present, follows then as the conclusion of this christological centerpiece. This Christ whom the audience crucified is to be acknowledged as the Lord and Christ appointed by God.

It is characteristic for the Hellenistic style of rhetoric that now in verse 37 the speech is interrupted with a parenthetical remark about the audience's reaction. The "burning pain" that the audience experienced is related to the incrimination pronounced in verse 36b. They are the murderers of the Messiah. Their helpless question to Peter and the other apostles leads to the concluding part of the speech: "What may we do?" Peter calls on the audience to repent and to be baptized in the name of Christ for the forgiveness of sins. Associated with this is the promise of the Spirit. In this passage, Luke links the speech artfully once more with the issuance of the citation of Joel 3. The statement from this prophet is interpreted as the promise of the bestowal of the Spirit to the Jews (and "their children") and the pagans ("those who are far away").

For Luke's typical use of the Old Testament, it is noteworthy that he understands this collection of texts chiefly as prophecy that has the purpose of pointing to and interpreting Christ. Therefore, while scriptural proof is cited from Joel, David is also viewed as a prophet. The existing Deuteronomic explanation of Moses as a prophet (Deut 18:15–20), however, assumes a role in Luke. The section of Peter's speech in 3:12–26 is especially rich in its use of Scripture, where he expresses himself basically about the significance of prophecy. According to Luke in verse 18, God proclaimed beforehand the suffering of Christ, which he now has fulfilled. Verse 22 cites the well-known verse (Deut 18:15) in which Moses announces the "prophet like me" whom God will send and identifies him in this connection with Jesus Christ. Verse 23 combines Deut 18:15 with Lev 23:29 to issue a warning of the consequences for all those who do not listen to this prophet. Verse 24 contains a general statement: *all* prophets of the Old Testament, beginning with Samuel, announced the present events. Acts 26:22–23 executes in its content something that is even closer: "that the Messiah must suffer and be proclaimed as the one first resurrected from the dead in order to be a light to the nations and the heathen." In addition, the speech of Peter in Acts 3 continues this process of the announcement of salvation for those who are the "sons of the prophets," a surprising and positive identification. The hearers are not only sons of the prophets but also those who belong to the covenant of Abraham, another scriptural citation, this time coming from Gen 22:18 (or 26:4). This identifies them with their successors to whom the key word "to bless" is applied in verse 26. The blessing consists in their conversion, which is fulfilled by those who await him.

In regard to the method of this use of Scripture, Luke differs very little from his contemporaries. In Luke we find evidence of mixed citations, already examined by us: the interaction with key words and the principle that the Scriptures are directed to the present. The theory that the Old Testament writers were essentially prophets, especially David and Moses, and that either they or God speaking through their mouths is customary in this developed form in Luke, which contains nothing that opposes this view. It is a form of personification that belongs to the Hellenistic historians. That the content of the prophetic announcements made before the present period are related to Jesus Christ in a central fashion is made even more explicit in Luke, although it is a common primitive Christian perspective. Luke knows that his christological interpretations, a process traditional for him to pursue, are to be supported by corresponding citations of Scripture.

While we are not able to go into all the details that emerge in the various questions that arising from Luke's speech of Stephen in Acts 7:2–53, we should look briefly at this special speech as our conclusion to examining Acts. It is an especially important piece because its form and content vary from most of the other speeches in the book of Acts and because there is a previous tradition that Luke very likely has appropriated. In addition, one should not exclude the possibility that the final form of this speech is the result of a number of editions, although the various views expressed in the scholarly examinations are quite different.

It is striking that the speech is barely associated with its narrative frame—the accusation against Stephen and his subsequent martyrdom (6:8–7:1; 7:54–8:3)—in contrast to the general case of Luke's speeches conforming quite smoothly with their present settings. In regard to the question of the high priest (7:1), one expects Stephen to present a rhetorical defense. Instead, there follows a lengthy account of the main features of Israel's history, which have no sensible place in a legal procedure. This account of history begins with Abraham's departure from Mesopotamia (see Gen 12:1–3) and ends with Solomon's building of the temple (Acts 7:47). One has the impression that the oldest form of this speech offered a thoroughly positive evaluation and narration of Israel's history. Even the temple was viewed positively at the conclusion. This type of respectful accounting of history could stem entirely from (Hellenistic) Judaism (see, e.g., 7:2: "our father Abraham"; 7:19: "our race"). This look back at Israelite history, however, contains, in addition to the positive recounting, resolutely negative criticisms, above all those in 7:39–40 and 51–53. It was probably edited by circles that favored the Deuteronomic tradition of the Old Testament prior to Luke's appropriation of it. These followed, thus, the critical view of Israel's history. One assumes that there were active Hellenistic Christians by this time. Verses 51–53 also deviate in style in another way from the preceding sections of the speech. The direct turning to the audience and the accusation of their murder of Christ (7:52) is similar to the speeches created by Luke. Thus, one can see perhaps his addition to this concluding passage. That this is possibly the case may be seen from the fact that he inserted scriptural proof into the previous tradition in two places. In one case (7:42b–43) Luke adds a citation from Amos that conforms to the context, while in the other case he draws on a saying in Isa 66:1–2 that contradicts the tendency of the earlier form of the text in its rejection of the temple. There is an alteration in the citation of Amos that obviously offers an adjustment to meet the contemporary situation of the audience. In the original text God threatens the Israelites with exile "beyond Damascus," but the name "Babylon" is inserted into the text in Acts. It may be either that Luke regarded the Babylonian exile as punishment for Israel's apostasy or that Babylon was a code word for the hostile world power Rome, an identification made elsewhere (Rev 14:8; 16:19; 17:5; 18:2, 10, 21).

In addition, the previous form of the historical recounting of the past is built around a large number of scriptural citations or allusions to Scripture. Most of these derive from the first two books of the Torah, given the period of history addressed in the speech. While Luke customarily follows the translation of the Septuagint, there is a variant textual form at the basis of four cases (Acts 7:4, 5, 32, 37) that also does not correspond to the Masoretic Text. This may be related to the similar observations one may make in regard to the authentic Pauline letters. In Acts 7:16, a change obviously occurs: in Gen 23, when Abraham purchases the cave of Machpelah, in Hebron it is reported to be a burial site. This is also where Joseph was buried (Gen 50:13). In contrast, Gen 33:19–20 narrates the purchase of a parcel of land by Jacob. According to Josh 24:32, Joseph was buried in Shechem. Perhaps the basic source of Acts 7 follows the speech of a later tradition concerning the location of the patriarchal graves in Shechem.

The fact that Luke can appropriate the historical recounting of the past and enable his purposes to conform, although imperfectly, to it demonstrates that for him the history of Israel is also the history of the church. Of the New Testament theologians, Luke most of all sees a continuous line through the history of salvation. Certainly the history of Israel is a history of salvation, only in respect, however, to the achievement of the victorious goal that is reached by means of God's activity. Israel's chief guilt resides in its responsibility for having killed the Messiah, although this sin already has been confirmed by the past events of its history. This is an essential expression of this history. Therefore, repentance and a turning to Jesus Christ manifested in baptism are necessary. This is because Jesus, due to his divine commission as Messiah (Christ), occupies the central place of the history of the people of God. His appearance and yet nonacceptance by the Jews leads to a break with the older history of salvation and introduces an entirely new one. Also, the Torah has been disregarded and has now become an unbearable burden that was placed upon the ancestors (15:10). It is difficult to determine the extent to which this speech has taken over the fundamental thoughts of the primitive Christian mission. However, there are archaizing rhetorical features in certain parts that reflect the style of a Hellenistic writer of Scripture who wishes to highlight the authenticity of the vitality of his scenes. Nevertheless, there may be still indications of an older practice that, at the time of Luke, who wrote the Acts of the Apostles presumably between 80 and 90 C.E., still had not been removed. It is worthy of attention that the intensity of this reaching back to the Old Testament had not been left behind even in Hellenistic circles. So for Luke, the Scriptures, the prophetic character of which he exalted, were an undeniable witness of revelation.

3.6. Christ Surpasses the Old Testament Institutions: The Epistle to the Hebrews

Of all the New Testament writings, the one that reaches back to use the Old Testament in the most extensive manner is the Epistle to the Hebrews. This surely occurs in line with its purpose of demonstrating that the Christ-event surpasses the validity of central institutions of ancient Israel. This presupposes, however, that those who received the letter gave indisputable authority to the Old Testament.

In modern criticism, the recognition that Paul could not have been the author of Hebrews is a commonly held position. On account of the distinctions in the diction and theology and, above all, to the situation compared to that of the authentic Pauline corpus, the only question is whether an unknown follower of the second or third generation of the Christian sect was the author (see 2:3). Complicating this matter is the fact that the circle of those who received this text is not clearly and conclusively transmitted. The superscription "to the Hebrews" is known from the third century, and whether the ones addressed are Jewish Christians who have a strong devotion to the temple cult and seek to know more of the other Old Testament concepts of faith or are Gentile Christians is a matter that is debated back and forth. A concrete community as the receivers of the letter is likely, even though the typical introduction to a letter is missing (see, however, the conclusion). The background points to the typical problems of second-generation Christians: weariness of and weakness in adhering to the faith. Indeed, a certain malaise seems to be widespread, corresponding to a decline in ethical behavior. Therefore, the author is driven by a strong pastoral concern. He seeks to strengthen the faith of his readers and to encourage them by setting before their eyes the decisive significance of the Christ-event. He wishes to make clear to them both the ominous consequences of any possible defection and their status as the "wandering people of God," who, even in the midst of persecutions, are able to approach in steadfastness and hope the heavenly goal (10:32–39; 12:3–13).

The interfacing of admonition and encouragement, which reaches back ever again to the different perspectives of the fundamental statements of Christian confession, determines the overarching structure of the Epistle to the Hebrews. This is difficult to overlook. Christology is without question the intrinsic theological center of this text. Hebrews develops this theological category in the customary fashion of drawing from the background of Old Testament forms and institutions. A frequently recurring schema, at the same time, is the evaluative comparison: the contrast is between the higher value and nobler character of the Christ-event and the Old Testament paradigms. Thus, the Christ-event has overtaken and replaced the Old Testament institutions with the result that the common salvation of the Christian community is now exclusively in and through Jesus Christ. Numerous citations from the Old Testament, which point to the author's closeness to the text, along with further allusions to its vocabulary and descriptions of biblical figures, are adduced as evidence for the theses of Hebrews. The citations are almost always anonymous. This obviously relates to the fact that Hebrews understands them as the directly given word of God (with the one exception in 2:6–7). More strongly than in other New Testament texts, where such assumptions have not been made, it may be that the author has used for certain doctrinal statements collections of Old Testament prooftexts (*testimonia*) that already existed when he wrote. This comes close to explaining those sections in the Epistle that point to a chain of existing traditional citations.

In place of the usual introduction to letters, Hebrews immediately begins with a fundamental statement about revelation present in both the Old Testament and Christ (1:1): God first spoke to the ancestors through the prophets, but now, at the end of time, he addresses Christians (the "us" includes both the author and the audience) through his Son. Therefore, both an association and a difference between the Old and New Testament revelations are made clear. It is the very same God who has spoken to the ancestors. However, for the Christian community, which is understood to be living in the end time, the word issued through Jesus Christ is the one that is determinative. The Old Testament revelation is evaluated differently by this author than by what is emphasized by the Jews. While they see the Torah as central, the author of Hebrews sees revelation through the prophets as decisive. In the title "Son," there may be concealed already an allusion to Ps 2:8. The identity of the Son at the right hand of God at the same time is blended with the concept of inheritance. The attachment to verse 3, which was presumably a hymn about Christ from the Hellenistic Jewish community, is a short citation from Ps 110:1 of the Son sitting at the right hand of God, something that signifies his superiority even over the angels.

With this introduction, the author has broached for the first time a conceptual sphere pursued throughout his entire letter: the distinction between the earthly reality and an otherworldly, heavenly one that is superior to all things mundane. This heavenly sphere is already invested with images in the Old Testament itself concerning God sitting on his throne in the midst of the divine council (1 Kgs 22:19–22; Job 1:6–12; Isa 6:1–8) and the heavenly temple (Exod 25:9, 40; 26:30). This presentation corresponds to a Platonic form of thinking that was widespread in the Hellenistic world. The uniqueness of Hebrews, however, exists in the fact that it binds closely the figure of Christ with the heavenly sphere. Christ assumes his eminent place in it.

In Heb 1:4 the author makes his initial transition to the main theme of Christology. He continues with a series of Old Testament quotations in 2:18 on the superiority of the Son to the angels. It is obvious that what moves this author to address this topic is the attraction of teachings about angels that had developed rather substantially in the Judaism of his time. In no way does he deny the existence of angels; however, he stresses their purely servant role to the power that was bestowed exclusively on the Son. In proceeding with this type of argumentation, he builds an artistically shaped structure in which he alternates citations having to do with the Son with those that, antithetically, deal with angels. An example is the traditional messianic verses of Ps 2:7 and 2 Sam 7:14 that establish the exclusive place given to the Son in his relationship to the Father. Over against this, the Septuagint's abbreviated translation of Deut 32:43 stresses that all the angels will serve the Son. Thus, the author of Hebrews seeks to characterize the angels both as the spiritual servants of God, a view that deviates from the primary Hebrew reading, and as messengers in Ps 104:4. In contrast to this, he speaks of Ps 45, which already had been given a messianic cast in both the Septuagint and the Targum, and points to 45:7–8, which tell of the "Son" sitting upon the throne as "God." Even so, this title read by the author appears entirely appropriate. Lordship is designated as eternal in this psalm, in opposition to the variety of services performed by the angels. A further citation is added to this, this time Ps 102:6–7, explained likewise as applying to Jesus. The author relates the title of the one addressed as "Lord" to Christ. The hymnic statements in the original text that praise Yahweh as the Creator means in the eyes of the author of Hebrews the one who mediates between heaven and creation (see also Heb 1:2) and who, at the same time, being eternal, will outlast the works of creation. Yet again he adds a citation from Ps 110 that belongs also to the traditional messianic passages: "To whom among the angels has he ever said: 'sit at my right hand...?'"

The operative method of the Epistle to the Hebrews is already clear in this first chapter. An antithetical, extended structure brings to the fore its leading thoughts. By means of the alternating positioning of the citations, the author establishes, on one hand, the servant role of the angels, but on the other hand, the absolute, sovereign position of the Son. With this line of argument, which is his own conceptual achievement, he interprets christologically Old Testament citations, which are taken especially from the Psalter. Through his messianic understanding of the Septuagint, he goes back to an interpretive tradition already shaped by the community. This may also apply to his use of Ps 8, which is cited in Heb 2:5–7, even though this Old Testament text actually treats generally the place of humanity in the world, not the Son of Man in a christological understanding. In Heb 2 the author also refers to the name of Jesus, which we encounter for the first time (2:9). His frequent use of the name (see 3:1; 4:14; 6:20; 10:19; 12:2, 24; 13:12) makes it clear how great a weight he places on the humanity of Jesus in addition to his heavenly grandeur. Jesus' humanity also serves the author's interpretation of Ps 8:6, which he understands as expressive of lowliness, in contrast to the original meaning. Although Jesus is the Lord over all creation, God has humbled him for a time ("for a brief time"; found only in the Septuagint translation), making him even lower than the angels. What drives this is the readers' faith having become weak. The anticipated return of Christ in glory is not the point of this particular citation, for Hebrews only has his lowliness in mind. According to Hebrews, this humility is in accord with the way that God determined for the Son.

Hebrews adds to this citation another from the Psalter: Heb. 2:10 remarks that it behooved the Lord God Almighty to "lead many sons to glory ... in order to bring them to perfection through suffering." This suffering, however, is suffering for the sake of brothers: the Son draws the sons to himself. From this point, then, the thought process at work in the author moves him to associate the key word "brothers" in Ps 22:23 and "children" in the Septuagint translation of Isa 8:18. This method of operation, which follows the grouping together of key words, corresponds to the exegetical method in the pesharim as we know it from Qumran. Theologically, Hebrews wishes to go beyond this in speaking of both the humiliation that Jesus Christ accepted for himself for his brothers and the conquering of the depravity of humans through his suffering of death for their sins (2:5–13, 14–18). Here (2:17) the key word "high priest" occurs for the first time, which provides the basis for the central concepts in the continuation of the letter.

For Hebrews, the motif of comparative eminence is customary: Christ stands higher than the angels, although temporarily he was made lower than them. Humans (Christians) are both his brothers and children as well as the sons of God. Therefore, the sufferings to which they are exposed are experienced as a means of participation in the suffering of Jesus. This is a necessary stage through which they are required to pass in order to participate in his coming glory.

The principle of increasing comparison, which is recognized in the rabbis to be a standard rule of interpretation, is asserted in the following section (3:1–4:13). In this section it is primarily (3:1–6) a comparison between Jesus and Moses. Moses was (according to the citation of the Septuagint in Num 12:7) faithful as a servant in his entire house, while Jesus is like a son who is *over* the house. This argumentation should comfort the readers and make certain their hope, for they have a part in the heavenly commission of Jesus, "whose house we are"!

The equation of the "house" with the Christian community makes possible the transition to the following argument, which compares the "wandering people of God" with Israel's wilderness journey. A fundamental thought molds this entire connection: an extensive citation from Ps 95:7–11 warns the community of the obduracy of the Israelites in the wilderness (3:7–11). After this, the key terms "today" and "rest" are highlighted in regard to both the situation and activity of the community. "Today" means, in this context, to experience once again a reprieve here and now through the working of the call of God. "Rest" refers to Israel's goal in the wandering through the wilderness, which, nevertheless, was denied and not fulfilled even by Joshua. This rest is offered once again, now to the author's readers and hearers, even though it also may be forfeited because of disobedience. In addition, the expression Sabbath "rest" is drawn from Gen 2:2: "There is a Sabbath rest that remains for the people of God" (Heb 4:9–11). With the admonition bound to the promise, the doubting community receives the certainty of the approaching salvation placed before their eyes. With this stratagem for interpretation, we possess a visible example for the type of preaching of the Old Testament that occurred at the end of the first century C.E.

In the main section that follows in 4:14–10:18, Hebrews unfolds its own particular christological teaching that will become the basis for the exhortations in 10:19–13:25. The key expression in this section is "high priest." Leaving aside the intervening exhortatory section in 5:11–6:20, the theme of Jesus as the high priest is developed according to several trains of thought. The Old Testament is used in a somewhat different way at this point in Hebrews: a few verbal citations shape the essential outline in order to set forth a few elaborate meditations. These are certainly much more strongly nuanced by Old Testament allusions and reminiscences than may be noticed at first glance. It is probable that here the author of Hebrews takes up previously shaped primitive Christian traditions.

Programmatic assertions about Jesus as high priest, found in 4:14–16, introduce this lengthy section of the epistle. It is decisive for the community that the high priest, Jesus, is, on the one hand, the Son who journeyed through the heavens, thus, as the preexistent Christ, and is, on the other hand, a human being who was tempted and could suffer with other people, although without sin. The thoughts attached to this key role of high priest have to do with the relationship between Aaron as high priest and Christ, who now serves in this office. These point to both the difference and the commonality between the two: the high priest who is taken from among humans must also offer sacrifices for his own sins, but Christ did not of his own accord enter into the office of high priest but rather is called by God to fulfill this role. In this passage, the traditionally understood citations of the Psalter, including Pss 2:7 and 110:4, find their place (Heb 5:5–6). The key expression the "priest according to the order of Melchizedek" is provided by Ps 110:4, which has been interpreted more precisely. In addition, the assertions in Heb 5:7–10, behind which one may assume there was a previously formed text, may reach back to the Old Testament's psalmic formulations; Ps 116 comes especially into consideration.

Connecting to the key expression from Ps 110:4, Heb 7 offers an interpretation of the well-known narrative of Gen 14:17–20 concerning Abraham's encounter with the legendary priest-king of Jerusalem. The essential ideas that occur here are the tithe, which Abraham contributes to Melchizedek, and the superiority of the priesthood that is "according to the order of Melchizedek" over the Levitical priesthood that stems from Abraham. According to Heb 7:3, one encounters the notion of the preexisting Son of God, presumably according to an Old Testament tradition to which, among others, the Qumran texts allude. Thus, the "priest forever" appears as the foreshadowing of Jesus Christ, who is presented in the image of Melchizedek. In the assertion about Melchizedek in 7:3, who appears as one who is "without father, mother, and genealogy," a rabbinic principle of interpretation assumes importance: "what is not in the Scriptures is not in the world." Since the genealogy of Melchizedek in Gen 14 is not mentioned, he cannot have had the normal experience of having parents! Melchizedek becomes, then, the *typos* for Christ, who conforms to him on the basis of the power of eternal life (7:15). In place of the former law, abrogated due to its weakness and ineffectiveness (7:18), Christ has become the guarantee of a better covenant (7:22), on the basis of an oath sworn by God. Christ occupies this type of priesthood forever (7:24). These expressions are so constructed that the language of the priest "according to the order of Melchizedek," the "eternal" oath of God, and "the just things" adopt the language of Ps 110:4, which the author of Hebrews uses in interpreting what he considers to be its important aspects. The homiletical style of the constructions clearly emerges. The concluding thought in 7:27 is that Jesus, unlike other high priests, does not have to perform sacrifices each day first for his own sins and then for the people but rather offers himself as a sacrifice once and for all. The significance of the event of the cross is brought out by the ideas of the forms of cultic sacrifice.

Another form of image and archetypal thinking is encountered in Heb 8:1–5. Here the author uses the idea already appearing in the Old Testament itself that Moses should prepare a tabernacle according to the model (type) of a heavenly archetype. That the earthly sanctuary is only a copy of a heavenly one is a common Oriental concept. This vertical typology is superseded immediately (8:6–13), however, by the concept of the ongoing periods of salvation history that follow one after the other. In this section one finds the longest of all the citations of Scripture in Hebrews: the well-known passage about the "new covenant" in Jer 31:31–34. This section also establishes the preeminent priesthood of Jesus, due to the fact he is the intercessor of a better covenant. Important is the concluding statement in 8:13, where Hebrews, in viewing the consummation of the "new covenant," explains that God has declared the first covenant to be obsolete.

Although the Old Testament is extensively quoted in Hebrews, an abrupt, negative attitude toward the question of the continuation of the old covenant and its orders is conspicuous. This is comparable to an attitude already expressed in Paul, particularly in Gal 4:21–31 and 2 Cor 3, thus pointing to what appears to be a previous tradition. However, the Old Testament's status as the word of God is in no way diminished.

In Heb 9:1–10:18, the cultic institutions dealing with sin found in the Old Testament are now contrasted with those of the New Testament (in Christ). The author presupposes of his readers a precise knowledge of the regulations of the temple and the functions of the priests, especially in the introductory section of 9:1–10. The description of the "earthly" sanctuary with its division into the holy place and the holy of holies, spaces that are separated by a curtain, and of the length of service of the priests and high priests serve as a visualization of the fundamental thought pursued here. This is the idea that Christ is the high priest in the tent in which this understanding of the sanctuary and its priests is actualized. Through this means the old statutes are made obsolete. He is the high priest in the greater, more perfect tent—the otherworldly tent—and removes sins and effectuates salvation no longer through the blood of animals but rather through the offering of his own blood once and for all (9:11–14).

That blood is necessary for the ritual of the sin sacrifice is made clear in 9:18–22 through reference to the ceremony of blood that Moses performed to conclude the covenant (Exod 24:8). Christ's entrance into the heavenly, not the earthly, sanctuary is an act that he does not have to repeat, since his single sacrifice removed sins (this is made clear in 9:23–28). All of this assumes a style of preaching in which repetition of important fundamental thoughts plays a role. Thus, it is not surprising when in 10:11–18 it is again mentioned that the priest brings a daily sacrifice, while Jesus through the one-time occurrence of his sacrifice has made superfluous all other sacrifices. Citations from Ps 110 group together these thoughts once again with the earlier appearance of references to "sitting at the right hand of God." In view of Ps 110, this place of honor is accorded to the messianic "Son" (see the previously mentioned citations of this psalm).

The complexity of this process of thought with its limited coterie of Old Testament reminiscences is shown in the additional citation of Jer 33:33–34 in order to demonstrate that in the period of the new covenant, when the law is written on the heart and sins are forgiven, sacrifice for sin is no longer necessary. In the foregoing, in 10:1–10, Hebrews had arranged in its customary fashion a section around Ps 40:7–9a. The writer obviously construes a speech of God to be one of the preexisting Christ before his descent into the world. Since there has emerged an antithesis between sacrifices, which God rejects, and the doing of his will, Hebrews can relate this to Christ becoming human. This is possible because Hebrews contains a mistaken reading, probably through a textual error, that transmits a key expression. Instead of the original reading, "ears you have given me," Hebrews reads "a body you have prepared for me."

As a meditation on the salvific work of Christ, the principal christological understanding in Hebrews as a whole is described by means of the background of the Old Testament's cultic institutions dealing with sin.

A moderately meditative and homiletical style is appropriate for a coterie of a limited number of Old Testament texts that are continually and partially cited and interpreted according to the theological concerns of the epistle. There are two sides to the relationship to the Old Testament. On the one side, there are texts that, according to the program in 1:1, are the uncontested word of God and have a continuing authoritative status. Their authority climaxes in pointing ultimately to Jesus Christ as the one who perfectly fulfills the salvific will of God. The cultic institutions of the Old Testament eventuate in this. For other texts of the Old Testament, there are, on the other side, those that have lost this authority. The earthly temple and the continually repeated sacrifices that are offered in it have become superfluous, since the sacrifice of Christ, given once for all, has washed away sins for all time. The old covenant is dissolved finally through the issuance of the new. The Epistle to the Hebrews is especially clear in stressing the break between the old and the new. The community receiving this teaching lives in the end time, which has broken into existence with the sending of Jesus and his sacrificial death.

In the last portion of Hebrews, the practical and theological consequences of the christological convictions are set forth for the life of the community. The transition is indicated in 10:19–21 through the bold statement that the community itself has access to the heavenly sanctuary through the blood of Christ, for its members are interpreted to be like a community of priests who have access to the holy of holies beyond the veil, understood allegorically as the flesh of Christ. This allegory remains an exception, however, in distinction to Philo and in spite of parallels to him, even though Hebrews is aware of the dualism of the heavenly and the earthly. There occurs in the following section the expression of holding fast to the hope, avoiding apostasy, and continuing in faith in view of the imminent consummation.

In the characteristic style of this exhortation there emerges in Heb 11 an entirely different use of the Old Testament. Under the key word "faith," the "ancestors," the great figures of the Old Testament's history of faith (see the "ancestors" in 1:1–2), attain an exemplary significance. Their faith, which corresponds to the definition given in 11:1, "faith is the reality of things hoped for, the conviction of things not seen," becomes the pattern for those of the present generation who lack this kind of unyielding belief. Thus, there appear in this series of figures of faith drawn from the Old Testament the ancestors Abel, Enoch, Noah, Abraham, Sarah, Isaac, Jacob, Joseph, Moses, Rahab, and, finally, prophets and martyrs who constitute the "cloud of witnesses." Also, this use of Old Testament figures as paradigms for the present corresponds to Jewish tradition (see especially Sir 44:1–50:21; 1 Macc 2:51–61; Philo, *Leg.* 2.57–59). In the concluding remarks in 11:39–40, this "cloud of witnesses" (12:1) is clearly lifted up before the addressees of this epistle, the Christians of the time of fulfillment. Here it is demonstrated that the "ancestors" have already seen the perfection: it was not yet concluded in their lifetimes, but they now see it occurring in the life and actions of Jesus Christ at the end of time, together with his community in whom they take part. Thus, the entire Old Testament history of faith stands under the promise of God that is coming to its conclusion.

Subsequently, in the Epistle to the Hebrews the relation with the period of the old covenant is not seen as lacking in didactic value. Its institutions indeed now are surpassed and discarded in the end time after the sacrificial death of Christ for all humans. Also, the faith of the ancestors was a precursory promise without immediate fulfillment. Thus, the ancestors are not excluded but rather are brought within the purpose of the ways of God.

Understanding the Epistle to the Hebrews, with its process of thought and its use of Old Testament images and ideas, comes at a significant cost for modern readers of the Bible. Also, one encounters in it a series of time-bound methods of execution encountered in other writings of the same period. The entire sphere of ideas of sins and sacrifices, of which Hebrews makes considerable use, may seem strange to us at first glance. Still, even with the concepts of substitution and sacrifice, dimensions are addressed that penetrate to the depths of religious thinking. The sacrificial death of Jesus as once and for all and for every sinful deed is a core statement of the Christian faith that one can never renounce. All exhortations to a hopeful trust and corresponding actions, which Hebrews also contains, are not thinkable without this fundamental foundation. This is why the writer of Hebrews has made Christology the center point of his preaching.

Although some maintain that there is often an approximation of Hebrews to Philo and to the Hellenistic Alexandrian milieu, which includes some shared methodological and cosmological views, this argument carries little weight. While the opposition between the heavenly and the earthly, the exegesis of key expressions, and the occasional process of allegorizing are similar in both writers, there is no evidence for direct influence. This is because the Hellenistic features in Hebrews satisfy the general Hellenistic character of Judaism in this period, which was also determinative for the community that received this epistle. The use of the Septuagint's translation of the Old Testament (with few variations) by the writer of Hebrews corresponds to this.

3.7. A Christian Visionary in the Succession of the Prophets: The Apocalypse of John

As a final example of the use of the Old Testament by the New, one should turn to the last book of the Bible to deal with the Apocalypse of John. Although the term *apocalypse*, which is used for a certain form of early Jewish literature, is found in the superscription of this New Testament book, "The revelation of Jesus Christ" (1:1), the Apocalypse of John is to be distinguished in important ways from the apocalypses in Jewish literature. While Isa 24–27 is an apocalypse and there are apocalyptic features of parts of the book of Zechariah, there is only one apocalyptic book found in the Jewish canon: the book of Daniel. In contrast to the Jewish apocalypses, which are in each case pseudonymous and attributed to the authorship of legendary figures of the past, including Daniel, Enoch, as well as others, the author of the Apocalypse openly names himself as John (1:4), a brother of the recipients of the text he has written and a participant in their oppression (1:9). In so doing, he abandons the fiction of speaking from the past: John does not present himself as having lived in the distant past (as does Daniel, e.g., in the time of the Neo- Babylonian king Nebuchadnezzar) and from there prophesying what is to happen in the reputed future, things that are already known. The Apocalypse of John also lacks the periodization of history that exists, for example, in Dan 2 and 7 in the description of the succession of world empires down to the expected final empire. It does certainly hold in common with Jewish apocalypses the purpose of granting comfort to those marginalized readers who are experiencing oppression and enduring an apparently hopeless position. In addition, there are also admonitory statements in the letters sent to the communities of Asia Minor mentioned in Rev 2–3, who experience both the threat of weakness and internal dangers. In addition, the crisis situation is entirely clear in some places (see esp. 13:11–18; 17:6, 8–14). Presumably these things were occurring during the last years of the rule of Caesar Domitian (81–96). The requirements of the totalitarianism of the Roman state are seen, for example, in the demand for the common religious observation of the Caesar cult, central to imperial ideology, by all inhabitants. While not occupying the center of imperial policy and action, there are still local areas of the persecution of Christians who refuse to participate in this religious activity.

In this situation, two mistaken attitudes threaten the readers. One involves, at least externally, participating in the consuming of flesh offered to idols during special social occasions or perhaps even taking part in the cult of the Caesars (see 2:12–18, 20), due, on one hand, to the fact that they have already realized their call to freedom from all such things; on the other hand, this participation results from a resigned hopelessness in the face of oppression (2:9–10, 13). In contrast to this, John seeks to make his readers aware of two apparent aspects of divine reality that are seen only by believers: the heavenly glory of Jesus Christ (the "Lamb"), which includes the salvation already realized by all Christians; the imminent judgment of the wicked powers, which has already transpired in the heavenly realm. However, this judgment will not be realized on the earth until the expected end time can break into history. It is then that the final salvation also will be realized along with the direct sovereignty and proximity of God. In order to demonstrate this, the author uses in a comprehensive manner images drawn from apocalyptic and vision reports ("and I looked," 1:12; 4:1; 5:1, 6, 11; 6:1, 12; 7:1–2, 9). Like a messenger (witness, 1:2; scribe, 1:11, 19) he imparts to the recipients of his letter the message he has received (22:6–10, 16) that is to be transmitted from Jesus Christ as its only author (see 2:1, 8, 12; 3:1, 7, 14). In so far as he continues in the role of the Old Testament prophet, for whom visions are directly characteristic (for the assimilation of the prophets Ezekiel and Zechariah, see below), he refers to himself as a "fellow brother" of the primitive Christian prophets (2:9) and designates his communications a "word of prophecy" (1:3; 22:7, 10, 18–19), yet he never calls himself a prophet. The letter-like character of the book of Revelation has recently been noted: it begins with the address of a letter (1:4–8) and ends with a type of concluding epistolary formula (22:21). The seven letters sent to the communities of Asia Minor (Rev 2–3) form an organic part of the whole. The visionary sections are distributed throughout the further course of the book. It is possible that the letter form signifies that the book of Revelation was meant to be read in worship.

The division of the book, on one hand, is clear: an introduction and the seven letters (Rev 1–3); the main apocalyptic section (4:1–22:5); and the conclusion (22:6–11). On the other hand, the arrangement of the main section creates difficulties that continue to be debated. The sequence of a vision of seven seals (4:1–8:1), seven trumpets (8:2–11:9), and seven plagues (15–16) may be recognized as the primary division. Each time (6:1–8:1 and the additional two sections) a series of plagues is unleashed against the earth, which in part run parallel to each other, there is still a progression leading to an execution of universal judgment in Rev 16, following the prelude in 6:1–8:1 and the adjacent section in 8:2–11:19. Further, it is clear that the vision cycles, which are interlocked with the sections that stand between them, are a conscious arrangement of the whole. The vision of the seven trumpets is attached directly to the opening of the seventh seal in 8:1; the seventh trumpet in 11:15–19 prepares the way for the eschatological consummation; and the vision of the plagues in Rev 16 prepares for the event of the judgment in 17:1–19:10. The author's precise attention to structure gives the book an artistic shape. Even so, this formation is accessible to the modern reader only when he or she has learned to understand the background of its tradition.

The Old Testament above all informs the background of this tradition. No other New Testament writing reaches back to Old Testament traditions and motifs to the same extent. The means by which this occurs, however, differentiates Revelation from all the others with which we have become familiar. An Old Testament text is not cited expressly a single time. Instead, there is a literary and imagistic world present in Revelation that is filled in a comprehensive manner with the Old Testament tradition.

Without recognizing the Old Testament tradition continued in Jewish apocalyptic and standing behind numerous images and symbols, it is impossible to understand what John the seer has to say. When one delves deeply into the origins of the encoded statements, there opens up a view of the rich and powerfully expressed world of theological thought that cannot be compared to other writings of the New Testament.

Many Old Testament books were especially influential on the Apocalypse of John, including Ezekiel, of which more than two-thirds of the New Testament passages that are recognized as especially similar to this prophetic book are deployed in the Apocalypse. Other Old Testament books that are obvious include Daniel, Exodus, numerous passages from the Psalter, words from Second Isaiah, and the vision of the heavenly throne in Isa 6. John is intimately familiar with the Old Testament and shapes his visions using Old Testament models well known to his hearers. However, he uses these visions in his composition with a great deal of freedom and independence. He clearly uses the primary Hebrew text or a Greek translation that is very close to it, but he does not use the Septuagint. Furthermore, he inserts into his text oral apocalyptic traditions of early Jewish origin in which Old Testament traditions were already explained in a particular way.

The usual impulse for his pervasive, new fusion of Old Testament motifs with his composition, however, is the Christ-event that makes up the central content of his message. As a Christian prophet and apocalyptic seer, he created a thoroughly independent work. It should not be denied that, in addition, motifs from his Hellenistic environment played a role. John openly draws from the background of the audience of his writing, an Asian community situated in Paul's earlier mission field, in order to express this type of thinking. This audience was made up mainly of Gentile Christians. Even so, in contrast to this, one has often asserted for John a Jewish Christian origin, especially noting the strong Hebraicized language of his work, which deviates considerably from Hellenistic Greek. It is a matter of question, however, how extensively there resides behind this a conscious proximity to Old Testament rhetoric.

There are many prominent examples of Old Testament motifs brought into view in the Apocalypse of John. This recourse to the Old Testament is already encountered in the introductory vision (1:9–20) about the mission that was given to John on the Isle of Patmos. Filled with the Spirit, John heard a mighty voice behind him that assigned him the task of writing to the seven communities. When he turned around, he saw seven golden lampstands (obviously representing these communities) and in the midst of them a form that was the figure of the resurrected Christ.

There is no reason to doubt that this was an authentic vision. However, visionary events and how they are described for the present audience are customarily stamped with traditional associative motifs. In this case, motifs from various chapters of the book of Daniel together with echoes of other Old Testament writings are mixed together. The visible form, compared to the Son of Man, depends rather closely on the vocabulary of Dan 7:13. Its appearance, over against this, is largely described according to the example of the depiction of the angel in Dan 10:5–6. In this regard, the later understanding of Dan 7 as an individual is already presupposed, while originally it was understood collectively to refer to the people of Israel. Furthermore, the body and face of the heavenly form is described as having a head and hair that signifies the appearance of God himself in the text to which allusion is made (Dan 7:6). This heavenly form possesses eyes like those of the figure portrayed in Dan 10:6. There are two Jewish apocalyptic parallels to the association with Dan 10 and 7 (Apoc. Ab. 11; Jos. Asen. 14), suggesting perhaps a traditional linkage that was already in existence. The robe with which Christ is clothed is probably the robe of the high priest (Exod 28:4, 31), for the high golden girdle on the breast conforms to his priestly garment (Josephus mentions this). Also, the description of the feet has been taken from Dan 10:6. In contrast, Ezek 1:24 stands behind the characterization of the voice of Christ "as the sound of many waters" and the sound of the noise of the wheels of the chariot supporting the royal throne of God. However, Ezek 1 had already worked its way into the formulations present in Dan 10, so that the Apocalypse of John is continuing here an interpretative tradition. While the seven stars in the right hand of Christ and likewise the seven lampstands are associated directly with the context (the seven communities to whom the letters are sent), the sharp sword that goes forth from Christ's mouth, signifying his power of judgment (see 2:12, 16), is an image taken from Isa 49:2 (see also 11:4). The concluding comparison of this form with the brightness of the sun comes from Judg 5:31.

It is clear that the seer has used the biblical images with relative freedom to describe his visions, even if he does on occasion take over a partially existing apocalyptic tradition in his literary sections. This is especially clear in his description of the form of Christ, who is provided a variety of conceivable attributes in order to circumscribe the features of his heavenly radiance. It is striking, on the other hand, that almost all of these images are taken from the Scriptures. Obviously, behind this stands the same unlimited recognition of the Old Testament as the word of God, a view that is also true of other New Testament writings. However, in the case of this book, the Old Testament is interpreted not as a document of revelation but rather as a series of visions from the prophets and other recipients of God's word from this earlier time. These visions are grouped together with John's own. Thus, the new Christian message directly continues that of the ancient people of God.

A second great vision, in Rev 4–5, builds to a certain extent the entryway to the apocalyptic episode in Rev 6. In this vision the seer is given a look into the heavenly throne. The inducement at the entrance, where a door into heaven is opened (4:1), is initially provided by pseudepigraphical texts (1 En. 14:13; 3 Macc 6:18). However, the idea of an opened heaven is already presupposed in Isa 6, Ezek 1, and 1 Kgs 22:19–23. Directly following is an invitation in a trumpet-like voice to the seer to ascend to the heavenly throne of God. This corresponds to the summons issued to Moses in Exod 19:16, 24. John sees in the heavens a throne set up and one who sits upon it, an image taken from Ezek 1:26. However, in opposition to Ezek 1:27–28, John does not bring into view an approximate description of the divine form but rather merely a portrayal of the radiant light that surrounds him. Each anthropological similarity to God is customarily omitted. Then follows the representation of the heavenly court with twenty-four thrones and twenty-four elders dressed in kingly robes (Rev 4:4). The mention of these elders may go back to Isa 24:23, which John has interpreted as referring to the heavenly court. Scholars have wished to see the number twenty-four as the same number of astral deities of the circle of animals according to ancient mythological thinking. Lightning, rumbling, and thunder already are found in Old Testament theophanies (see Ezek 1:13, Exod 19:16). In the continuing course of the description, the four creatures who bow down (Rev 4:6–8) are taken from Ezek 1. Their function in this prophetic passage is to bear the divine throne, but this is missing in John's text. Rather, they bow down before the throne (5:8; 19:4). In John's text they vary from Ezek 1:10 in that they assume four distinctly different forms (Rev 4:7): a lion, a bull, a human, and an eagle. Presumably the great astral deities who were associated with the four seasons were in the background of this portrayal, although John was not conscious of it. Later they became symbols of the four Evangelists. In the depiction of the four creatures, suddenly (Rev 4:8) the temple vision of Isa 6:2 plays a role, where the creatures (as was the case with the seraphim in the prophetic text) have six wings. The difficult phrase "full of eyes in front and behind" is explained by the appropriation of the image in Ezek 1:18. In the conclusion, the three occurrences of the word "holy" allow Isa 6:3 to come back into view. The hymnic praise of the seraphim in Isa 6 is modified in the Apocalypse of John, however, with the typical naming of God as "the Almighty" (1:8; 11:17; 15:3; 16:7, 19:6; 21:22; see also 16:14; 19:15) and the divine name given to Moses in Exod 3:14 (already occurring in Rev 1:4, 8; 11:17; 16:5) being understood according to the Greek transmission encountered in the Septuagint to mean in its essence "being." To this John adds the twofold statement "who was" and "who is to come." This occurs presumably under the influence of an original Greek formula inserted into the Jewish interpretation of Exod 3:14 and Deut 32:39. It is also the case that different influences of contemporary interpretation are active in John, even if they are frequently hidden behind very customary formulations that only may be inferred.

The scene is continued in Rev 5 with the description of the scroll written on the "inside" and on the "back." Many interpreters wish to see in this chapter the form of a type of early document (a two-part document that is inscribed on the inside and yet also has writing on the outside) that was common during that time. The vision of the call of the prophet in Ezekiel mentions a scroll covered with "alas and woe"; this would have served as the formulation of a pattern. The reference to the seal might be taken from Isa 29:11. The scene of Ezek 2:8–9 is once again taken up in the commission of the seer renewed in Rev 10, especially the manner in which the prophet is to dispatch the scroll (10:9–10). It is made especially clear in the vision that no one is worthy to open the seal. This serves as the introduction of the symbolic figure for Jesus Christ, the Lamb, who now appears between the figures of the traditional scene of the heavenly throne (5:5).

The Lamb lacks a direct Old Testament metaphorical archetype. One is able at most to think of the comparison of Isa 53:7, according to which the "Servant of Yahweh" is led like a lamb to the slaughter. However, in this Old Testament text this is only an image for the humility of the Servant, who does not protest. In addition, there is no other allusion or reference to the Servant of Yahweh in the entire book of Revelation. Or, one may think of the Paschal lamb (see 1 Cor 5:7) whose blood is understood as the means for removing the guilt for sin in the Jewish tradition (see Rev 5: 9). However, the importance of the image of the lamb may be seen in comparison to the significance of the image of the lion in Gen 49:9–10, which is designated as coming from Judah (Rev 5:5), or as the "root of David" (see Isa 11:1, 10), which has symbolic attributes of the seven horns (an Old Testament symbol for power) and seven eyes (according to Zech 4:10), which are explained as spirits of God sent throughout the entire world. Therefore, the lamb who appears as the Lord is found only in the Apocalypse of John. With this image the seer John speaks out of his personal commitment to Christ. For John, the worthiness of the world ruler (see 17:14) is produced in part on the basis of his sacrificial death, the wound of which he still carries around his neck. This Lamb alone is worthy to open the seven seals of the scroll that contains the plagues unleashed beginning in 6:1.

The Old Testament provides both in structure and content the essential background for the threefold series of plagues that are an essential element in the construction of the expectation of the eschatological judgment in John's Apocalypse. The Egyptian plagues from the plague narratives of Exodus are used as the archetype for the first and second visions inaugurated by trumpet blasts (8:7–8: hail and fire, changing water into blood; see Exod 9:23–26; 7:20–21) and in most of the paired visions. These are ulcers in Rev 16:2 (see Exod 9:10–11); water and blood in 16:3 and 16:4 (see Exod 7:17–21); darkness in 16:10 (see Exod 10:21–23); frogs in 16:13 (see Exod 8:1–3; 16:21); and hail in 16:21 (see Exod 9:22–26). The structure of these visions also follows a scheme already appearing in the Old Testament: (1) the authorization (15:1; 15:5–16:1); (2) the carrying out of the commission (e.g., 16:2a, 3a, 4a); (3) the execution (e.g., 16:2b, 3b, 4b); (4) the extent of the impact (e.g., 16:3c, 9a); and (5) the reaction of those affected (e.g., 16:9b, 11). The freedom that the seer exercises in his use of material is shown in the fact that he decreases the number of Egyptian plagues to the symbolic number seven and introduces an altered sequence of plagues, as in the paired visions. Thus, the first pair corresponds to the sixth plague in the Egyptian sequence, the fifth pair to the ninth in the Egyptian list, and the seventh pair to the seventh of the Egyptian plagues. In addition, the opening of the first four seals in Rev 6:1–8 presents an image of the four horsemen of the apocalypse that is certainly taken from Zech 1:7–15. The description of the opening of the sixth seal, which unleashes an earthquake and its results in 6:12–17, is infused with an entire range of allusions to and citations of Old Testament prophetic texts.

The last vision, found just prior to the conclusion of the book, is the view of the New Jerusalem in 21:9–22:5. Once again the seer reveals his masterly work of taking up an Old Testament tradition in this section (which possibly was based on an original created by Jewish editing). It is especially the case that the book of Ezekiel served as an exemplar of this description. The motif at the beginning (21:10) of the seer being removed "to a great and high mountain" originates in Ezekiel's temple vision in 40:2. Even so, the city is not on the mountain itself but rather descends out of heaven to a flat-appearing earth. It is an open city, never closed (21:25). In addition, the city lacks a great sanctuary because God himself and the Lamb (Christ) are present in it (21:22). This contrasts with Ezekiel, who depicts the temple of the future as the midpoint of the land. In the New Jerusalem dwells the glory of God (21:11; see Ezek 43:2; Isa 60:1). The city wall, according to an ancient idea, has twelve doors, making it square (21:16), with three gates pointing in each of the four directions of heaven (21:13). The angels at the doors are obviously the watchmen whom God has positioned there (Isa 62:6). As in Ezek 48:30–35, they are named after the twelve tribes of Israel. Also, nowhere else is it so clearly expressed that the seer consciously appropriated the heritage of Israel for the Christian community of the end time. If he attributes to the city wall twelve foundation stones with the names of the twelve apostles, it becomes clear how Jesus himself regarded the appointment of the apostles. It is doubtful that the number twelve, which recurs in the following verses, signifies cosmic and astronomical features. The measuring of the city by the angel of revelation follows again Ezek 40:3–49, although this time the measuring rod is made of gold. Furthermore, the city possesses tremendous dimensions, encompassing approximately 1,500 miles. Thus, the city measures 12,000 stades (1,000 x 12), and its wall is 144 (12 x 12) cubits (about 75 yards). The number twelve is perhaps symbolic of perfection. In the description, the city is built out of costly materials (21:18–21), causing one to think of Isa 54:11–12 and Tob 13:16–17. The foundations are either adorned with jewels (21:19a) or made of them (21:19b–20), thus reflecting the twelve stones on the breastplate of the high priest (Exod 28:17–20; 39:10–13) that bear the names of the tribes of Israel. Once more the church of the end time is compared to the heritage of Israel. Only one who knows well the Scriptures is able to understand this intimation!

When it is stated in Rev 21:23 that the new city needs neither the sun nor the moon, since it receives its eternal light from the glory of God and the Lamb, reference to Isa 60:19–20 is made. Thus, there is an eternal light to rule, and there is no more darkness (21:25; 22:5; cf. Zech 14:7). In the same verse it is stated that the gates are never closed, for the city is always open, made possible only by the presence of eternal peace. In addition, the remaining statements in 21:24–27 are taken from Old Testament texts that likewise address the time of salvation encompassing the city of Jerusalem, if not also around the Jerusalem of the eschaton. It is in our experience illogical to describe nations walking about in the radiance of its light and kings bringing to it their treasures (Isa 60:3, 11; see also 62:10–11), since according to Rev 19:19–21 and 20:9 these kings and nations of the earth were destroyed long before, and the old earth had passed away. However, the ancient motif is used in a particular way. According to 21:27, all who are unclean, the worshipers of idols and the heathen, are not allowed to enter; only the redeemed (whose names are in the "Lamb's book of life") shall make up the future population of the eschatological Jerusalem that consists of the Christian communities of Jews and non-Jews.

Concluding the vision of the eschatological Jerusalem is the river of life that flows out of it (22:1–2). Once again a section from Ezekiel serves as the exemplar for the vision of the prophet concerning the water source of the temple (47:1–12). The "tree of life," mentioned in Rev 22:2, introduces into the text the concept of paradise of Gen 2. The connection of city and paradise is somewhat challenging (the street in 22:2 causes some difficulty), although this image is also found in contemporary Jewish apocalypses (4 Ezra 7:26; 2 Bar. 4). In distinction to the previous tradition, the river does not flow out of the temple, as it does in Ezekiel, for there is no longer any temple in the Jerusalem of the end time (21:22). Rather, it flows from the throne of God and the Lamb (22:1; see likewise 21:22). The particularly Christian position of John the seer therefore comes to expression also here.

Comparing the statements of John's Apocalypse to the traditions reworked in it as well as to contemporary Jewish apocalyptic materials, it is evident that the Christian seer was indeed in a position to make clear his message to those who received his letter. This was due to all of his connections to the world of biblical language and images, which go far beyond the comprehension of the modern reader to perceive, at least at first glance. That he succeeds in this clarity for the ancient audience is to be explained only by the fact that the Christian community, in spite of the fact that it was largely composed of Christians from a pagan background, were still shaped by the Old Testament. These Christians searched and found in the Holy Scriptures the key for understanding their contemporary situation. John understood himself as a prophet who continued the message of the prophets of the Old Testament and was able to address it in new ways to the Christian communities existing in a fundamentally altered situation. However, all that is new corresponds to the old. Thus, ancient Babylon of old can serve as the symbol of the contemporary global city of Rome, whose encoded announcement of collapse can be taken from the lament uttered over fallen Babylon (Rev 18). The Roman Empire, which persecuted the Christians, also can be described by adopting motifs from Dan 7, as the beast that rises up from the sea (Rev 13:1–8) and the beast from the land (13:11–18), who causes the inhabitants of the earth to come and pay homage to the cult image of the creature from the sea. This example from the Old Testament background derives from Dan 3, in which the Babylonian king Nebuchadnezzar fashioned a golden image and causes it to be worshiped (3:5, 15). In John's Apocalypse, this is a reference to emperor worship, specifically that of Hadrian, for he was the first emperor who caused others to worship the image of him as a God while he was still alive. The Old Testament is not the only source for the seer. It is possible that ideas from an obviously ancient astral mythology play a role in the description of the figure of the heavenly woman in 12:1–17. However, for the seer the Old Testament still remains an essential authority. He never quotes it as a dead book but rather allows it to speak anew. This signifies for him an awareness of its extraordinary power that shapes him. This power rests on the fact that Jesus Christ himself authorized the vision and the seer wrote down what he was allowed to see through Christ's angel (1:2–3, 11, 19; see also 19:9; 21:5; 22:6). Therefore, the seer can add at the conclusion a solemn threat (22:18–19) that makes use of the exemplar of similar Old Testament formulas (Deut 4:2; 13:1), to defend against anyone who would alter or falsify a canonical writing.

The Apocalypse of John has a significant history of influence in the church. Even if extremist circles and sectarians have often made use of it, they overlook that fact that John the seer, in his imagistic language, seeks to announce nothing other than the general Christian truth. To him this has to do with the building of the church, made concrete in the communities in Asia, to which he himself turns in order beyond all else to enable them to hear what one reads in the Scriptures or what is recited in worship. He seeks to admonish, to enable his readers to trust, and to strengthen the community so that they may persevere through the time of persecution in order to experience the coming salvation. He does so in the form of preaching about the Old Testament, which in its form is matchless. Yet he shows in his own special way that the new message is the same as the old and that the word of God continues to go forth in its continuity. This occurs because God, who sits upon the heavenly throne, has seated on his right hand the Lamb, Jesus Christ. Therefore, the new message may not be understood without the old.

3.8. A Refutation in the New Testament: The Letter of 2 Thessalonians

This chapter, which concerns the interpretation of the Bible in the New Testament, should not conclude before we ask if there is a New Testament text that bases its interpretation on another book in the Second Testament.

Some books that could be expected to do so, when considering them under the key word "interpretation," must be excluded immediately on methodological grounds. The significance of Jesus in the Gospels, including his activity and his preaching, which are examined in the so-called criticism on the life of Jesus, cannot be regarded as having anything to do with the interpretation of Scripture, since Jesus did not leave behind any written witnesses. Another subject area in connection with the origins of the Gospels is the matter of the sources that could have been used in their descriptions. This includes the matter of which of the Synoptic Gospels (Matthew, Mark, or Luke) may be the oldest, an issue that cannot be addressed here. The basic presupposition of our entire investigation is to proceed by examining the sacred Scriptures that are recognized as binding at the time of the interpretation and to investigate this status of the time of the various Gospels. Whether Mark, as most critics think, or Matthew is the oldest is not at issue here. Even the relationship of the Gospel of John, which according to the standard view is the latest of the Gospels, to the older Synoptic ones falls outside the scope of our study. It is clear that the Synoptic traditions were often parallel to each other in their edited versions, but each one was still written according to a redactor's own disposition, without having been aware of the existence of the others. In contrast to these, the Johannine community, which originated in a circle outside the gospel of the Synoptic writers, obviously possesses its own tradition of Jesus. There is no written model of this tradition that existed for the writer to use. However, the problematic enticing of a person to engage in a closer examination in order to determine the religio-historical influences that may have influenced John's Gospel and formed a part of his unique theology, possibly a Hellenistic form or Judaism or an early form of gnosis, resides outside the scope of this study. Nevertheless, there is at least one text in the New Testament that has used another from the same canon. Even if this kind of usage falls outside what we already have examined, it is still valuable to describe the things that connect to New Testament interpretation. This approach belongs in a situation of transition, when writings later placed into the New Testament had acquired a certain authority, even if there were still some doubts about them. In my view, 2 Thessalonians, which engages in a disputation with 1 Thessalonians, is the key example of one New Testament book referring to another.

In more recent biblical scholarship, which includes Catholic criticism, the prevailing opinion is that 2 Thessalonians, in spite of the superscription ascribing the letter to Paul and his associates, does not stem from Paul but rather from an unknown author. In addition, 2 Thessalonians is not an actual letter but rather a document of instruction that examines contemporary theological problems.

The pseudo-Pauline origin of 2 Thessalonians is clear from an investigation of the relationship between this text and 1 Thessalonians. The theme of 2 Thessalonians is inserted into the beginning of chapter 2. The author is uneasy about the false expectations that have led the audience astray. They consider the return of Jesus Christ (the parousia) to be close at hand. One could attribute these expectations to three different possibilities: (1) the prediction of one who filled with the Spirit (probably a prophet); (2) the word that possessed another content that had been imparted orally; and (3) a letter. The following formula is worth noting: "by word or by letter, as though from us" (2 Thess 2:2). Thus, if the letter were indeed from Paul (in that case certainly one would expect the vocabulary to be far more complex), two possible understandings of this statement are to be considered: this language could point to a letter that ostensibly was from Paul but instead had been forged; what is meant is an authentic letter of Paul that has such an intensified expectation of the end so as to lead to an incorrect understanding.

In considering which of the letters of Paul would have come into question, one thinks of 1 Thessalonians. The most serious difference between the two letters is represented in the different views they have about the anticipation of the end time. The central position of 2 Thessalonians is to impress upon its readers the point that the return of the Lord (the parousia) and the gathering together of the pious are not close at hand. Before that occurs, in accord with apocalyptic expectation (see 1 John 2:18), the "man of wickedness," the antichrist, first must come and establish his reign. In 1 Thess 4:13–14 Paul became involved in a question of the Thessalonian community (located at Solonica) that had led to vehement discussion. At issue were the return of Christ and the fate of those in the community who had already died. Would the dead not participate with the community in the parousia, when, as expected, the coming of Christ would soon occur? That Paul, both before and now again, anticipated the parousia to be imminent is seen in his statement "we who are still alive." However, joining the living would be the dead, whose resurrection would occur at the same moment as the parousia. As concerns the precise time when the parousia would occur, Paul states that no one could possibly know (1 Thess 5:1–2), for the "Day of the Lord" will come like a thief in the night.

Subsequently, if many now read Paul's comments concerning the nearness of the end, they would not have completely misinterpreted 1 Thessalonians. A considerable span of time had elapsed between the writing of this Pauline letter and others of his uncontested writings and when the unknown author of 2 Thessalonians undertook to compose his letter. The expectation of the immediate return of Christ eventually abated within the young church during this intervening period, and its members had begun to learn that a lengthy stretch of time would pass prior to the completion of the present course of history. However, there continued to be circles that, appealing to Paul's understanding, held fast to the expectation of the imminent return of Christ.

The author of 2 Thessalonians opposed this view. The method appropriated is one common to antiquity and early Christianity: pseudepigraphy. That is, 2 Thessalonians gave the appearance of having originated with Paul. To that end, the introduction to the letter names Paul and his co-workers as the authors. In addition, there are a series of references that point back to Paul, such as "from us" in 2:2 (see also 3:6). The literary conformity between the introduction to the letter in 1 Thess 1:1 and that of 2 Thess 1:1–2 is the most striking parallel. Another example of comparison includes the variety of individual features found in the expression of 1 Thess 1:2–10 and 2 Thess 1:3–12. Then there are echoes of 1 Thessalonians found in the later letter: the motif of the expression of thanks is repeated in each letter (1 Thess 2:13; 2 Thess 2:13), as are the wishes for blessings that conclude the main part of each letter (1 Thess 3:13; 2 Thess 2:17). The same expression "finally," which makes the transition from the main part to the section of exhortation, occurs in both letters (1 Thess 4:1; 2 Thess 3:1). The comparisons between the two conclusions also demonstrate remarkable parallels: the formulae of blessing in 1 Thess 5:28 and 2 Thess 3:18 correspond word for word in both texts. Above all, the author of 2 Thessalonians has set forth a feature that is especially noteworthy: he imitates the concluding comment of Paul that he has composed the letter in his own hand, a characteristic found in other authentic letters (1 Cor 16:21; Gal 6:11). Thus, this unknown author emphasizes that Paul has written this letter, because the letter concludes in the traditional way that the apostle's other letters do. This is not found, however, at the end of 1 Thessalonians.

Therefore, each of these considerations supports the view that the author of 2 Thessalonians has undertaken to refute the calamitous opinion held by those in his own situation who point back to the expressions made by Paul about the imminence of the coming parousia in 1 Thessalonians. His own written text is composed as an epistle to the Thessalonians. Those who assembled the texts for the New Testament canon were certainly under this impression when they included the letter in this collection, having concluded it was the second Pauline letter to the Thessalonians. Already in the second century (see Marcion in the following chapter), its place in the canon was uncontested. Even to the present day, there are people who support the letter as Pauline. We have shown that this is not very probable. Paul would not have contradicted himself in this way by engaging in a refutation against his own letter.

We thus have to do with a pseudepigraphon, a writing that purports to originate with a writer endowed with great authority. We should not bring into consideration our own intellectual views of propriety about matters of copyright. In antiquity, including early Judaism and Christianity, pseudepigraphy was widespread. When a text experienced such an assignation, it was customary to place its content within a particular tradition, which would be regarded by both the author and his readers as binding. In Jewish apocalyptic, it is often one of the great persons of the past, such as Daniel or Ezra, who is said to be the author of a pseudonymous text. The Gospels were all ascribed to apostles, although they originated with people from the second generation. They are endowed with the same authority as that given to the first disciples of Jesus, who are viewed as those who transmitted the authentic apostolic tradition. The additional writings attributed to John and to Peter are further examples.

The author of 2 Thessalonians perpetuated no deception either in his own eyes or those of his readers when he wrote under the name of Paul. He believed that he was the true transmitter of the Pauline tradition. Other New Testament writings have a similar disposition, including letters to the Ephesians and the Colossians that are very probably letters of the Pauline tradition, although not from the apostle's own hand. They continue, however, his message and enjoy therefore the same authority. In terms of 2 Thessalonians, one certainly does not discover the theological teaching of Paul. This author had his own very narrowly defined purpose.

The letter of 2 Thessalonians, along with other writings that refer to Paul, belong to a period of transition, inasmuch as there was at the time still no recognized collection of New Testament writings. The letters of Paul, as well as the other writings of the later New Testament, did not possess the same biblical standing. The Holy Scriptures at that time were still regarded as referring to the so-called Old Testament. The New Testament writings came to have the same rank as the Old Testament only when this second collection had been formed. This is a later development about which we shall hear from many different sources in the following sections. Even so, one sees in the occurrence of the growth of the Pauline literature the modification of additional letters that were to be included among those that go back to the apostle. Thus, one realizes that the canonization of the New Testament was not a sudden development but rather presupposes a lengthy development. The true worth of the apostolic heritage, like the letters of Paul, including those later ones alleged to be his, is the preparation of the eventual collection and final canonization of the texts that today we call the New Testament. Thus, many writings were either rejected or recognized in individual communities. This led to New Testament apocryphal writings similar to the Old Testament Apocrypha that could not be included in either the Masoretic or the Greek canon. Thus, in regard to the New Testament Apocrypha, one finds, for example, the Gospel of Peter. In the example of Marcion, we catch a glimpse of the battle fought over the New Testament canon.

4

THE EARLY CENTURIES OF THE COMMON ERA

4.1. FURTHER DEVELOPMENT OF THE TORAH:
EARLY RABBINIC INTERPRETATION OF THE BIBLE

Judaism had a variety of expressions during the time of Jesus and the early Christians: apocalyptic circles who awaited the end of the present age and the coming of the one at the end of time; Essenes, whom we encountered in their strictly secluded community at Qumran; and zealots and other nationalistic groups who attempted to rebel against the power of Roman occupation. In addition, official Judaism in Jerusalem, whose internal judgments were decided by the high council (Sanhedrin) under the presiding official, the high priest, consisted of two main parties: the Sadducees, whose course was conservative, for they included the priests and the aristocracy who provided the tone of the sect; and the Pharisees, that is, the "scribes." The meaning of "Pharisees" both then and now remains uncertain, although this identification expresses the central concern of this group. Originating among the laity, the Pharisees sought to discover and to carry out in the most comprehensive fashion the will of God as set down in the Torah. The Torah was the center of the Tanak and, in the view of the Pharisees, consisted of the five books of Moses. In order to be able to fulfill the Torah, it was necessary, above all, to study the books of Moses. Furthermore, the other books of the canon, which presumably was approximately fixed in its current form in the Hebrew Bible quite early in the Common Era, was investigated by the Pharisees in its most exact details.

Even before the Roman destruction of the temple in 70 c.e., the Pharisees had gained an ever-increasing public influence because of their exemplary fulfillment of the law and their comprehensive knowledge of the Bible. However, they refrained from engaging in political questions. Their only task was to study and fulfill the Torah. Their concentration on the religious sphere was the most important reason that they became the only group in Judaism to survive the destructive assaults of the Romans during the two Jewish rebellions in 66–70 and 132–135 C.E. By contrast, the Sadducees met their end with the destruction of the temple in 70 C.E., while the Zealots and messianic groups together with the Essenes were finally undone during the catastrophe of 135 C.E.

The influence of the Pharisees rested on two institutions: the synagogue and the house of study. Gathering in the synagogue (the house of assembly) for worship possibly reached back as early as the Babylonian exile. However, it was fully ensconced in the communities of the Jewish Diaspora and even spread to Palestine itself. Synagogues also existed in Jerusalem even when the temple was still standing. After the destruction of the temple, the synagogue continued on, and it is still today the only place of worship for Judaism throughout the world. Prayer, the reading of Scripture, and a sermon each Sabbath constituted worship in the synagogue. The sermon interpreted the section of Scripture (pericope or parash) that was read. Because the preachers were laymen, this provided the Pharisees, who were knowledgeable about Scripture, the opportunity to instruct the congregation in their teachings. The second sphere of activity in which the Pharisees worked was the school. While we do have a significant amount of information about the school in the early period, it was presumably only loosely organized. Thus, the process of teaching was conducted on a private basis in that students gathered together to learn under a well-known teacher in different places in Palestine and probably also in Babylon. Later on, there were regulated houses of study or academies. The earliest school was likely located in the vicinity of the Sanhedrin, which existed from 70 to 135 C.E. in Yavneh (in the proximity of modern Jaffa) and later was relocated to successive places in Galilee. From the third century on, there were obviously several of these centers of learning both in Palestine and in Babylonia.

While we are provided with insufficient information about the early history of these houses of instruction and remain unaware of many of the details of their instructional operation, we are able to have somewhat more precise ideas about their instructional materials and methods. Some of the early commentaries on the books of the Torah (midrashim) provide information about the content of their interpretation of the Bible. These commentaries, we are reasonably sure, originated during the so-called Tannaitic period (the Hebrew term is *tanna* "teacher," with the image of compressing into the mind materials to be learned by rote memorization). This period began in the early part of the third century C.E. These commentaries normally expressed the oral tradition in the form of the sayings of known or not so well known rabbis whose interpretations of certain biblical precepts often conflicted. These sayings, partially anonymous, had been transmitted orally over what was obviously a very long time.

A routine system was established over the course of time for the education of rabbis. After 70 C.E., the designation rabbi (lord), which originally was merely a title of respect, became the name of an office to which one could enter successfully only after having completed a regularized course of study. In addition to the memorization of sayings, the youth studied under recognized scholars. The purpose of this study was to acquire the ability to make independent decisions about disputed questions in the sphere of religious law. In Palestine, one acquired the qualification to make these judgments through a regularized ordination with which the title of rabbi was connected. It is uncertain as to whether the same also was the case in Babylonia.

The main attention of the rabbis was directed to the further development of the order of law. For rabbinic Judaism, the chief principle was to live a life according to the will of God as he had set it down in the commandments of the Torah. The Sadducees, in accord with their conservative orientation, regarded as sufficient the sentences of the Torah set forth in the books of Moses and thus opposed any alteration, but the Pharisees already recognized that the biblical prescriptions were incapable of meeting every actual situation and that there were gaps that could lead to contradictions and thus needed clarification. Consequently, this required explanation, if the Torah was to have an unconditional validity that could be followed also in the present. Therefore, they added to the written Torah their own legal materials, which at first were transmitted through oral tradition. Later on, these were collected and arranged according to topics. The collection of all of these tractates is designated the Mishnah (Hebrew *shana* "to repeat, teaching"). While in the Mishnah reference was also made to biblical statements, it did not present itself in the form of actual commentary because of its different way of arranging the material. The method of early rabbinical interpretation of the Bible, thus, is better studied by examining the midrashim.

One may divide the material contained in the midrashim into two subject areas. The first area comprises the further development of prescriptions of the law through rabbinic casuistry, called the halakah (Hebrew *halak*, "to go, to conduct a change in the way of life"). Since the content of the halakah was often already fixed before its relation to the Bible was established, one perhaps should speak of biblical grounding instead of interpretation. This is because the usual efforts of the rabbis, which they developed and defended against other types of proceeding, was to discover a good example for a manner of behaving that found support in the Bible. The other area was the haggadah, which is made up of narrative materials that the rabbis would use to develop biblical narratives. These additional materials led to often imaginative discoveries of new details, usually for the purpose of edification. The first examples of this were already found in the Old Testament, above all in the books of Chronicles (see earlier). Since the halakah stood at the midpoint of the interests of the rabbis, it is understandable that the older midrash is concerned with the books of the Torah. It is also the case that the books of Moses contain narrative sections in addition to the books of law and priestly prescriptions. Corresponding to these, narratives are also found in the rabbinic commentaries in the haggadic sections.

Since the halakah touched on provisions issued by the rabbis, they developed above all precise principles for interpretation. In part, these rules were similar to the interpretive principles developed in Hellenistic exegesis in Alexandria, although the debate among scholars over whether rabbinic principles were dependent or not on those found in Hellenistic circles has not reached a consensus. One is not able to point to evidence for direct dependence, due to our sparse knowledge. Still, the rabbinic methods are not capable of being understood apart from the intellectual background of the Hellenistic period, even if these principles originated from Judaism itself.

The rabbinic rules for interpreting the sacred Scriptures were collected together in catalogues that continued to be expanded over the course of time. The oldest list of seven rules was put together and placed in the tradition under the name of Hillel, who worked in the second half of the last century before the Common Era. These had to do with the rules that, in essence, were common to the ancient period. These seven rules were expanded into the traditional number of thirteen, mostly through a subdivision, which was ascribed to Rabbi Ishmael (taught ca. 135 c.e.) and still today have an established place in the Jewish Morning Prayer and even were regarded as having been received by Moses at Sinai. Later still, although the date is not clear (the earliest appear to have originated in the sixth to the eighth centuries c.e.), is a list of thirty-two (or thirty-three) rules.

The methods of rabbinic biblical interpretation in the Tannaitic period should be demonstrated by examples occurring in a midrash, the early origin of which is as good as certain, rather than by many more far-fetched examples whose emergence may not always be clear. Thus, the Mekilta of Rabbi Ishmael, a commentary on the book of Exodus, is one that may be examined. It is not accidental that this commentary does not deals with the entire book of Exodus but rather begins with the celebration of the Passover festival and only brings into consideration other selected sections. Even so, one recognizes fairly clearly the connection of the interpretation with the passages that were read in worship, especially certain festivals. Although the Mekilta primarily handles halakic materials, it does not leave out purely narrative sections of Exodus. These latter passages also contain haggadic material.

In the interpretation of biblical statements by the rabbis, their remarkable knowledge of the Bible plays a decisive role. In their readings of certain verses, many other verses also come into play that oftentimes stand in places of the Bible far removed from what is being immediately discussed. However, due to the occurrence of the same key term or expression, these other passages are brought into consideration in order to fashion an explanation. The basic presupposition is that the entire Bible exists essentially on the same broad plain. A historical understanding of development reflected in some texts is entirely missing in the rabbis. Therefore, morally repugnant statements, when they are present in biblical narratives, must be explained away. Things that are unclear, gaps, and contradictions must also be set aside by means of corresponding explanations. It is presupposed that all provisions of the Torah are unconditionally binding. Often the direct obligations of biblical provisions are held only in theory. In reality, it is the responsibility of the rabbis to confirm a tradition of law from the Bible that has become binding through convention.

One example is the Jewish custom to bind on the left upper arm the small scrolls of writings (mezuzah) that have on them the texts of Exod 13:1–10, 11–16; Deut 6:4–9; 11:13–20. This prescription is deduced by the rabbis from the passage in Exod 13:9: "It shall serve as a sign on your hand." Their reflections on this passage—that the hand may signify the "upper arm" and that a single, small scroll of writing must contain the four texts—leads to the discussion of the question in the Mekilta as to why the left arm is the correct one. "You say it is the left, but perhaps this is not true, but rather it is the right." There is no direct evidence given in the passage for such a "sign of remembrance." Thus, the following texts are quoted: "For my hand has laid the foundation of the earth, and my right hand has stretched out the heavens" (Isa 48:13); and "she [Jael] grasped in her hand the tent peg, and with her right hand the smith's hammer"

(Judg 5:26). Obviously unaware of the rules of *parallelismus membrorum* (that is, placing two words meaning the same thing parallel to each other), the rabbis concluded from the explicit mention of the right hand in the second position in both verses that only the left hand can be intended. The analogous conclusion may be extended to Exod 13:9, due to the fact that the same key word, "hand," occurs, although there is no factual connection or any other type of relationship between these verses and Exod 13:9 that may be recognized. That these similar entities may be compared to each other may be found under the rules of Hillel: similarity rests on the occurrence of one or several of the same words.

Another rule that similarly is appropriate for the Hellenistic art of interpretation, the conclusion from the easy to the most complex and vice versa (*a minore ad majus*; Hebrew *qal wahomer*, the first rule of Hillel) may be illustrated in the Mekilta in the expression "in the land of Egypt" in Exod 12:1.

> This means outside of the city. You say it means outside of the city. Perhaps it means within the city. However it reads: "And Moses spoke to him: as soon as I have left the city, I will stretch out my hand to the Lord" (Exod 9:29). Should we not, therefore, use the rule of *qal wahomer*? If, in respect to the prayer, which is of less significance in terms of Moses speaking outside of the city, it is only a logical implication that in regard to the divine word, which is more significant, he speaks it outside of the city.

In the dialogical form of this section, it is already clear that we can visualize the dispute occurring within the rabbinic academy (the "house of instruction"). There the arguments for and against are exchanged, and whoever can point to the most convincing of the parallel texts from the Scriptures has the last word.

The rule *qal wahomer* can be used both for the halakah and the haggadah. Thus, with respect to the ordinance in Exod 22:30 about the flesh of cattle that has been mauled by animals in the wild, it is said that one should not eat it "but rather throw it out to the dogs." To this the Mekilta says:

> Before the dogs and those who are like dogs. However, must one literally take it to mean, "Before the dogs"? The Scriptures read: "You shall not eat an ass; you may give it to the stranger in your city, since he may eat it, or sell it to a foreigner" (Deut 14:21). Now, in using the method of *qal wahomer* may we not argue that it is an ass who makes one unclean?

If so, then why is it that the one who is carried by it does not become unclean or when it is used in any other way? Therefore, what must the Scripture mean when it says "you shall throw it before the dogs," that is, "the dogs and those who are like dogs"?

With the help of the argumentation of the more difficult to the less difficult, the provision of Exod 22:30 becomes clear. The provision appears to forbid an economic use of what is torn by animals by annulling it. The law is further developed and thereby perpetuates the fiction of the lack of contradiction within the Torah.

In a direct connection to this halakic discussion, we discover a haggadic expansion:

> From this you are able to follow that the dog receives more honor than the foreigners, since the piece of a cow that has been torn apart by wild animals was assigned to the dog and the ass to the stranger. This is to teach you that the Holy One, blessed be he [i.e., God], does not deny his wages to any creature. As it is said, "However, against Israel no dog shall wet its tongue" (Exod 11:7). The Holy One says, blessed be he, "Give him his wages!" Now, if we use the method of *qal wahomer* we can conclude: if God does not withhold the wages owed to an animal, shall he all the more not withhold the wages owed to humans.

Two citations out of Jer 17:10–12 conclude this discussion.

The distinction in the setting forth of the purpose with the same logical scheme of argumentation falls into view. In the first, the halakic discussion of the prescriptions of behavior have to do with the cultic and ethical sphere, therefore, instruction in the law, while, in the second, the haggadic discourse, the topic appears to have to do with edification as it takes its place in a sermon.

The rabbis precisely analyze the wording of a proscription. For example, Exod 12:19 says (in connection with the proscriptions for the Passover week): "Seven days long shall no leaven be found (in your houses)."

> Through this I know only that what is forbidden is "to find." Do we not know also that it also may not be seen? The Scripture says: "And there shall be no leaven seen with you" (Deut 16:4). As far as I know, the leaven is forbidden to be found and to be seen. How does this relate to the bread that is made out of leaven? The scriptural passage says, "Neither leaven nor leavened bread shall be with you" (Exod 13:7). This means that leaven is compared to leavened bread, and leavened bread with leaven. Neither one should be found or seen.

From the different scriptural statements there emerges a net of proscriptions that complement each other.

An especially important rule of analogy (the second rule in the list of Hillel) is the *qal wahomer*. It is utilized only according to strong proscriptions of tradition and may be rigorously applied only in regard to situations when two comparable statements possibly have the same expressions, and possibly only in these locations, and are also indispensable for understanding them. An example of this occurs in the Mekilta in regard to a sentence in Exod 19:11 (in connection with the preparation of the people by Moses to receive the commandments on Sinai):

> "And he (Moses) spoke to the people: be ready, etc." However, we have not heard that God has spoken directly to Moses, that they should keep their distance far away from a woman (as an ascetic practice). However "be ready" (19:15) and "be ready" (19:11) are the basis for a *qal wahomer*. Exactly as the expression "be ready" means there (19:15) to keep one's distance far removed from a woman, thus the expression also here (19:11) that is used, "be ready," is to keep one's distance far removed from a woman.

An additional model of interpretation (Hillel's rules 3 and 4) is the "establishment of a family" (Hebrew *binyan 'ab*). This has to do with the comparison of different contents of biblical passages that belong together. Here a particular ordinance may be used to explain the other that occurs in another place or two. One example of a *binyan 'ab* is found in two places in the Mekilta that refer to Exod 21:27:

> "and if he knocks out the tooth of his slave": I could understand this to mean that it is only a milk tooth that he knocked out. However, it also reads an "eye" (21:26)—as the eye is formed it could not grow back. Thus, it must also be a tooth that cannot grow back. As far as I know the passage deals only with the eye and the tooth, which are expressly mentioned. How about other main organs? See, you reason and construct a general rule on the foundation of what is common to both.... What is common to both is that this passage describes a continuing loss. These are main organs that are visible. And if the lord has purposefully destroyed them, then the slave for this reason goes free.... Therefore, I can include only those parts of the body the loss of which signifies continuing harm. The major organs are visible. When they are purposely destroyed by a lord, his slave is to gain his freedom.

This commentary has less to do with the meaning of the text itself than something that is emphasized much more. This is the scope of its usage. From the largely accidental mention of the two organs of the eye and the tooth in the Torah, a system is developed that allows analogous bodily injuries not named in the text to be handled in the same way and that adapts the sphere of the validity of the Torah to different and various forms of experience. The interest resides in the exercise of the law and corresponds to casuistic differentiations observed in other cultures as concerns the development of law, to subsume under the proscription additional possible offenses. The content of the decisive trait that is common to both sentences is worked out. This is the procedure at work in the interpretation of the biblical text. On this basis, then, the generalization can follow.

Hillel's fifth rule is concerned with the relationship of the general to the particular and the specific to the general (Hebrew *kelal uferat ukelal*). The general becomes recognized through the special, if the latter is mentioned in the second position and is closely linked to it. If the general follows the specific, it expands the particular. An example of the first case is the Mekilta's interpretation of the change in Exod 21:18, "and when men fight."

> I know this is something only about men. But what about women? Rabbi Ishmael tends to say that all prescriptions over injuries that (occur) in the Torah are not decided about this, although Num 5:6 expressly says that women are to be regarded in the same way as men. This expressly stated sentence indicates the laws concerning injuries in the Torah are to take both women and men into consideration.

As the following sentences show, however, this interpretation certainly did not lack for debate among the rabbis.

In addition, this principle's reversal, in which the general follows the particular, may also be demonstrated in the Mekilta. On the expression in Exod 22:9 pertaining to the attribution of responsibility for the custody of a livestock animal, "an ass, an ox, or a sheep," the interpreter remarks:

> I find here only an ass, an ox, and a sheep mentioned. What does this passage have to say about other animals? It reads: "all animals that are kept." It would be sufficient if I read "all animals." Why are the "ass, ox, or sheep" also mentioned? Because, if only "all animals" had been used there, then I would have to understand that the keeper is accountable only if all animals had been entrusted to him. Therefore, the passage

reads "an ass, an ox, or a sheep" in order to declare that he is accountable for each animal. And what does the Scripture teach (in which it says): "all animals"? This is only written down in order to teach you that a general statement attached to a specific one includes everything.

The rabbis customarily interposed something into the Hebrew text if it appeared in their eyes to have a meaning from which they could extract something that conformed to it. This type of alteration usually appeared when the vowels of a word in the consonantal text were under consideration. "Observe the proscription of the unleavened Bread" is read in Exod 12:17. However, Mekilta suggested an altering of this text. "Rabbi Josiah says: Do not read the text in this way. Rather read: 'Observe the commandments.'" In Hebrew, the consonantal text allows the possibility of both readings: unleavened bread (*matswot*) and commandments (*mitswot*) are distinguished only by the vowels. From the context, the understanding mentioned first is clear. However, Rabbi Josiah wanted to attach an edifying interpretation (haggadah) to this passage: "Thus, even as one should not be slow in the preparation of unleavened bread, so that it does not become leavened, thus, one should not be slow to fulfill a religious responsibility." Actually, the rabbi did not deny that the text, when read literally, deals with leaven. However, he could not allow to pass by the opportunity to include an almost playful preoccupation with its expressions, the consonantal text of which allows the provocation of an approximate association.

An interpreter normally turns to the art of dissecting a Hebrew word in order to derive another edifying meaning. An example of this is found in the interpretation of Exod 14:22: "And the children of Israel cross over the sea as on dry land." Rabbi Meir gives an explanation of this when he says that the tribes had fought over which one should descend into the sea. The question of which tribe actually did this first is solved by recourse to Ps 68:28, which in actuality has to do with an entirely different situation: "There is Benjamin, the youngest of them, who is their lord. Read not 'their lord' *rodem* but rather *rodyam* 'defies the sea.'"

On the other hand, the rabbis attempt in a way that appears thoroughly modern to ascertain the exact meaning of an expression. Thus the proscription of Exod 12:6 contains the statement that the community, "between the two evenings," should slaughter the Passover lamb. Even modern interpreters have pointed to Deut 16:6, the parallel text: "You shall slaughter the Passover sacrifice in the evening." To this the rabbis said:

If "in the evening," I can say [it] signifies after it is already dark. However, it says "when the sun goes down" (Deut 16:6). Perhaps the phrase "when the sun goes down" belongs to the statement "you should cook and eat." However, the intervening statement, "at the time when you left Egypt," concludes the theme of the time for the slaughter. The following commandment (at the beginning of 12:7) "and you shall cook and eat" is then what follows, when it is already dark.

A discussion is elicited from the formulation in Exod 17:13: "And Joshua defeated [*wayyakhalosh*] Amalek and his people." "Rabbi Joshua says, He descended and cut off the heads of the warriors who were with him (Amalek), those who stood at the head of the battle lines. Rabbi Eliezer says of the word *wayyakhalosh*, that it may have to do with an abbreviated statement for 'he weakened, quaked, and broke.'"

In Hebrew, the idea of "notary" stands for "abbreviation." This is a foreign term from Latin *notarius*, one who takes dictation, a stenographer. The abbreviated writing already is present in antiquity with the shortening of words. The explanation of Rabbi Eliezer understands the word *wayyakhalosh* as a compression of three words: *wayekhal*, "he weakens"; *wayese*, "he made to quake"; and *wayyishbor*, "he broke." In its most developed form, this method understands each individual letter of one word as the beginning letter of another. This allows the association, then, quite naturally to have a vast array of meanings. Related to this is the method in the haggadah, seeing that, in regard to the quoted example, it serves the purposes of its demonstration in preaching and in the process of interpretation.

The sequence of words is also closely observed. For example, Exod 12:48 reads, "If a stranger who resides with you and will celebrate to the LORD the Passover, every male who belongs to him is to be circumcised, and then he shall draw near and celebrate it." The Mekilta remarks in regard to this verse: "See, if someone had to fulfill two commandments, that of the Passover and the other of circumcision, I would not know which of them has priority. However, when it says 'every male who is his is to be circumcised, and then he shall draw near to celebrate it,' this shows that the commandment of circumcision has priority over the Passover." However, the most important thing can also stand at the conclusion. Thus, Exod 12:35 reads: "And they (the Israelites) had been given by the Egyptians treasures of jewelry made of silver and treasures of gold and clothing." "It makes no sense to say 'and clothing' outside of indicating that clothing had more value for them than silver and gold." This type of explanation is not always convincing!

The Scriptures are for the rabbis "rich" in the meaning of each passage. Each text offers statements that are able to explain other biblical passages. There are also other passages that are "poor." Their meaning must be sought elsewhere, usually outside of the Torah. An example of the "richness" of a passage is indicated by the Mekilta to Exod 15:3: "The Lord is a man of war."

> Rabbi Judah says: See, this is a passage of Scripture rich in meaning that is explained by many texts. It teaches that he has appeared armed with all the weapons of war. He appears as a warrior girded with a sword, even as it is said, "Bind your sword around your hips, you are a strong hero!" (Ps 45:4). He appears to them as a rider, as it is said, "And he rides upon a cherub and flew yonder." He appeared to them in armor and places "the helmet of salvation upon his head" (Isa 59:17). He appeared to them with a spear, as it is said, "in the light of a spear of lightning" (Hab 3:11). It also says, "Draw the spear and battle axe against the one who pursues me, etc." (Ps 91:4). He appeared to them with bow and arrow, as it is said, "He shot his arrow and dispersed them" (2 Sam 22:15). He appeared to them with buckler and shield, as it is said, "His truth is a buckler and shield" (Ps 91:4). It also says, "Grasp shield and buckler" (Ps 35:2). I can understand that he has no need of these things, therefore it says, "The Lord is his Name." He does battle with his name and has no need of all these things.

Conversely, a passage of Scripture can be "poor" and require supplementation from other texts, such as the commandment in Exod 20:15, "You shall not steal."

> Do you understand this as a warning against stealing from persons. Perhaps this is not so, but rather it is a warning not to steal money? When it says "You shall not steal" (Lev 19:11), see, there you have a warning against stealing money. Therefore over what does the sentence speak, "You shall not steal" (here in Exod 20:15)? Over the one thing a person steals.

The presupposition is entirely clear that the entire Torah depicts a unity. When the commandment in Lev 19:11 uncovers a reference, the parallel text in Exod 20:15 can mean only one thing. In conclusion, there certainly are other ways that enlighten us from the context out of which Exod 20 argues. These include the fact that this commandment stands in a series of other ones that threaten the death penalty, so that here it is capable of dealing only with a crime that is worthy of death.

The succession of words also pay attention to the ways that separate explanations find apparent double meanings. A descriptive example is the explanation of Exod 12:6, "the entire assembly of the community of Israel shall slaughter it": "(The rabbis) said of this, The Passover lamb is slaughtered by three groups, an assembly, a community, and Israel."

Obviously efforts are made to explain contradictions.

> One passage (Exod 12:40) says: "Four hundred and thirty years" (the Egyptians tarried in Egypt); one text (Gen 15:13) says, "And you shall serve them, and they shall afflict you for four hundred years." How can these two passages be reconciled? Thirty years before Isaac was born, this decree was enacted between the parts of the sacrifice (separated by this occasion). Rabbi (Judah the Prince) says, One text says "And they shall serve them, and they shall afflict them four hundred years," and another passage (Gen 15:6) says, "In the fourth generation they shall return here." How can these two passages be retained together? The Holy One, blessed be he, said: "If you shall repent, then I will redeem you according to the number of the generations, and if not, I shall redeem you according to the number of years."

The allegorical interpretation cultivated by Philo and the church fathers and that played an important role in their interpretation was seldom found among the rabbis. They opposed it openly by means of their common orientation that was aligned with their interest in the real meaning of the text and with their matter-of-fact approach. Rabbi Ishmael interpreted allegorically only three passages in the Torah pertaining to the halakah (*mashal*, "parable," twenty-fifth rule of Eliezer): Exod 22:2; Num 21:19; and Deut 22:17. We cite from the Mekilta for Exod 22:2, "'If the sun rises over him (the burglar who is caught by the owner of a house and killed),' Rabbi Israel says, 'Does the sun rise only over him? Does it not rise over the entire world? What does the sun signify? Peace in the world. Therefore, if it is known that this burglar had friendly intentions toward the owner and still the latter one killed him, he is guilty of murder.'"

Even so, this meaning is also debated, for the Mekilta continues, "Perhaps it is not so, but rather does this case make a distinction between day and night, in that it says to you, if the owner kills the burglar, he is guilty, but if he kills him at night, he is free?" One marvels that this interpretation is not the only one that rules in so significant a case.

In contrast to this, it is often a matter of either an explanation of historical issues with regard to the Torah or another spiritual explanation.

One example comes from the interpretation of Exod 15:22: "And they wandered three days in the wilderness and found no water." Here also there are two fundamental interpretations. "Rabbi Joshua says, This is to be taken literally." The allegorical interpreter says, "They found no word of the Torah with which water is compared. And from where do we learn that the word is compared with water? It is said, 'Now then, everyone who thirsts comes to the water, etc.' (Isa 55:1)." In fact, this is a passage where the idea is used metaphorically. According to the system of comparison of passages, the allegorical interpreters of Exod 15:22 proceed accordingly. The specification of the content quite naturally is that the Torah is the actual source of life. However, a piece of wood can also be explained allegorically as the Torah, thus Exod 15:25, "And the Lord showed him (Moses) a piece of wood [Hebrew *'ets*]." The allegorical commentators say, "He showed him the words of the Torah with which a tree *'ets* is compared, as it is said, 'She is a tree of life to all who grasp it'" (Prov 3:18, this verse is also reinterpreted, since there the discussion has to do with wisdom!).

These explanations belong to the area of edifying explanation (haggadah). There the entire thought of the rabbis encircles the Torah, and their edifying statements are concentrated on it. Day and night the Torah is contemplated. It is regarded as their task with which they complied in the house of instruction as well as in their casuistic interpretation of the Torah proscriptions (halakah). It is also their task reflectively to guide their audience into the sphere of life of the Torah, with the help of the interpretation of Scripture. The result of both kinds of activity is the comprehensive literature from which we are able to set forth only a small slice. All essential forms of this type of scriptural exegesis are recognized in the Mekilta.

4.2. THE APOSTOLIC FATHERS

Scholars since the seventeenth century have subsumed a collection of early Christian writings that were not placed in the New Testament, even though they still belonged to the apostles of the following two generations, under the designation "Apostolic fathers." The designation is slightly erroneous, since only Ignatius of Antioch (died after 110 C.E.) and Bishop Polycarp of Smyrna (died after 155 C.E.), whose writings were included in this collection, can be identified. In other cases the ascription is mostly legendary. Thus, the Letter of Barnabas, beginning in approximately 200 C.E. (mentioned first by Clement of Alexandria), was attributed to the companion of Paul and the apostle who bore the name Barnabas. Clement, whose name emerged as the third successor of Peter in the Roman list of bishops, is considered to be the author of the Letter of 1 Clement, a writing of the Roman community. Others, such as the Didache (The Teaching of the Apostles), are anonymous.

The question of authorship, however, is not especially central, as has often been the case in interpretation. Much more significant for these writings is that they are frequently considered to be literature of communities. Formally placed in the form of a letter, the text contains a tractate that expresses theological and ethical interpretations that were considered influential in either a Christian community or a particular group. This tractate imparted instructions for the life of both the community and the individual. The form of these texts' engagement with the sacred Scriptures is what most concerns us. The Holy Scripture of this early period is still without doubt the Old Testament, as it was later known. Each theological interpretation must have its authority established and legitimated by Scripture. Further, the apostolic fathers' intimate knowledge of the New Testament writings often may be demonstrated. The words of Jesus command the same authority as the Scriptures. For examples of developing literature, there is the assembling of the Pauline letters, which obviously already existed in a number of different collections. Even so, there was still no discussion of a New Testament canon.

The type of encounter with the Scriptures found in the apostolic fathers should be understood only in relation to the types of exegesis practiced at the time and the methods appropriate for this context. We have already examined a variety of these methods in their Jewish and Christian formations.

The background of the unquestioned authority given to the Old Testament and a contemporary methodology that was used everywhere indicates even more clearly the objectives of diverging theological and practical purposes of the early Christian tractates and the distinctions that emerged from them. These differences are seen in the significance of the content that is derived from Scripture.

We shall examine two examples that clearly point to the nature and context of the apostolic fathers: the Epistle of Barnabas and l Clement.

4.2.1. The Old Testament Is Only for Christians: The Letter of Barnabas

We have already indicated that the tradition that frequently attributes the letter to Barnabas in the history of the early apostles is relatively early. Indeed, one can find echoes of this attribution in the beginning and conclusion (1:20–2:8) of the ancient letter formulas, including the use of the autobiographical form in the author's address to his audience. However, neither the author nor the audience is mentioned by name. In reality, this text is not an authentic letter but rather a tractate similar to the example of the Epistle to the Hebrews in setting forth theological themes. Hebrews and the Letter of Barnabas share a common form of argumentation that is composed of numerous Old Testament citations. However, their points of departure are completely different. While Hebrews argues from the basis of the Christ-event in its selection and use of Old Testament foreshadowings, Barnabas sees the corpus of the Old Testament, including its entire portfolio of texts, as a document of revelation in which are found valid propositions for the present. The upshot of the latter method leads, however, to the conclusion that the entire history of salvation and all the institutions of the Old Testament are theologically negated in order to set forth a polemic directed against Judaism's claim to sacred Scripture. This view is surpassed only by Marcion in the early church (see below).

In addition, the understanding of Barnabas is complicated by the fact that the exact circumstances of its origins, including the time and the place of its composition, are contested. Suggested as places of origin are Egypt, Palestine, and Asia Minor. Its chronological placement swings between 95 and 135 C.E. Debated is the point in time when, according to 16:4, the temple, destroyed in 70 C.E., would be rebuilt. This is the only chronological notice possibly providing valuable information that is mentioned in the entire book. The location of this letter is especially difficult to identify, since the Hellenistic culture of the Roman Empire spread over so much of the East. Indeed, different traditions continued to be maintained, as, for example, in Egypt and Syria, that certainly influenced the intellectual milieu of the upper class's Greek education.

The purpose of the writing is stated by its author in 1:5, in which he notes his desire to impart to his audience the tradition that was being transmitted through him (see also 9:4). By this it is already clear that he does not represent a personal, special knowledge. In fact, the traditional character of the explanations of the Scriptures developed in the following chapters soon transpires, interrupted by several places where the author inserts his remarks.

An early form of the explanation of the Scriptures is announced already in the introductory sentences with a foundational remark: "The Lord (God) has permitted us to know through the prophets the past and the present and the beginnings of a foretaste of coming things" (1:7). The terms "prophet" and "prophecy" are key words that make clear that the scriptural passages appropriated by Barnabas are prophetic in nature. This means that the letter regards the entire Old Testament as prophecy. Individuals such as Abraham, Jacob, Moses, David (the psalmist), Isaiah, Jeremiah, Ezekiel, and Daniel are designated as prophets. Even so, a particular feature characterizes this key expression: "The prophets ... have prophesied about him" (5:6). The writings of the Old Testament as words of the prophet are in their central meaning explanations of Jesus Christ. They are the previous announcement of his coming—and his alone! That inner Old Testament fulfillments are entirely excluded is one of the particular features of Barnabas. Although the schema does not occur in the same form in Barnabas as it does in Matthew, we are still reminded of the Gospel writer's fulfillment citations. Barnabas can always in the same breath speak of the promise given before to the ancestors and their fulfillment in the Lord (the *kyrios*, Jesus Christ; 5:7). A central subject of this prophecy is the passion of Jesus: "Because he should also appear in the flesh and suffer, his suffering has been revealed beforehand" (6:7). The assertion "that the true Lord of all has been revealed in the past" (7:1) is, among other things, demonstrated through the discovery of the correspondences in the Scriptures to the Christ-event.

A section explaining individual features of the passion story is found in the conclusion to this fundamental commentary in 7:3–11. Already in 6:6b the casting of lots by the soldiers over the robe of the crucified one is explained as the fulfillment of a prophecy of Ps 22:29 (a traditional explanation; see already Mark 15:24; John 19:24). Here the discussion revolves around the two goats mentioned in Lev 16:7, 9, one of which is selected to be a burnt offering and the other to be sent into the wilderness to Azazel. In regard to the second goat, which is intended for Azazel, Barnabas reports a considerable amount of what is obviously oral tradition. The goat is spit upon, pierced, and crowned with a wreath of red wool, which later in the wilderness is covered with briars. Barnabas explains this chain of motifs as referring to the crucified one, who, following the suffering of many things ("mocked, pierced, and spat upon," 7:9), will return in a purple cloak (Mark 15:17; Matt 27:28; John 19:2) as the world ruler. The red color of the wool and the cloth is obviously the point of comparison. Afterwards (7:1–2), the feature of the wool being covered in thorns is explained as a paradigm of Jesus for the community. They are able to reach his kingdom only by experiencing his suffering. The word "red" in 8:1, 5, however, is also an indication of the suffering of Jesus.

The key word "wood" is understood as the cross (8:1, 5; 11:8; 12:1–7, but also the spreading out of the arms of Moses during the battle against the Amalekites: Exod 17:8–13; see Barn. 12:2 in a midrashic form). "Water" is understood as baptism (11:1, 8, 11). Though Barnabas often uses the word "typos" in this connection (7:3, 7, 10, 11; see also 8:1; 12:2, 5, 6, 9; 13:5), the method approaches allegory. One speaks of typology when the precursor has an appropriate historical meaning. This is not true in this case. The method of gematria, a recognized approach of Jewish interpretation (the reckoning of the value of the numbers of letters of the alphabet in a word and the meaning attributed to numbers) occurs in 9:8, which deals with the circumcision of the 318 servants of Abraham (a free combination of Gen 17:23 with 14:14). From the number "eighteen" (the letter *yod* or *iota* equals ten; *eta* means eight), the abbreviation for the name of "Jesus" is read. "Three hundred," that is, *taw* (t), signifies the cross.

Obviously, there were previous collections available to the author of Barnabas that were arranged according to the principle of the key word. One example is found in 9:1–3. In 9:1 Barnabas speaks of the ears that had been circumcised, metaphorically speaking, and the heart, by which we hear a word and are able to believe. He traces these thoughts, occurring again in 9:3, to the end. In between there is a chain of citations in which the key word "hear" (once as "circumcise") occurs. Although they are not related to the theme that has been addressed, Barnabas brings them full circle before finally returning to link them to the beginning. In the middle of the collection in 6:2–4, which centers on the key word "stone," found in Isa 28:16; 50:7; and Ps 118:22, Barnabas offers his comment. The meaning of the "stone" from Isa 28:16 and Ps 118:22 was already traditionally interpreted as referring to Christ (see Rom 9:33; 10:11; 1 Pet 2:4, 6; Mark 12:10 par.; Acts 4:11). Thus, Barnabas is therefore also transmitting a tradition of the community.

Also in its use of mixed citations one finds nothing especially unique in the Letter of Barnabas. We have seen similar examples in the Pauline corpus. Many of these may be attributed to mistakes of memory, while others are consciously constructed. One example is the previously mentioned connection of Gen 17:23 and 14:14, which is found in 9:8. The mixed citation in 6:13 (Deut 1:8/Gen 1:28) concludes a summary that began in 6:8. This section, bringing together a combination of passages, presents a meditation on Christ as the new creation that makes use especially of Gen 1:26–28. This demonstrates that for Barnabas, like others, the entire Bible resides on the same plane.

In one place (11:9–11) we find also a continuing exegesis with the stereotypical formula "this means," which is found also in the pesher interpretation in Qumran. Still, it does not treat a running text as we find in the Habakkuk commentary in Qumran but rather individual citations, not easily identified due to the fact they are freely altered. These are held together by the common reference to baptism.

While Barnabas does not essentially deviate from the prophetic and typological-allegorical uses of Scripture, as are common to Christian usage and occur in significant quantity in the New Testament, his own uniqueness clearly emerges in the two other uses that are grouped closely with each other.

A contemporary situation that stands at the forefront of the epistle is visible especially in 4:6: "Do not make yourself like certain (people) who say … to you: The covenant to those is also ours." These "certain people" are representations of the common Christian interpretation who see a relationship in the history of salvation between Israel and the church. They find an act of God performed for Israel to which the Old Testament gives witness as a precursor to the Christ-event. In contrast, Barnabas seeks to demonstrate (4:7–8; 14:1–2) that the Jews have "forever forfeited" the covenant (4:7) and indeed did so beginning at Sinai, when Moses broke the tablets of the covenant due to their apostasy to the idols (Exod 32:19). That Moses subsequently made intercession and once again received forgiveness for them (Exod 32:30–31) and fashioned new tablets (Exod 34) has no effect. Thus, the fact that Israel forfeited the covenant even at the beginning means that their common institutions as such are worthless. This was made clear, for example, in regard to circumcision, which should "not be carried out in the flesh" (9:4). "However, they have gone astray because an evil angel has tricked them." The literal interpretation of the Old Testament as invalid is seen, for example, in the Sabbath commandment (Barn. 15) among others and the temple (Barn. 16). Only in the end time shall one be rightly healed, for one's present healing is without validity. Instead of the Sabbath, the Christians point to the eighth day as the day of resurrection and the ascension of Christ (15:9). It is an error to place one's hope on the building and to limit God's holiness to the temple (16:1–2). That the literal interpretation is a misunderstanding is expressly shown in respect to the commandments concerning food (Barn. 10).

In what sense these different aspects may be encountered in their interaction is seen in the example of circumcision, which is especially striking. While in 9:4–6 the invalidity of a literally understood commandment, the commandment of circumcision, is made clear, there is added the statement directly following in 9:7 that Abraham carried out his circumcision (literally?), "because he looked forward in the Spirit that came upon Jesus." The "prophetic" explanation legitimates the execution of the deed, which was not fundamentally rejected. It is wrong to conclude from this a literary lack of conformity, for the contradiction is apparent only to modern observers.

The polemic against a literal understanding of Old Testament ritual proscriptions, it may be assumed, goes back to a similar situation that provided Paul the occasion to write his Letter to the Galatians. In the community that Barnabas seeks to instruct, it is probable (although we cannot go beyond only making assumptions) that some advocated remaining in compliance with a variety of customs, such as Sabbath observance, circumcision, and kosher laws. The position of Barnabas, by contrast, is much more radical. While Paul abolished Jewish ritual proscriptions as required for Gentile Christianity, Barnabas maintains the invalidity of the Old Testament for the Jews from the very beginning. He thus came close to the position represented by Marcion and the gnostics.

Barnabas shares with the gnostics the concept of dualism, which differentiates between the lower realm of matter and the higher world of the spirit. Only in the latter region may one find truths that are eternally valid. In philosophy, Platonism incorporates this typical Greek way of thinking. We found this already in Philo. However, the assumption that Philo influenced Barnabas cannot be confirmed. The purpose and method determinative for Barnabas are very different in Philo. Dualism appears in Barnabas particularly in the polemic against the cult.

Barnabas provides a key remark about his fundamental understanding in 10:2 (see also 10:9). In respect to the prohibition against food, he writes that God's commandment is not involved in this, that is, not to eat certain things (e.g., pigs and other animals). "Much more Moses has spoken in the Spirit [*pneumati*]." Subsequently, the commandment involving the enjoyment of different impure animals, taken in a literal sense, produced the transitional explanation that has to do with a moral and edifying meaning. Thus, in regard to the commandment "You should not" prohibiting the consumption of pig flesh, Moses means to adhere to certain people who are similar to swine. This means that if they live in opulence, they forget the Lord. However, if they live in need, they know the Lord. "Even as the pig devouring its food ignores its master but when it is hungry cries out and receives something and then is still" (10:3). A spiritualizing meaning of the Old Testament proscriptions concerning the cult, which almost appears as their negation, is already present in part in the Old Testament. Well known especially are the anticultic polemics in different prophets, whose views have been examined rather often in recent scholarship. Some of these assessments, however, have led to the erroneous conclusion that these prophets rejected the cult entirely. Barnabas adopts all of these words in his own criticism of the cult. Thus, the expressions in Barn. 2 take up remarks concerning the Old Testament sacrifices in Isa 1:11–13; Jer 7:22–23a and Zech 8:17a (a composite citation); and Ps 50:19. In Barn. 3 the fasts are regarded as, according to Barnabas, unwanted by the Lord, thus Isa 58:4b–5, 6–10. Also in Barn. 3 are statements regarding the temple that cite Isa 40:12 and 66:1 (a composite citation). The depiction of the temple is as a "spiritual temple" (16:10) and is explained as individual Christians (16:6–10) who are "built up" like a "dwelling" in Barn. 2, through forgiveness of sins, faith, and repentance. Paul already was familiar with this depiction of the temple (1 Cor 3:16–17; 6:19; 2 Cor 6:16), in which the thought of the individual's belonging to the community is imbedded.

A leading principle of interpretation in Barnabas is disclosed in 2:1, where the author depicts for his audience and himself the momentary, current situation, which he understands to be the time for the eschatological rule of the wicked. Here he assesses critically the "legal demands of the Lord." Practical virtues such as reverence, perseverance, humility, and self-control are thus enumerated as the presupposition for "wisdom, understanding, knowledge, and awareness" (2:2–2). This practical, ethical aim, which reaches its climax in the teaching of the two ways (Barn. 18–20), stands already in the background of the Epistle's biblical exegesis in Barn. 2–17. It should be noted at this point that here Barnabas is not to be identified with the speculative objective of Philo. There are additional discussions of the "requirements of the law" of God (see 10:2). Thus one should rejoice in them (4:11; 10:11), and their wisdom forms the character of Christians (16:9). Chapter 14 makes it clear that not Israel but rather Christians have received the covenant from the Lord himself (14:4). The covenant, however, consists of the tablets of the law (14:2–3; see 4:7–8). The entire Old Testament's ritual proscriptions are invalid, and the Old Testament is not a history of salvation. Rather, Barnabas understands it to be a law book. The legal basis of Barnabas is clearly expressed in 21:1. "It is therefore good to learn all of the legal requirements of the Lord as they are written down, for they direct the way of life for people to follow. Whoever complies with these shall be exalted in the kingdom of God. Whoever chooses to follow the other path of the two ways shall perish, along with his or her works. Hence resurrection and hence retribution." For this purpose, the formula "the new law of our Lord Jesus Christ" also may be used (2:6). Sure enough, Paul had already admonished the Galatians to fulfill the "law of Christ" (Gal 6:2). However, this isolated statement is to be understood in connection with the theology that becomes clear in his letter. In Barnabas, this theology is brought into conformity with his legal thinking.

It is certain that Barnabas did not dismiss the teaching of the forgiveness of sin. The passion of Jesus, the prior proclamation of which he sought to demonstrate was found in the prophetic witnesses of the Old Testament, served this function for him. "For this reason the Lord even took upon himself to consign the flesh to destruction in order that we might be sanctified through the forgiveness of sins, that is, through the shedding of his blood" (5:1; see 5:5; 7:2–3, 5). By means of his suffering, the Lord has demonstrated to Israel its unworthiness to receive the covenant that he gave to Christians as the people of the inheritance (14:4). Barnabas then turns to the forgiveness of sins in baptism (11:1; see 6:11; 11:11; 16:8), which signifies a new creation (16:8; see 6:11). For the new Christians whose ears are circumcised in order to hear the word (9:1, 3), fulfilling the requirements of the law of the Lord is no longer required (11:11: "in that we bear fruit with the ear, because we are comforted from the fact we have in our heart the fear and hope that comes from Jesus").

In the teaching of the two ways in Barn. 18–21 (which Barnabas has in common with the apostolic teaching, Did. 1–5), these commandments are explicated in numerous admonitions for concrete actions. Here are visible traditions of moral instruction for the community that were already provided for the two texts.

A review of the Letter of Barnabas shows that it shares numerous methodological features characteristic of biblical interpretation of that time. Barnabas uses this tool, however, to fashion an extreme position. For this reason, one may thus only appreciate the later decision of the church not to accept Barnabas into the New Testament. At the time, however, the letter appears to have been highly valued, as one may determine from the fact that it directly follows the New Testament found in the famous Sinai Codex of the monastery of Saint Catherine's (fourth century; discovered in 1859 by Count Tischendorf).

4.2.2. A LETTER OF EXHORTATION BASED ON THE OLD TESTAMENT: THE
LETTER OF 1 CLEMENT

A second document of the early church is the letter of 1 Clement. It too
is an important witness for early Christianity's use of Scripture. Approximately a fourth of the entire text consists of Old Testament citations.

The exact dating and the authorship of 1 Clement are debated. It is
traditional to attribute the text to Clement, who emerged as the third successor of Peter in the oldest list of the bishops of Rome (in Irenaeus). This
list, nevertheless, is presumably a stylized one in as much as the authentic
constitution of the early church in Rome at the end of the first century
C.E. probably had no monarchical office of bishop; rather, the leadership
of the community was vested several presbyters or bishops who would
have been equal in authority. It also remains unclear as to whether the
frequently accepted origin of the bishop of Rome is dated appropriately
in the last years of Caesar Domitian (around 95 C.E.). Although several
indications of a relatively early period of composition make it likely that 1
Clement was composed at this time, this continues to be debated.

The occasion of the composition concerns events in the community
of Corinth, who are mentioned as the audience addressed in 1:1. Accordingly, the letter is treated as an official communiqué to the Corinthian
community from its sister community in Rome. Although only a few
indications are present, one can still conclude that there were in Corinth
a few (1:1; 47:6) younger (3:3) members of the community whose boast-
ful and reckless behavior is condemned (13:1; 14:1). They have risen up
against the presbyter and leader of the community and have instigated
a revolt (1:1; 14:2; 51:1; 54:2; 57:1; 63:1) that was still continuing at the
time of the writing (46:9). The purpose of the writing was to restore the
office of the legitimate leader of the community and to lead community
members to subordinate themselves to his authority (57:1–2; see 1:3;
38:1). However, it is often assumed that there were other purposes of the
author residing in the background, since in the discursive movements in
the tractate there are also themes that appear to have little to do with the
major occasion prompting the writing. The frequency of these excurses,
which obviously are a part of the writer's style, belong to the opportunity
he took to instruct his readers in a series of basic Christian confessions
that were significant to him. Many of these may have been treated in the
sermons that Clement cherished.

The explanatory role played by the Old Testament in the entire argumentation of the letter of 1 Clement is striking. Figures from the Old

Testament, appearing for the first time in chapter 4, are introduced as examples of warning for the damnation that derives from jealousy and envy: Cain and Abel (cited from Gen 4:3–8), Jacob and Esau (Gen 27:41–42), Joseph and his brothers (Gen 37), Moses' flight out of Egypt (Exod 2:14), Aaron and Miriam (Num 12), Dathan and Abiram (Num 16), and David's persecution by Saul (1 Sam 18–29). Noah and Jonah (Jonah 3), who in pseudepigraphical writings offer sermons of repentance, are mentioned because the occasion of the rebels provided the opportunity to issue calls for repentance. Indeed, these sermons by these two well-known figures, when they were heard, created the possibility of salvation (Jonah 3). Indeed, for Clement, the blood of Christ has been poured out in order to offer to the entire world the opportunity to repent. There follows in 1 Clem. 8 scriptural language about repentance that, according to 8:2, "the Lord of All," has spoken himself. Difficulties that occur in 8:3 make it difficult to know which texts are intended. Since Ezek 18:30 and especially 33:11 are echoes (in addition, Ps 103:10–11; Isa 1:18), one is led to think that Clement used free association in his citation of texts or depended on an unknown apocryphal text of Ezekiel. Subsequently, Clement sets forth a clear citation from Isa 1:16–20, in which the textual form of the Septuagint, which he mainly used, varies from the one he normally used and that enjoys the witness of the great manuscripts. The call to repentance, which now is directed expressly to the rebels (9:1), supports a lengthy series of examples that extends over chapters 9–12. These are mentioned because of their faith, obedience, and especially hospitality, which made them well known. The striking emphases placed on hospitality appear to elevate an earlier proverbial virtue of the Corinthians (1:2). In this series, Enoch and Noah (9:3–4), Abraham (1 Clem. 10), Lot (1 Clem. 11), and Rahab are encountered. The question that this raises is whether the tradition had already formed such series of examples (testimonies). Of course, this cannot be answered.

The following chapter calls on the rebels to be patient and obedient, while in 1 Clem. 14–15 (for 1 Clem. 13, see below) one finds once again an entire chain of Old Testament citations, this time strung together by the word "again." These are encountered by reference to a positive key word, "charity," in 1 Clem. 14, and a negative expression, "hypocrisy," in 1 Clem. 15. A central chapter in the letter is 16. Jesus Christ is set forth as an example of proper humility, which characteristically is introduced by a citation out of the fourth Servant Song in Isa 53:1–12. This is called a dictum of the Holy Spirit. Again this occurs in the variant form of the Septuagint text that the author used. The "Servant of God" can be none other than Jesus Christ, something one would expect in primitive Christianity. However, this lengthy citation contains within it an additional one: a section out of Ps 22:7–8, a passage that is traditionally connected to the passion (see above).

In this chapter, Clement appears also to follow entirely the usual understanding that interprets these passages as prophecies about Jesus Christ. At the same time, he introduces his own special concerns. He concludes with a sentence addressed to his readers: "See, beloved people, who the example is who has been given us!" (16:17). This basic motif permeates his entire letter.

Such is also the case in 1 Clem. 17. When Elijah and Elisha are expressly mentioned, along with Ezekiel, as prophets who announced the coming of Christ (17:1), this occurs in conformity with the early Christian interpretation that the announcement of the coming Christ was in the prophets. However, they are quoted here because they "traveled about in goat and sheepskins" (see Heb 11:37) and thus were examples of pious humility to be emulated. It is similarly so with Abraham, Job, Moses, David, and all other examples of those who were highly honored as righteous before God and at the same time were meek. The examples of these righteous ones serve, obviously, as a pedagogical contrast of behavior. In the case of David (1 Clem. 18) Clement expressly cites Ps 51 (vv. 3–19) in the Septuagint translation as an expression of this humility. That David is regarded as the author of all the collected psalms is once more a traditional understanding.

One of the values of the Old Testament and of Old Testament Israel is the ability of this series of exemplars to provide summary observations that are markedly enlightening for the topics at hand. "The humility and modesty of these so great and illustrious people have not only made us better through obedience but also all the generations that have gone before us, namely, those who have received his (God's) words in fear and truth" (19:1). In contrast to Barnabas, who declared the history and institutions of Old Testament Israel as completely finished, the examples of faith present in the ancient covenant receive a higher value in Clement. He can thus formulate the relationship of Christians by attaching these Old Testament examples to his observations. "We have part in many, great, and glorious acts." They are present in the background and in the following exhortation: "let us race to accomplish the objective of peace that is set before us since the beginning." Thus, he uses the ancient idea of a contest (agon; see 2:4 and earlier 1 Cor 9:24–25; Phil 3:14; Heb 12:1). The content is also significant here as the writer spurs on his readers to emulate these examples.

Above all, however, he sees behind them an unbroken succession of witnesses of faith. There is no break in salvation history; rather, at least as far as the paradigmatic saints of the Old Testament are concerned, a great communion of faith binds together the generations. Also in 1 Clem. 32 it is clear that "all the priests and Levites who serve the altar of God," "the Lord Jesus Christ according to the flesh," rulers and princes of Judah, and above all the tribes that descended from Abraham are placed in a series that attains honor through the will of God.

Certainly, as the following expressions show, the circle for Clement is extended outward. He continues: "let us direct our eyes to the Father and Creator of the entire cosmos and hold fast to his great gift he has given to us." What many interpreters have regarded as an excursus—the insertion of a consideration of the wonderfully arranged order of creation that God has set forth—actually is consistent with the apologetic universalism characteristic of Clement. Stoic formulations echo in some passages (as, e.g., in 19:3), and there is a view of the cosmic phenomena that corresponds frequently to ancient conceptions of theistic creation already widely present in Hellenistic Judaism. These may provide the actual theological background of Clement's expressions. In the conclusion (20:11–12), the process of thought indeed links again especially with the Christian readers, "who have taken refuge in his compassion through our Lord Jesus Christ." In the concluding prayer (1 Clem. 59–61), which is saturated with motifs from the Old Testament psalms, creation motifs once again play a powerful role. In the request for the forgiveness of all sins, which also includes the role of the (heathen) authorities, there may be reflected a typical practice of the Roman community (see Rom 13).

The second part of the writing (1 Clem. 21–28) also includes paraenetic admonitions shaped for the ethical behavior of the Christians and instruction about the basic content of the Christian faith, which is able to motivate hope in a resurrection (1 Clem. 24–26) and set forth the behavior consistent with this. Also here we confront many texts that in part expressly include Old Testament citations. Thus, 1 Clem. 33 takes up once again the theme of creation and cites verses from Gen 1:22–28. In 1 Clem. 31, Abraham, Isaac, and Jacob are again mentioned as paradigms of humility. Judith and Esther emerge in 55:4–6 as examples of women and their actions who are strong in faith. Chapter 35, with its introduction, "For the scripture says," leads to the warning of the fate of the godless, using the language of the Septuagint. The citation of Job in 1 Clem. 39 (Job 4:16–5:5, with an insertion from 15:15) is interesting not only because the book of Job is rarely quoted in early Christianity but also because the words of Eliphaz in the dialogues, who at the end of the book is refuted for his adherence to the teaching of retribution, is cited by Clement in a positive way: as speaking of the impurity of all people. The book of Job is thus quoted to offer support to Clement's argumentation, not simply because the text was little cited in early Christian literature. The original function of the citation of Eliphaz in this context has only been determined by modern critical interpretation; this understanding was not evident in the traditional interpretation practiced by Clement. Also later, when Clement deals with chastisement and repentance (1 Clem. 56–57), another lengthy citation from the speech of Eliphaz appears (Job 5:17–26 = 1 Clem. 56:6–15). In 57:3–7 one also discovers the presence of traditional wisdom that characteristically is expressed Prov 1:20–33.

Characteristic for Clement's view of the unbroken connection between Old Testament Israel and the Christian community is 1 Clem. 40–44. In this context God establishes the cultic orders (behind the idea of orders stands an ancient concept, as, for example, already noted in 1 Clem. 19–20). Clement is clearly distinguishable from the expressions of Hebrews, which refers metaphorically to the Old Testament orders of sacrificial worship and priesthood. Hebrews sees the high priesthood of Christ as superior, making the Old Testament view outdated. Clement, however, approaches the order of offices as necessarily fixed, thus providing a valid analogy for those of the Christian communities. Clement values the distinctions in the duties of priests, Levites, and laity (the concept is met here for the first time in early Christian literature), for they correspond to the differences between the offices of bishops and deacons and their establishment over the hosts of laity. The law that sacrifice may be offered only in Jerusalem on the altar of temple becomes an example for the validity of fixed rules for the worship of God (1 Clem. 41). An additional analogy exists between the installation of bishops and deacons through the apostles (1 Clem. 42) and those of the Old Testament offices established by Moses. One is especially able to recognize such a correspondence in the provisions that Moses established during the strife of the tribes over the priestly office (see Num 17:16–26, set forth in 1 Clem. 43:2–5 with some midrashic expansions, presumably from Jewish tradition) and in the introduction of the occupant of the office of bishop through the apostles (1 Clem. 44; apparently Clement traces this introduction in 44:2, which corresponds to 42:3 back to the direct mandates of Christ). It is striking that none of these places says anything about the Old Testament cultic and priestly orders no longer being valid!

For the first time since 2 Tim 3:16 one encounters in 1 Clement a conception of the inspiration of Scripture. The writer often indicates that the Holy Spirit is active directly (13:1; 16:2; 45:2) or indirectly (22:1; see 16:15) as the one who speaks in a scriptural text. In 22:1, however, it is Christ himself who speaks through the Spirit in the Scriptures. Even more frequently a citation is introduced as the Word of God (of the Lord, in the sense of sovereign; see also Barnabas).

The nondialectical form of recourse to the Old Testament's ethical paradigms and even cultic proscriptions was obviously typical for the Roman community, as it had developed in the Roman community and presumably also in the Corinthian fellowship toward the end of the first century C.E. One should, however, not lose sight of the writing's purpose to admonish ambitious persons to cultivate humility and submission to the legitimate authorities. Nevertheless, the distance of this text from the theological profundity of a Paul is obvious.

One may ask which of the texts by Paul were familiar to the author. Obviously, he knew well the letter of 1 Corinthians, which was directed to the same community and presumably was also read in worship services outside of Corinth. In 47:1 he certainly speaks rather generally of "the letter of the blessed apostle Paul." This can mean only 1 Corinthians, since 47:3–4 mentions the parties in Corinth named in 1 Cor 1:10–4:21. These include, with the exception of the party of Christus, the names of Cephas (Peter) and Apollo. In 37:5–38:1, Clement takes up the topic of love and its many facets for the community. Although there is no specific quotation, there is an allusion to 1 Cor 12 (see also 1 Clem 46:7; 37:3). In 24:2, he speaks of the actions of God from the "beginning" to the resurrection of Jesus Christ. This key word is found in a similar way only in 1 Cor 15:20, 23. Also, there are many allusions to this letter of Paul. The list of vices in 1 Clem. 35:5, together with the concluding sentence in 35:6, clearly rests on Rom 1:28–32. There are also many other possible intimations of passages from Romans. Clement's possible knowledge of other letters of Paul is less certain. As for the letters produced by the school of Paul, 1 Clement presumably knew Ephesians (see 1 Clem. 46:6: "Have we not a God and a Christ and a Spirit of Grace who is poured out on us and a calling in Christ"; see Eph 4:4–7, in another arrangement, which still allows one to suggest an orally transmitted formula of confession) and possibly others, although this is uncertain.

The allusions to the Scriptures of Israel, while not always clearly identified, permeate the epistle and point to the fundamental role of the Old Testament citations. Most of these are cited literally from the Septuagint. His arguments undergirded by the sacred Scripture point clearly to their authoritative status. Perhaps the audience of his writing knew well 1 Corinthians and other letters of Paul. However, it is not always the case that these New Testament texts shared the same level of authority that Scripture did.

One particular place accepts only the "words of the Lord Jesus," who is the "teacher of gentleness and generosity," as the basis for the warnings in 1 Clem. 13 against boastfulness, anger, and rashness. Certainly the introductory formula, "be conscious of the words…," is different from that of other citations, including the preceding one of Jer 9:22–23, which has the double formula "what is written" and "the Holy Spirit says." The following are seven briefly composed maxims that have more or less six or seven correspondences with passages in the Sermon on the Mount:

Be compassionate in order that you find compassion!
Be forgiving in order that you may be forgiven!
As you act, thus it shall be done to you;
As you give, so it shall be given to you.
As you judge, so you shall be judged.
As you are benevolent, so shall your benevolence be returned.
With the standard by which you measure, so shall you be measured.

The similarities with the Sermon on the Mount, or the Sermon on the Plain, are apparent. The parallels certainly do not occur all together in these sermons (see Matt 5:7; 6:14, 7:12; 7:1–2; 7:2b/Luke 6:36; 6:37a; 6:38c; see also 6:35c) and are not set forth in such a terse form structured by means of parallelism.

The position that the writer of 1 Clement knew and used one or more of the Synoptic Gospels cannot be proven. Rather, his variations from them would speak against this. In addition, the correspondences are not found entirely in one of these Gospels. The terse form of his statements, which would enhance the process of memorization, points rather to an oral tradition. Originally the remarks appear to have involved two series of sentences: two members in the first and five in the other.

Further, the "words of our Lord Jesus" are cited in 46:8. Similar statements are found in Mark 14:21b/Matt 26:24b and Mark 9:42/Matt 18:6/Luke 17:2, but this particular combination is found only in 1 Clement. The position that he knew these three Gospels is less probable than the view that he was familiar with an oral tradition that would have sayings like the shorter form in 1 Clement.

Strongly debated and difficult to decide is the question whether 1 Clement also knew and used the Epistle to the Hebrews. The decision is difficult because the dating of Hebrews is unsettled. The effort to substantiate the use of Hebrews by 1 Clement has often been attempted. Others contest the view that these contacts are to be explained as citations. In the end, the problem of a circular argument cannot be resolved.

The strongest agreement is indicated by the common vocabulary about Christ found in 1 Clem. 36. Already in verse 1 Christ is designated as "the high priest of our sacrificial gifts," which is also found in Hebrews. In 1 Clem. 36:2 there is a chain of hymnic praises in the "we style" that is introduced by the expression, "through this." The verse closes with a relative clause, the formulation of which is very close to Heb 1:3–4: "whose reflection of his glory is even more illustrious than that of the angels, for he has inherited a more excellent name." The three following citations of the Psalms (104:4; 2:7–8; 110:1) are also found in Heb 1:3–4. In spite of this correspondence, the results are difficult to interpret. The hymnic statements in verse 2 echo various New Testament writings, hardly Hebrews alone. The Psalm passages are common to early Christian usage in their interpretation of Christ. The relative clause could originate in an influential passage of confession (perhaps taken from the liturgy of the Last Supper). It is uncertain, however, whether the series of examples of Old Testament piety in 1 Clem. 9–12 is dependent on the "cloud of witnesses" in Heb 11. Also here, too, many differences are can be noted. One may wish to identify a series of other examples of dependence, but certainty cannot be reached. There are clearly numerous possible allusions but nowhere a citation.

However one interprets the connections between 1 Clement and Hebrews, even when one takes into consideration the mistakes made in a precise citation, if 1 Clement knew this book, the same rank was not given to this New Testament writing as to the Old Testament books. With 1 Clement we are led into a period in which there was still no New Testament canon in the sense it came to have later on, only a canonical Old Testament. When Clement speaks of "Scripture" (23:5; 34:6; 35:7; 42:5; 62:2), he means, as did Barnabas, the Old Testament. In some places he uses the plural "the Holy Scriptures" (45:2; 53:1).

It is typical for 1 Clement not to see a disruption in the history of salvation between the old and new people of God. The figures of the Old Testament, in so far as he treats paradigmatic people of piety and ancestors of the faith, appear in a series with believers of the present. Also, Christ "according to the flesh" belongs to Israel. The institutions of Israel, including the cultus and its orders, are patterns for the order of the community.

How this particular characteristic is to be explained is difficult to say. As was true throughout the entire Roman Empire, the community in Rome presumably originated in a synagogue located in the city. Thus, the first Christians would have been Jewish Christians. Eventually, Gentile Christians also entered into this community. This situation is reflected already in Paul's Letter to the Romans. His passionate battle waged for the gospel of justification coming only through faith was a matter of concern to opponents, who were inclined to extend the enforcement of the Jewish law upon all Christians. In 1 Clement there is no evidence of any direction opposition to Paul. As we saw, he is in fact highly valued. In 32:4 we discover, if anything, the statement of justification through faith. Besides this there appears, moreover, in 30:2 the exhortation to the readers to seek justification through works, not through words. In 7:4; 12:7; 21:6; and 49:6 we find the statement the blood of Christ in part brought about the redemption of the believer. However, it is still characteristic that this redemption is interpreted directly in 7:4, corresponding to the context, as the "grace of repentance." In 49:1 the statement is formulated: "Let the one who possesses love in Christ adhere to the commandments of Christ!" Clement knows to speak of the significance of the grace that has occurred in Christ in many passages. Still, as in 7:5, this is qualified by those features earlier noted, for he states, "the Lord (has issued commandments) to those who from generation to generation have wished to convert to him."

On the whole, there is reflected in 1 Clement a community piety that turns back to a certain extent to everyday life. The well-honed features of Paul's theology are not maintained, even though it is not abandoned. To a certain extent, there is a christological reading of the Old Testament in 1 Clement, which, lacking in antagonism, allows the author to call upon paradigms and exemplary orders from this sacred text.

4.3. EARLY APOLOGETICS: JUSTIN MARTYR

Justin was born in Samaria, in the city of Flavia Neapolis (the present city of Nablus) sometime around the turn of the second century C.E. He became familiar with several directions of Greek philosophy before finally finding his place of "rest" in Platonism. He himself narrates the history of his conversion to Christianity (in his dialogue with the Jewish scholar Trypho, in *Dial.* 3–8). This leads us immediately in an important direction to his interaction with the Bible. He met by accident an old man who pointed him to, among others, the prophets, who may have been earlier than the so-called philosophers and who had spoken in the divine spirit and announced the future events that would take place, "what now has come to pass" (*Dial.* 7.1). The Holy Scriptures, understood as prophecies, appealed to the Hellenistically educated young man who had sought the truth residing with the pagan philosophers and convinced him of the superior truth of Christianity. He was an intellectual who allowed himself to accept the evidence of the enlightenment of Christianity. When he sought to attract others to believe in these Scriptures, he brought forward the same arguments that had won him and others who stood apart from the Christian community to the young religion.

Justin was the author of a series of writings of which essentially only two have remained. Both apologies (writings of defense) appeared shortly one after the other (between 150 and 160 C.E.), although they are directed to different audiences. The so-called first apology (*1 Apol.*) was issued to Caesar Antoninus Pius (138–161 C.E.) and his two adopted sons, along with the leading groups in the Roman Empire. The dialogue with Trypho was issued to a reader to convince him of the truth of Christianity over against Judaism. In both writings, the internal and external position of the young church is reflected, especially regarding the manifold dangers to which it was exposed. Because the Christians rejected the Caesar cult, the Roman authorities considered them "godless." Indeed, the very thought of making confession in Christ threatened the believer with the punishment of death. Even if persecutions were not carried out everywhere at the same time and were seldom pursued in a systematic fashion, many Christians still suffered martyrdom, among them Justin himself in Rome, likely in the year 165 C.E.

Difficulties also emerged in the mission field. In addition to the Jews, Christian missionaries also announced their message to the "God-fearers": Gentiles who were close to Judaism without having formally made the transition to identity with their community, because they balked at the strong Jewish proscriptions. However, they could easily be won to a monotheistic faith. They sought to achieve a greater freedom, which provided them the motivation to join this religion. There were, then, conflicts with contemporary Judaism, which, alarmed at the enticements that were issued to its supporters, already had developed a hostile attitude against the Christians. It had disseminated rumors about reported atrocities and vices (cannibalism, group sex, *Dial.* 10.1; see also *1 Apol.* 26.7). Trypho, who is characterized as a gentleman, stressed that these matters were contrary to human nature (*Dial.* 10.2). Since there were many people who were uncertain, Justin was concerned to convince the God-fearers of the truth of Christianity and of the errors of Judaism.

The two major writings of Justin that we have are examples of a model for the literary defense of Christianity. They are examples in so far as they both contain arguments that refer only in a limited fashion to Justin's personal, theoretical efforts. While he certainly composed the whole of these two texts, he gave them only a small degree of a tightly organized argument due to his many digressions. However, the material in its details is very traditional. It presents generally well-known reasons for the truth of Christianity that existed in the communities of the time.

This is the case especially for the evidence shaped from the Bible. Following the initial section of *1 Apology*, which contains Justin's rejection of the allegation that Christians are atheists, the second section (*1 Apol.* 30–60) offers biblical proofs. In the introduction to this section (*1 Apol.* 30), Justin makes his arguments against charges that a so-called Christus had performed his miracles through magic and thus incited the Christians with the mere appearance that he was God's Son. Justin produces his evidence from witnesses who would clearly be regarded as truthful by the ones addressed. Thus, the evidence to which he refers are the words issued from those who long before the events transpired had prophesied about them and thus must be given the necessary credence. Therefore, these chapters concern evidence for Jesus as the Christ (Messiah) from the predictions of the Old Testament prophets.

Obviously, long before Justin Christians had read certain statements of the Old Testament as predictions of Christ. In their center are passages that already had been understood as messianic prophecies in Jewish exegesis. Christians related these to Jesus Christ. In the earlier chapters of this study, we already provided examples in the writings of the New Testament. Nowhere, however, have we encountered the argument from prophecy that is made with the same frequency that it occurs in this section of Justin's *1 Apology*. In *1 Apol.* 31, Justin introduces his evidence from prophecy with a reference to the tradition of the Septuagint. Here he repeats the well-known legend of Aristeas about the origin of the Septuagint, although he wrongly places it in the time of King Herod. He remarks that it is in the Greek interpretation of the Old Testament that there exists a written source that a Hellenistically educated audience can read for themselves. The role that the Greek translation of the Bible had already played in the promotion of Christianity to Jewish proselytes in the mission of the early church is once again a key matter. When reviewing in precise detail the biblical citations contained in the *1 Apology*, it is important to notice the varying textual forms of the interpretation before us. These deviations may best be explained by the assumption that Justin appropriated cited texts already present in the scriptural evidence that had already been compiled to a large extent.

In *1 Apol.* 31.7, Justin provides an overview of what he wants to demonstrate in his Old Testament evidence concerning matters that had previously been predicted:

> In these books, then, of the prophets, we have found that Jesus our Christ (1) is coming, (2) being born of a virgin, (3) becoming a man, (4) healing every disease and illness and raising the dead, (5) being hated, not recognized, and crucified, (6) and dying, rising again, and ascending into heaven and called God's Son (7) and that he sent out from himself certain people into every nation in order to proclaim these things (8) and that people among the Gentiles rather would believe in him more.

Obviously, this is a primitive confession of faith in a form used in the area of the mission among non-Jews.

This program is carried out in *1 Apol.* 32–35 and 48–53. In *1 Apol.* 32 Justin begins to present his evidence with a citation from Gen 49:10–11 (in a translation that does not come from the Septuagint). The saying concerning Judah in the blessing of Jacob is interpreted as a prediction that this tribe will never lack for a ruler until the Messiah comes. "Our task now is to investigate and to learn how long Judah has produced its own lord and king." In this regard, one comes to Herod, who was the last king of Judah before the coming of Jesus. Then follows an individual exegesis of the sentence that points to the explanation of Jesus Christ (see already Mark 11:2–11 par.); attached to the citation are several formulas: "that means"; "that was an interpretative symbol for that"; "was a prediction that." A short report that follows the citation is the third feature added to what is announced. This technique reflects the pesher exegesis of Qumran (see above). A combined citation comprises Num 24:17 ("Star from Jacob"), Isa 11 ("sprout from the root of Jesse"), and Isa 51:5 ("hope of the nations") and concludes with the interpretation of Gen 49:10–11. This combined citation is constructed as a parallel to Gen 49:10. It is ascribed entirely to the prophet Isaiah and is designated as fulfilled.

In *1 Apol.* 33 the second proof follows with an elaborate interpretation of the announcement of the birth of Immanuel in Isa 7:14. The form of the text (*parthenos*, "virgin") facilitates the desired meaning of the virgin birth, while in *Dial.* 84 Justin presents the rendering as *neanis* "young woman," which comes closer to the meaning of the Hebrew term. One may recognize the appearance of the elements of this verse that are found in the prehistory of the interpretation, including Luke (1:35; 1:31, 32; 2:2) and Matthew (1:21; 2:6; 2:1). Thus, there is a lengthy tradition standing behind Justin's christological use of Isa 7:14. Perhaps the Evangelists, however, are directly cited.

The third line of evidence concerns the concealment of the identity of Jesus as the Messiah, which was maintained until he was grown. Justin reads a translation of Isa 9:5a that does not come from the Septuagint: "A child is born to us; a young man is given to us." The rules of interpretation operating at the time caused Justin to overlook the principle of parallelism present in this statement. The exact attention to these individual expressions resembles to us already-recognized Jewish examples.

The healings that the Messiah Jesus performed and his awakening of the dead are the fourth consideration. Justin (*1 Apol.* 48:1–3) finds this announced in Isa 35:6, 5, where the text, in order to allow the mention of the awakening of the dead, has been correspondingly altered. This was a prevalent practice that we have already frequently noted.

The suffering of the Messiah is Justin's fifth proof, which is substantiated in *1 Apol.* 50.1–51.6 through a lengthy citation from the Septuagint's translation of the song of the Suffering Servant in Isa 52:13–53:12.

For the resurrection and exaltation of Jesus, Justin's sixth element of proof, *1 Apol.* 50.1–51.6, the passage of Ps 24:7–8 serves as a witness (although the translation does not come from the Septuagint). To this, also briefly, is attached a scriptural proof for the return of Christ. The citation is from Dan 7:13, notably introduced by Justin as a citation of Jeremiah in *1 Apol.* 52.10–12.

The recognition of Jesus by means of his parousia by "the tribes of the Jews" (see also the eighth proof) is introduced as a citation from the prophet Zechariah that in fact is basically structured by 12:10–12. This citation, found in *1 Apol.* 52.10–12, is a combined one consisting of other texts (Isa 43:5–6; Joel 2:12–13/Isa 29:13; Isa 63:17/64:10) placed within this outer structure and then shaped into an artistically formed, three-strophe poem that obviously had already existed in the traditional material that Justin used:

(10) I shall call upon the four winds,
to gather the children who are scattered;
I shall command the north wind to bring them back,
And the south wind not to hold them back.
(11) And then in Jerusalem there shall be a great lamentation, not a lamentation

of mouths or of lips,
but rather a lamentation of the heart;
and they shall not tear to pieces their garments
but rather their hearts;
tribe by tribe they shall mourn.
(12) Then they shall look on him who they pierced,
And they shall say:
"Why, O Lord, did you make us stray
From your way?
The glory, which our fathers have praised,
Has been for us turned into shame."

This has to do exclusively with Israel and its eschatological fortunes. The vital interest that the primitive church, still partially Jewish Christian, took in the fortunes of Judaism is clear in this testimony. In *1 Apol.* 53 Justin attached yet another argument constructed out of three scriptural citations (Isa 54:1; 1:9; Jer 9:25) that the Gentiles, rather than the Jews, come to faith. This is his eighth proof.

Also important for Justin's apologetics is the teaching of the twofold coming of Christ, in order to reject and then dismiss from discussion objections by non-Christians that the fulfillment of the biblical promises could not be realized in the poor, earthly appearance of Jesus and his failure on the cross. This theme, which appears more frequently in the *Dialogue with Trypho*, is broached briefly in *1 Apol.* 52.3: "The prophets had announced previously that there would be two comings by him: the one that has already occurred, when he appeared as an unseemly and suffering person; the second, however, when he shall return in glory from the heavens with his army of angels."

Justin (and the traditional material that lay before him) therefore appealed to the Scriptures (the Old Testament) as a prophetic witness for the Messiah, Jesus Christ. May this occur without further ado? It is remarkable that Justin himself had posed this question in a lengthy excursus in his *1 Apol.* 36–49. His citations in *1 Apol.* 35 had led him to the question: Is this matter handled completely by the genuine prophetic passages that are traditionally explained as referring to Christ? Must these not speak *about* the Messiah and in the future tense? Justin introduces his detailed answer with the conviction that his hearers (readers) should understand the words not as those of inspired prophets but as the words of the divine Logos who moved them to say these things. Justin participates, thus, in the general, primitive Christian interpretation of the inspiration of Scripture. He is able also to say expressly that the Holy Spirit had already spoken in the Old Testament: "It happens that the Holy Spirit worked so that something that happened, which was a paradigm for us if something should happen to occur, and that he also spoke words concerning future events, in that what he spoke about had already happened or was to happen" (*Dial.* 114.1). "From time to time he (the prophet) as the one who had been sent before knows what will happen, often as though he were in the role of the Lord of all and God the Father, often, however, as though he were in the role of Christ, and often as though he were in the role of the nations who answered to the Lord or to his Father" (*1 Apol.* 36.2). The following chapters offer examples for the different manners of speaking. In *1 Apol.* 37 there are utterances of the Father (Isa 1:3, 4; 66:1; 1:14, 13, 12, 15, etc.), and in *1 Apol.* 38 there are utterances of the son (65:2; 50:6–8; Pss 22:19, 17; 3:6; 22:8, 9), and similarly *1 Apol.* 49.1–4 (Isa 65:1–3). Finally, *1 Apol.* 47 offers utterances of the people (Isa 64:10–12). By contrast, in *1 Apol.* 39.1–42.45 there are side by side future and past manners of expression in the prophets. The entire section in Justin is presented somewhat like an early Christian hermeneutic, that is, a teaching concerning the understanding of the Bible.

One section in *1 Apology* reflects the particular way Justin grasped the situation and the form of the scriptural evidence: *1 Apol.* 47–49. When Justin wrote his texts, the events of and bloody conclusion to the Bar Kokhba revolution of the Jews (132–135 C.E.) against Roman domination did not reside too far back in the distant past. A consequence of this revolution was the edict of Caesar Hadrian that prohibited Jews any future presence in the city of Jerusalem, which had been reconstructed as Aelia Capitolina. Indeed, it is debated how extensively the prohibition was actually followed. Still, Aelia Capitolina was now a city dedicated to the practice of a pagan cult, where the temple of the Jews lay in ruins. A Christian community was, by contrast, soon able to be established there.

The objections of the Jews raised against the Christians are formulated by Trypho in *Dial.* 8:3–4. He accuses Justin of abandoning God and of having placed his hope in a human being. He exhorts him first to obey all the proscriptions of the law (circumcision, Sabbath, festivals and New Moon), in order to receive God's compassion. Finally, he states the validity of the Jewish interpretation of the Messiah: "The Christ, when he is born and wherever he exists are not known, and not even he himself knows and has not the power until Elijah comes and anoints him and makes known to him all these things."

Justin formulates the chain of his argumentation in correspondence to these contested points. In *Dial.* 11–29 Justin deals with the new law and the new covenant, in close correspondence to what he wrote in *1 Apol.* 37.39–49 and which presumably was present in similar traditional materials. Embedded in this section are polemical expressions dealing with the Jewish ceremonial practices. The traditional passages for the new covenant and new law—Jer 31:31; Isa 51:4–5; 55:3–5—are also found in his introduction to *Dial.* 11–12. In *Dial.* 24 the central passage of Isa 2:3–4 is followed. Already in *Dial.* 11, in which Isa 51:4–5 is first cited, the combination "law" and the "light of the pagans" makes the decisive identification: Christ is the new law and the new covenant! The same theme is taken up once more in *Dial.* 122. It is clear from rabbinic sources that the image of light stems from the Jewish activity of missions and was related to the conversion of proselytes to Judaism, that is, those who were interpreted as moving from the kingdom of darkness to the kingdom of light. Justin introduces the same arguments against his opponents. Among the polemical passages there comes into view the contrast between Jewish rituals of washings, which are connected to the blood of goats and sheep, the ashes of rams, and gifts of meal (said by Justin not to have the power to wash away sins), and the blood of Christ, which alone is capable of removing sins. This he derives from the mixing together of the passages of Isa 1:11, 13 and Heb 9:13–14. Serving as a more comprehensive scriptural proof is the citation of the Septuagint's rendering of Isa 52:10–54:6 that follows in the remainder of the chapter. An additional noteworthy passage is found in the section of 15.7–17.2. Remarks about the true baptism (*Dial.* 14) and the true fasts are supported by a lengthy citation of the Septuagint's translation of Isa 58:11 (*Dial.* 15.1–6). Here Justin argues that the Jews have killed the righteous one (Jesus Christ) and now persecute and slander his disciples (Isa 52:5; 3:9–11; 5:18–20). They are driven out of the land (Lev 26:40–41), which has been transformed into a wilderness (Isa 1:7). However, the punishment consists above all in corporal bodily circumcision that the Jews practice, for this marks them. This sign of their identity keeps them from wanting to oppose the prohibition and to return to the land. The background to this, already mentioned, is the edict of Hadrian. The Christian feelings of revenge, however, are called forth through the practice of the Jews described in *Dial.* 17.2. This practice is to send out of Jerusalem emissaries throughout the entire world who defame the Christians as an atheistic sect.

The section *Dial.* 19.3–4 in combination with 23, 27.5, and 92.4 produce yet another argument against circumcision. Even the ancient ancestors from Adam unto Abram did not have to be circumcised, yet they were still considered to be well-pleasing to God. The same is true of women, who cannot be circumcised (23.5). In contrast to these, Egyptians, Moabites, and Edomites are also circumcised, an act that proves of no value to them (28.4).

Justin indicates in *Dial.* 19.5–6 that God gave to the Jews the ceremonial laws only because of their preference for the worship of idols and their apostasy, as the example of the golden calf shows (Exod 32). In *Dial.* 20–22 Justin interprets the scriptural evidence that is appropriate for the food laws (*Dial.* 20 refers to Exod 32:6; Deut 32:15), the Sabbath (*Dial.* 21 refers to Ezek 20:19–26), sacrifice (*Dial.* 22.1–11 refers to Amos 5:18–6:7; Jer 7:21–22; Ps 50), and the temple (*Dial.* 22.11 refers to Isa 66:1).

In *Dial.* 24.3 Justin exhorts his readers with a series of scriptural expressions (Ps 128:4–5; Isa 2:5b; Jer 3:17; Isa 2:2–4; 65:1–3) to come to Jerusalem in order to see God's salvation there. The people he has in mind are the heathen nations, from whom the new people, the church, shall be made up. The one who issues this call is Christ. Chapter 30 (with allusions to Ps 19, esp. v. 10) presents Christ as the new law. With this Justin introduces an entire section (*Dial.* 30–39) that discusses this theme. The theme, the "new law," dominates also the long concluding part (*Dial.* 108–141) of the dialogue. We are able to single out and comment on only a few of these.

The section *Dial.* 40–42 has within the sphere of "law" a special point of view. In these chapters the typology of Old Testament proscriptions concerning the law are given a Christian content. According to *Dial.* 40.1–3, the Passover lamb (Exod 12:7) is a type of the passion of Christ. The two goats on the Day of Atonement (Lev 16:5–15) are, according to *Dial.* 40.4–5, signs of the two comings of Christ; the Lord's Supper is prefigured by the final meal offering (Lev 14:10), according to *Dial.* 41.1–3; and circumcision on the eighth day is a type of the true circumcision, that is, baptism (a frequent comparison). Finally, the twelve small bells on the high priest's garment (Exod 28:4, among others), according to *Dial.* 42.1–3 signifies the mission of the twelve apostles in all the world. An additional chapter (*Dial.* 86) specifies the types of the cross (key word "staff"). Typologically presented in *Dial.* 90.4–5, 91.3, and 97.1, among others, is the battle with Amalek (Exod 17, a typology of the cross), while in 91.4 and 94.1–4, among others, is the brazen snake (Num 21:9, another typology of the cross). These are likewise traditional. Striking, however, is the recognition that typology as a *method* plays a very small role in Justin, as seen from the cases we have already treated. By contrast, the evidence of prophecy is assumed by him and given from this time on as the standard argument of Christian apologetics.

The comprehensive middle part of the *Dialogue* (48–107) is devoted (in correspondence to *1 Apol.* 30–60, often on the basis of the same traditions) to the demonstration that Jesus is the Messiah.

One example that allows one to track the discussion between Jewish and Christian interpretation of the Old Testament is especially impressive, that concerning the virgin birth (Isa 7:14). That this theme in the traditional Christian scriptural evidence had already played an important role can be recognized in the occurrence of the citation from Isa 7:10–16 (+8:4) in *Dial.* 43.5–6. Thus, the theme appears to stem out of appropriated material in which already there was a recognition of a relationship with the law. One recognizes how important it appears to Justin in his remarks in *Dial.* 120.1. Here he speaks of the (salvific) economy of Christ through the Virgin Mary. Obviously, to Justin the virgin birth presents a focal point in the history of salvation.

The actual treatment of this theme begins in *Dial.* 63.1, where Trypho demands evidence for the virgin birth. After several digressions to deal with other questions, Justin returns to the theme in *Dial.* 66. He brings to bear once again the citation of Isa 7:10–16a (combined with 8:4) and concludes with the sentence: "Now, since there is among the descendants of Abraham according to the flesh no one who has been born of a virgin and also nothing is said to that effect, it is obvious to all that this one is our Christ."

To this Trypho answers: "The Scripture has not said, 'See, the virgin [*parthenos*] will become pregnant and will bear a son' but rather 'a young woman [*neanis*]…,' and in the remainder of this series nothing accords to what you have said. The entire prophecy has addressed Hezekiah and in a way that indicates to him what is happening concerning this prophecy" (*Dial.* 67.1). The Jewish interpretation therefore differs in two decisive points from the Christian.

First, the interpretation differs in the forms of the text. While Justin uses the textual form of the Septuagint, which favors the explanation of the virgin birth, Trypho draws on a translation that is in line with the term of the Hebrew original. In fact, one is able to observe how during the second century the Septuagint began to diminish in usage within Hellenistic Judaism. Other translations that were closer to the Hebrew text, which was in the meantime understood to be the authoritative text, replaced it more and more (up to that of Aquila). Above all, there were, however, places, that were altered usually in regard to content and were interpreted by Christians as referring to their Messiah Jesus. In the case of Isa 7:14, modern exegesis says that the rendition is, as a matter of fact, more appropriately "young woman" and corresponds to the statement of the primary text. The thesis of the virgin birth is exegetically no longer capable of being supported, at least in a literal sense, and can no longer be supported by reference to Isa 7:14.

Second, the Jewish interpretation refers the prediction to the Jewish king Hezekiah, son of Ahaz, both of whom were contemporaries of Isaiah. The explanation of the verse as appropriate to this earlier audience, and not to the distant future, is not strange to modern exegesis. It belongs to the different suggestions of a historical identification of the mysterious child Immanuel that various scholars have made. The virgin birth may not be appropriate indeed due to chronological reasons but it is not absurd a priori.

A special chain of argumentation concerns biblical proofs for the preexistence of Christ (he exists from eternity). Since this theme is not touched on in *1 Apology*, one may assume that a special tradition resides in the background that Justin was the first to have brought together with other materials. The corresponding material is found in *Dial.* 55.1–62.75 (par. 126–129). In *Dial.* 56 Justin begins with the demonstration that in the Old Testament, in addition to the one God, the Creator, there is an additional God who may be mentioned. Thus, one of the three men to appear to Abraham in the grove at Mamre (Gen 18:1–3) and to stand with him before Sodom and Gomorrah was no angel (Gen 19:27–28) but rather was God. However, this God is not God the Father, the Creator God, as Gen 19:24 shows. The same holds true for Gen 21:9–12. Likewise, a comparison of Ps 110:1 with 44:7–8 reveals that the discussion is about two "Lords," that is, "Gods." According to different texts from Genesis (Gen 18–19; 31:11, 13; 32:22–30; 28:10–19) that speak of divine appearances to the exalted fathers, including Moses (Exod 3 = *Dial.* 59–60) addressed by a God in the burning bush, Justin comes to speak of what he wished to demonstrate from the Scriptures:

> that in the beginning before all creatures, God had created a word like [*logos* like] power from himself, who is named also the "glory of God" by the Holy Spirit and many times "Son," frequently "Wisdom," repeatedly "angel," also "God," and many times as "Lord" and "Word" [*logos*]. Often he even names himself as the one who holds the position, commander-in-chief, when he appears in human form, as he did to Joshua, son of Nun [Josh 5:14]. (*Dial.* 61.1)

One also recognizes this in the following comprehensive citation of Prov 8:21–36, in which Jewish wisdom speculation contained in the early chapters of the book of Proverbs is appropriated. These tell of the presence of personified wisdom at creation. Also, the plural manner of speech in Gen 1:26–28 and 3:22 is evidence for the duality of God (*Dial.* 62).

Justin comes then to his real aim at the end of *Dial.* 62 with a citation from Josh 5:13–6:2 and in *Dial.* 75 with a reference to Exod 23:20. The "angel" sent by God to make a promise to Moses is identified with Joshua, the Greek Jesus. He seeks to demonstrate that it was Jesus who is mentioned in all these places as the other "God," the "Lord," or "Angel." Jesus was the one who appears in the Old Testament in the theophanies to the recipients of revelation.

In the writings of Justin we confront a form of apologetic literature that emerged from the missionary encounter with educated pagans, especially those who comprised the God-fearers, who were familiar with the Old Testament and conversant with Jewish tradition. The material used, in particular the ever-recurring prooftexts, is largely traditional. However, in a more precise analysis, older collections may be sensed to have existed as well as different tendencies that no longer can be traced and that, in spite of penetrating examinations, cannot be clearly identified. Still, the examples that we have examined may provide an impression of the exegetical wealth found in this literature. Incidentally, Justin in his *Dialogue with Trypho* used the Septuagint extensively, from which he brought forth frequently comprehensive citations. This led to the expression of a greater independence from the tradition.

The Old Testament in Justin is without question recognized as the Scripture of the Christians. Especially the book of Isaiah and the Psalms offered the most scriptural proofs for him. He also took statements out of the New Testament and alluded to others. However, the New Testament is not actually interpreted. Its character as "Scripture" does not appear to have been held. Especially in the *Dialogue* it frequently is used in relation to the ones being addressed. Demonstrations of the Christian truth, however, are capable of being obtained only from the Bible held in common with the Jews.

On the other hand, Justin carried out a sharp separation between Christianity and Judaism. Thus *Dial.* 24.3 exhorts the Gentiles to come to Jerusalem to assume the inheritance of Old Testament Israel. The Christians are the new people of God. According to Isa 26:2–3, they are a righteous people who hold to the truth and grasp hold of peace (*Dial.* 24.2), a holy people (citation from Isa 62:12 in *Dial.* 26.3), and another nation that has flowed together from the many nations (Zech 2:15, cited in *Dial.* 119.3). The equation of the Christians with "Israel" is found for the first time in Justin. In *Dial.* 119.4–121.1 Justin indicates that not all children of Abraham, not the Arabs, the Egyptians, and the Idumeans, are the children of promise and are the people proclaimed to him in Gen 15:5. The blessing in Gen 12:3 is not valid for all his descendants but rather only for Isaac (26:4) and after him only for Jacob (28:14). However, the descendants who take part in the promise are not according to the flesh but rather have the same faith that Abraham had. This is the line that goes from Judah (Gen 49:10) to Perez to Jesse to David. David renewed the blessing, according to Ps 72:17, to his seed (singular!). Here Christ is meant, through whom all the nations are blessed, so that the blessing of Abraham is fulfilled. Obviously, the meaning of these expressions, which set forth Christians as those who are successors to Christ, results in the designation of old Israel as the people of God who have now been replaced. In *Dial.* 123.5–6 Justin brings to light Jer 31:27; Isa 19:24–25; and Ezek 36:12, which are to be understood as speaking of a "new Israel." Obviously, this is the response to the Jewish polemic against Christian claims to be the true children of Abraham, a position held by Paul. The Jewish opponents held that Jews are the true children of Jacob. Justin rejects this claim. Christians are the true Israel. From today's perspective, this view is to be lamented. It emerged necessarily out of the situation that obtained at that time. The earlier hope, to be able to convert all Israel to recognize Jesus as the Christ, as it is expressed in Rom 11, was obviously abandoned by the Christians. They turned their view around and began to regard the Jews only as enemies. This blazed the trail for estrangement lasting for two millennia.

4.4. The Abrogation of the Old Testament? Marcion and His Program

In his *1 Apology* Justin twice mentions the name of a famous heretic:

> After the ascension of Christ, the demons advanced certain people…, to wit, a certain Marcion out of Pontus, who even now is alive and teaching his disciples to believe in some other God greater than the Creator (the Demiurge). And he, by the aid of the demons, has caused many from every nation, who have allowed themselves to be convinced by him, to speak blasphemies so as to deny that God is the Creator of this world and to believe that there is another greater than he, who has done even greater works. (*1 Apol.* 26.1–5)

In the second mention of Marcion (*1 Apol.* 58.1), Justin repeats these remarks but adds to them that Marcion in his teaching also denies that "the Christ predicted by the prophets is his [i.e., the Creator God's] son."

These statements are the oldest that mention the name of Marcion. As the date of *1 Apology* may be determined approximately (around 150 C.E.; see above), this offers us an indication for the unknown dates for Marcion's life. By this time he must already have reached an advanced stage of life, and his teachings must have been found throughout the Roman Empire. As with other notorious heretics, the orthodox polemic must have obfuscated and mystified his person with legendary features. It is certain only that his origins were in the Black Sea port city of Sinope in the former kingdom of Pontus (since 64 C.E. a Roman province), found in present Anatolia. There, in Asia Minor, he openly proclaimed for the first time his teaching. That he may have come to Rome at the end of his life and, as Irenaeus reported (*Haer.* 3.4.3), was there during the time of Bishop Anicetus (154–166 C.E.) cannot be confirmed by the evidence we possess. This report is suspicious because it appears to describe an effort to reconstruct an encounter with the famous martyred bishop, Polycarp of Smyrna, in Rome. He was there to take up the issue of the date of Easter with Anicentus (celebrated at different times in the East and the West). Irenaeus reported in another passage (*Haer.* 3.3.4), without mentioning the name of the place, that in a meeting between Polycarp and Marcion, when the heretic asked the bishop, "Do you recognize us?" Polycarp answered: "I know you, O firstborn of Satan!" This statement may have made the rounds, passing from mouth to mouth, until it reached Irenaeus, before he wrote his work against the heresies around 180 C.E. A more correct background appears to be that Polycarp in his community in Asia Minor had engaged in a fierce battle against the influence of Marcionite teaching. As the protector of the apostolic tradition (he was viewed as a student of the apostles; *Haer.* 3.3.4) and the defender of orthodoxy, who yet suffered a martyr's death in his old age, he stood in high regard in the ancient church.

As is the case with other teachers damned by the great church, we are in the unsatisfying position for a historian to have to depend on the reconstruction of Marcion's arguments by his opponents. Among these are found also citations from his own known writings, the "Antitheses," which contrast Old and New Testament passages in order to demonstrate the lesser value of the Old Testament God. Outside of Irenaeus, the most important source for Marcion is the North African Tertullian (ca. 150–post 220 C.E.), who wrote an apology against him entitled *Adversus Marcionem*.

Already from the remarks of Justin we are able to derive some of the central characteristics of his teaching. Most objectionable for the great church was Marcion's insistence on the existence of two deities: the world Creator (Demiurge), who was at the same time the God of Old Testament Israel and thus assumed a lower status; and the Savior God who was revealed in Christ. The teaching of the two Gods by Marcion is, however, only the consequence of a fundamental dualism that permeated his entire thought: "The separation of the law and the gospel is the particular and main activity of Marcion" (Tertullian, *Marc.* 1.19.4).

Because of this separation, Marcion openly considered himself to be a student of the apostle Paul. Marcion is the first to have set forth a canon of early Christian writings for his own particular sect. These books, coupled with others, became widespread in the greater church. Thus, in the New Testament writings seen by him to be canonical, Marcion placed at the center the ten letters of Paul. The Pauline dialectic of law and gospel was obviously the beginning point of his thought. He wished to bring into prominence the practical implications of Paul's teaching, which had been neglected. He was interested in setting forth his interpretation of Paul initially in the more restricted area of his own homeland and then later in his appeal to a much broader public. As may be seen in the Marcionite prologue written in Latin that introduced the Pauline corpus, Marcion and his disciples saw, in the churches founded or addressed by Paul, his gospel being corrupted by "false apostles" who sought to return these early communities to the Jewish law. Therefore, Marcion and his disciples wished to continue the battle that Paul, especially in his Letter to the Galatians, had waged against "Judaizing" groups in the communities. "False apostles," however, had appeared even in the communities of Corinth, Rome, and Colossae.

In opposing them, Marcion appeared with the claim that he was bringing once again into full validity the authority of the apostle Paul and his gospel. He wished to found the Pauline gospel radically and exclusively on his letters alone and sought from them the explanation of what this gospel was. In his radical views, he separated into two entities that the Pauline dialectic had kept together: the law and the gospel.

For his understanding of Paul, Marcion taught that the Pauline gospel declares that the coming into the world of the Savior Christ was an event not previously prepared for or developed but rather a revealed event to which witness is made by a specially developed Marcionite gospel. This gospel received its meaning by considering as valid only the ten letters of Paul and an attenuated Gospel of Luke (e.g., by the removal of Luke

1–3). This gospel explains an unlimited liberation of humans through the salvation effected by Jesus on the cross, which is an act of God. This God is a Savior who possesses the unending will to love humanity. Without preparation and anticipation, Christ came suddenly into the world: "In the fifteenth year of Tiberius, Christ Jesus was honored by his descent from heaven" (Tertullian, *Marc.* 1.19.2; see also 4.7.13). The view that the event of the cross had not occurred as a culmination of an orchestrated event was condemned by the interpretation of the church, which believed the historical events had been previously preached by the prophets or typologically prefigured through the Old Testament. These events, in the view of the church, were previously set forth. Even more, for Marcion, the God who was preached in the Old Testament Law and the Prophets and the "unknown God" (see Luke 10:21–22) of the gospel (see Tertullian, *Marc.* 4.25.10), who is exalted over the world, have nothing in common with each other. Indeed, they are two different Gods. The God of the Old Testament is the one who created the world; at the same time, he is the God of judgment and punishment, the God of the Law, which is directed toward Israel and its members, who are not saved by the God of redemption. The unknown God, by contrast, does not engage in judgment. He is the incorporation of all things that are plainly good, thus love itself. This "strange" God has nothing to do with the creation as such. Humans as creatures are the "possession" of the Creator God. When the Creator God is designated as "righteous," he is still not good, but much more the "author of evil" (Irenaeus, *Haer.* 3.12.15). The passage in Isa 45:7, restricted to the statement "I create evil," is the decisive evidence for Marcion (see Tertullian, *Marc.* 1.27.2, alongside the mandate of hardening of the heart given to Isaiah in 6:9; see *Marc.* 4.19.2; 5.11.9). Other characteristics of the Old Testament God are that he is angry, seeks revenge (see Tertullian, *Marc.* 1.27.2), and is warlike. These features bring Marcion to the conclusion that this God could not be identical with the God of Jesus Christ. The moral tone of these accusations anticipates the biblical criticism appearing in the Enlightenment.

In addition, the anthropomorphic form of the appearance of the Old Testament God demonstrates he cannot be the highest God exalted over the world. For example, he must descend from heaven in order to carry out his judgment (Tertullian, *Marc.* 2.25–26), or he must ask in paradise, "Adam, where are you?" as though he did not know (2.25.1–2).

Although the problem of evil or the righteousness of God (theodicy) does not appear to have been the starting point of Marcion's theology and did not materialize as a central theme in his teaching, one should not fail to recognize the presence of dualism in his thinking. Good and evil cannot dialectically and conceptually be brought together in expressing the unity of God. For Marcion, they can be treated only as belonging to two separate Gods (apparently the beginning point for this is the passage in Luke 6:43–45, which Marcion read as meaning that Jesus meted out blindness to the apostles concerning the gospel, who only knew the Old Testament God; Paul is the first one to have taught the gospel; Marcion reached this conclusion from the opposition of Paul to the first apostles noted in the Letter to the Galatians).

With respect to this study, we are interested especially in Marcion's encounter with the Old Testament, which was regarded by the early Christians as the only Holy Scripture. For the first time we meet someone who contrasted his own canon, which mainly consisted of the Pauline Letters, with the Old Testament (although he never uses the term *canon*). We have already made clear that for Marcion the Old Testament forfeited its rank as the Holy Scripture of the Christians. In this regard, then, he inclined his radical thinking to explicit alternatives. The Old Testament cannot be Holy Scripture because the law of the Creator God, which exists in the books of Moses, is morally inferior, foolish, and absurd, as clearly noted above all by the proscriptions concerning food and the teaching of an "eye for an eye" and a "tooth for a tooth" (see especially Tertullian, *Marc.* 5.5.10). The salvation offered by the "distant" God consists especially in freedom from the law. On account of the distinction between the two Gods, it holds true that the Old Testament prophets spoke on behalf of the Creator God who was the God of the law, not on behalf of the "distant" God (see Irenaeus, *Haer.* 4.34.5). Therefore, the christological understanding of the Old Testament that was central to Justin was fully abandoned. An example is the treatment of the passage of Isa 7:14 plus 8:4 (which we already have seen brought together by Justin). Here Marcion rejects the common Christian understanding of the virgin birth of Jesus and points rather to the belief that the wealth of Damascus and the booty of Samaria is promised to Immanuel: "However, the one who is to come would neither be issued this name nor become active in a military action" (cited in Tertullian, *Marc.* 3.12.1).

The rejection of the christological significance of the passage leads, therefore, to a historical interpretation (we should remind ourselves of the Jewish equation with Hezekiah that is articulated by Trypho). The literal understanding of the Old Testament directs Marcion to the assumption that there must be a second Messiah who is proclaimed by the Old Testament prophets, who is, however, not yet come but rather will first appear in the end time (see already Justin, *1 Apol.* 58.1; see further Tertullian, *Marc.* 3.23.6; 4.6.3–4; 4.3.4; 4.4.1ff.). This "Christ of the Creator" will reconstitute Judah when he comes (Tertullian, *Marc.* 3.6.3; 3.24.1). However, the text does not presage that he must suffer and die on the cross (see 3.18.1).

Similar to his teacher Paul (see esp. Rom 9–11), he was faithful to the thinking of the church by not becoming an opponent of the Jews. However, Marcion stressed that the Jews had rejected the salvation offered to them (Irenaeus, *Haer.* 1.27.3) and persisted in their preference to remain in the fold of Abraham (Tertullian, *Marc.* 3.6.8). Still, they themselves were not actually at fault. Because they could not know the Father, they could also not know his Son (3.6.8). They could not know "something that had never been proclaimed, yet they could have known something that had always been announced" (3.6.9). Guilty rather is the God who made his followers blind and thus delivered them to corruption (2.28.3). Even the apostles remained in ignorance and thus could not have preached to the Jews any other God than the one in whom they had believed (see Irenaeus, *Haer.* 3.12.7).

On this basis, Marcion strictly rejected the inclusion of the Gospel of Matthew in his corpus of Scripture and could include only a truncated Gospel of Luke (without the Old Testament references). It is characteristic of his teaching—and understandable probably only from Marcion's opposition against the orthodox opinion—that the "strange" God does not save the children of the lesser God; that is, Marcion offered the view that the Old Testament persons of piety had known only of their God, who continually seduced them, and therefore as a result mistrusted the coming of the God of salvation (Irenaeus, *Haer.* 1.27.3).

It is thus false, as has been commonly asserted, to blame Marcion for opposition to Judaism. He was in a certain sense thoroughly positive toward the Jews and assigned to them salvation, which was expected to take place at the end. However, this view still required a rejection of the Old Testament. Because Marcion could not have the same understanding as did Justin that prophecy pointed to Jesus, seeing that a literal interpretation was applicable for everything, the Old Testament lost for him any quality of a continuing, valid revelation. The book of the law of Moses and the prophets sent only to Israel became for him a type of customary law peculiar to a past historical period. Finally, this view was in line with his ahistorical approach: the Christ-event was something that lost all historical associations. It was an event that was unprepared and unforeseen. His interpretation of salvation rested upon this and also upon his teaching of the lower Creator God (Demiurge), bringing him close to gnostic teaching. Even so, he was rather different from the real gnostics. Gnosticism also rejected the Old Testament, as did Marcion.

It should also be mentioned that Marcion, in keeping with Greek thinking, attached salvation only to the soul that heard the message of the spirit, not to the body, because it comes from the earth (Irenaeus, *Haer.* 1.27.3). The orthodox opponents of Marcion clearly saw what the consequences of his teaching were for Christianity. Christianity would no longer be understood in the sense of the fulfillment of the Old Testament (the Law and the Prophets), so it would lose its roots in history and become an ancient mystery religion. This insight is also decisive for the modern discussions over the role of the Old Testament. There are modern voices that have recommended a dissociation of the Christian message from the Old Testament. The famous theologian Adolf von Harnack, who has written the best-known book about Marcion, belongs to these. His voice played an important role in the discussions about the Old Testament prior to 1933, when a politically conditioned and, unlike Marcion, anti-Jewish campaign was launched that led to a well-known and terrible result.

4.5. HARMONY OF THE TESTAMENTS: IRENAEUS OF LYON

In the second half of the second century C.E., gnosis developed into an ever more threatening danger for the church. The origins, provenance, and forms of the appearance of gnosis have been debated and continue to be. The Greek idea signifies "recognition" and designates a personal claim of gnostic teachers, through the transmission of esoteric knowledge, to point to the way to salvation for the initiated. For the most part, we do not possess any authentic sources that are able to provide information about Christian gnosis. Nonetheless, gnosis appears to have been in its origins, in essence, contemporary with early Christianity and in competition with the church's fundamental character. The foundation of gnosis was a dualistic approach from which a corresponding dualistic teaching of salvation developed. There is a fundamental opposition between the material world and the sphere of the spirit. The gnostic myth, which exists in various formulations, offered a corresponding teaching of the origin of the world and developed a systematic teaching about this. It explained how humanity came from the sphere of the spirit into the material world and how humans could find the way back to their origins. Cosmology and soteriology, therefore, correspond to each other.

As an example of this system, which presumably dealt with the most far-reaching and developed form of Christian gnosis, is the teaching of

Valentinus and his disciples, called the Valentinians. According to Valentinus, the upper world, the pleroma (Greek for "fullness") in the form of aeons (worldly regions) originated from the ultimate source of being through emanations (proceeding streams). One of these aeons, Sophia (Wisdom) initiated a mistake. She originated the Creator of the world (the Demiurge), who proceeded to create the material world. It is the nonexistent, in contrast to life, that is both incorporated and desired by the Divine Father who encompasses all things. There is present in the material world an element from the upper world that originates with Sophia that must be redeemed and returned. Humanity, in an analogy to the Greek understanding of anthropology, is comprised of three different entities—spirit (*pneuma*); soul (*psyche*); body (*soma*)—and divided into three classes: the pneumatics (among whom the gnostics understand themselves to be, who come into this life with a knowledge of the true God); the psychics (normal Christians, who may partake in a limited way in salvation by means of their corresponding ethical behavior); and the hylics, who are completely bound to the material world (*hyle*) and remain incapable of redemption. Christ is the one from above who dwelt in the Pleroma with the "Unknown Father," the "invisible" and "strange" God. The Father sent the Christ as the Savior into the world, the sphere of nothingness. This Christ was the one in whom the true God himself dwelt. Salvation occurred in a dual manner: through the destruction of the nothingness, accomplished by the crucifixion of the body of the Savior on the cross, but especially through the process of enlightenment in which the knowledge (gnosis) that leads to salvation was revealed.

The battle between gnosis and the theology of the church was carried out on the basis of the Bible. The gnostics felt that they were Christians. They accepted the writings of the New Testament and consciously made it the basis of their teaching, but they appealed, similarly to Marcion, to Paul. They based their hypothesis, however, likewise on the Old Testament as the "Scripture" that was valid also for Christians and recognized indirectly its authority, even if they compared the God of the Old Testament, the God of the law, to the Creator God (Demiurge), whom they associated with the lower God of matter. The standard by which they explained the Scripture, however, is the typical myth in which are clothed their specific views of the origin, structure, and purpose of the world. Their opposition to the teaching that was held in the great church and their crass transformation of biblical traditions marked them as an extremist sectarian movement, in which their hatred of life, their mythology that stressed the mysterious, and the central role that was accorded "awareness" (gnosis) for the salvation of humans accommodated widespread ideas of Hellenistic late antiquity. The apologetics of the church followed the twofold direction in which they must defend the correct teaching of the faith against gnosis: (1) to point to the fantastic character and internal discrepancies of the gnostic myth; and (2) to oppose the form of the treatment of the Scripture that dwelt at the foundation of the gnostic interpreters' system by indicating the divergent, true meaning of Scripture. This could happen, however, only if the church developed its own genuinely Christian understanding of Scripture. Orthodox Christians were forced to move beyond the previously predominant limitation of "Scripture" to the Old Testament, as represented as late as Justin, although he did use citations of Paul and the Gospels already in his debate with his dialogue partner Trypho. This antignostic apologetics defended the difficult issues of their teaching by reference to New Testament texts (as the parables of Jesus and the correspondence of Paul). Even if an official New Testament canon still lay in the distant future, also all of the "apostolic" writings that later belonged to it, the second half of the second century saw the development of the authority of these texts, which were comparable to a "Scripture" found in the great church and in the heretics.

Through their frontal attack on the teachings of the church and the traditional understanding of Scripture, the gnostics provoked a fundamental reflection over doctrine, that is, what was to be believed as the content of the Christian tradition and to be preached on the mission field. They unintentionally offered the impetus to the development of a systematic, reflected Christian theology, which one may first speak about in the work of Irenaeus of Lyon.

Relatively little is known of the personal life of Irenaeus. He obviously grew up in western Asia Minor, where he could hear an aged Polycarp preach in Smyrna. Later he came into southern Gaul, to Lugdunum (Lyon), at that time the center of the Gallic Province and a wealthy trade hub. There he became a presbyter and as such was commissioned and sent to Rome to Bishop Eleutherus (ca. 174–189). When, during a persecution in Lyon in 177/8, Bishop Photinus lost his life along with other martyrs, Irenaeus became his successor. We know nothing precisely about his death, which occurred shortly after 200 c.e. While his writings were originally in Greek, outside of a few fragments nothing more has survived. His main work, *Refutation and Overthrow of Knowledge Falsely So-Called*, exists in a Latin translation (*Adversus haereses*; see earlier). A great sensation was caused by the 1904 discovery of another writing, called the *Epideixis* (*Demonstration of Apostolic Preaching*), in an Armenian translation.

In *Adversus haereses,* a rather detailed apology consisting of five volumes, one can recognize a planned overarching structure in spite of the fact that it is not always easy to discern the individual arguments. The standards for doing so often follow the rules of ancient rhetoric. In book 1 Irenaeus brings forth the "knowledge" of the heretics: a critical description of gnostic teachings, where the Valentinians, above all their main representative Ptolemaeus, stand in the center, and the summary of the different gnostic systems, especially the contradictions between them, is delineated. The "repudiation" of the gnostic teachings individually set forth follows in book 2: Irenaeus places critical questions to his opponents and wishes to make clear to them in this way the problems and contradictions in their own teachings.

Indeed, already in the sphere of this doctrinal controversy a position of Irenaeus echoes that will become the actual subject of his remarks in the following books. In the foreword of book 1 (preface) Irenaeus repudiated the gnostics: "Through means of a deceptively constructed probability they mislead the understanding of those who are inexperienced and imprison them with the words of the Lord that either are falsified or, in regard to those words that have been well preserved, are falsely interpreted." In this regard, he notes on one occasion that they take up the parables of Christ, which in fact are very difficult to understand, and argues: "all their meaning cannot be grasped, although their mysteries have been revealed through the parables to those who could understand them" (1.3.1). This is true for the Scripture as a whole in all of its parts:

> not only from the Gospels and the apostle [Paul] do they seek to produce their arguments in which they provide deceitful interpretation and falsify explanation, but also from the Law and the Prophets. For these also contain many parables and allegories that can be pointed in many directions. They also make texts conform in deceptive ways to their own explanations. (1.3.6; see also 1.8.1)

After this, he still often comes back to his aim, which he presents at length in books 3 and 4 of his work.

Before we concern ourselves with a more detailed examination of Irenaeus's biblical interpretation and to understand his arguments about biblical texts in their context, it is important to make clear what exegetes consider to be his primary interests in his inquiry into the Bible. He himself addresses repeatedly and expressly these interests, since they emerge in the leading position of his debate with the heretics in his apologetic work. Marcion and the gnostics, with whom he occupies himself, both maintained the existence of two Gods: one who is above, far removed from the world, spiritual, and redemptive; and a lower Creator (Demiurge). In opposing this position, Irenaeus states: "I have already shown that God is one. I shall demonstrate this yet again from the apostles and the speeches of the Lord. What would it be, were we to forsake the voices of the prophets, the Lord, and the apostles and turn to those who say nothing that is reasonable?" (2.2.6).

Irenaeus's central concern is to demonstrate the unity of God. This is set forth as the basis of the description he provides in book 1 in regard to the teachings of the heretics. Their purpose was not so much to present a teaching about God but much more to articulate a teaching of salvation, as we know from the gnostic writings that have been preserved. By the same token, refutation becomes the form dominating book 2. However, Irenaeus's central approach is a theological concern that raises the only red flag in his entire understanding of the Bible. At the end of the second book he remarks:

> Our statements conform to the preaching of the apostles, the teachings of the Lord, the announcements of the prophets ... and the service of the law, which all praise the one and the same Father God and not the one and another.... That I believe I have already sufficiently demonstrated. However, with this we do not seem to evade the proof that occurs of the Lord, since the writings themselves precisely proclaim much more explicitly and clearly this matter, at least to those who do not turn to follow their [the heretics'] false path. In a special book that follows [book 3], we shall explain these writings and from these divine Scriptures present evidence to those who love the truth. (2.35.4)

However, which are the texts he includes in these writings? When we survey book 3 of *Adversus haereses*, it is striking that the greater portion of the passages mentioned come from the New Testament writings. On the whole, we find in Irenaeus approximately twice as many citations from the New Testament as from the Old. The only texts he does not seem to know are the 3 John, Philemon, and Jude. Although the thought of a New Testament canon is still not developed in him, it is nonetheless clear that he concedes first place in the witness of the Scripture to the "writings of the apostles" and the "words of the Lord." The picture in *Epideixis* is different. The presentation of the teaching of God and Christ does not contain a polemical purpose here but rather proceeds in a traditional way by referring to the world of the Old Testament prophets. Thus, this difference appears to confirm that the preponderance of the New Testament citations in Irenaeus's main work is a reaction against the heretical claims made about these writings. Above all, heretics such as Marcion and the gnostics forced church theology to give a more fundamental consideration to the authority of the early Christian writings.

More precisely, there are two major themes that Irenaeus takes up in book 3 of his work: (1) he demonstrates that there is a single God who is the Creator of all things (*Haer.* 3.6–15); and (2) he shows that there is a single Christ, the Son of God who became a human and the incarnation of the Word (*Haer.* 3.16–23). After a general overview that surveys the use of the terms "God" and "Lord" in the Old Testament, in Paul's letters, and in the words of Jesus (*Haer.* 3.6–8), Irenaeus moves into a more precise investigation of the witness of the Gospels concerning the one true God (*Haer.* 3.9–11). The series of texts from which he cites are Matt 1–3; Luke 1–2; Mark (1:1–3, combined with Mal 3:1; Isa 40:1; he also includes a reference to Ps 110:1); and the Prologue of John, on which he especially offers a lengthy commentary. In respect to the authors of the Gospels, he follows a tradition that understands the term "apostolic" in a narrow sense (and now in Irenaeus is this form attested).

Disputes over the authority of one Gospel over against another, which involved the tendency of the heretics to select and then abridge the Gospel that corresponded to their own idiosyncratic teaching, led Irenaeus subsequently to his much-considered statement over the necessity of having four Gospels, found in 3.11.8: "Why, then, are there neither more nor fewer Gospels [translation of a Greek fragment; formulated as a declarative statement in the Latin translation]? Because there are four parts of the world, four principal winds, and the church is scattered throughout the entire world, the gospel and the spirit of life are the pillars and columns of the church. Thus, it follows that there are four pillars breathing out immortality from all sides and vivifying human beings." Obviously, in this remarkable formulation are entwined two images of the columns that sustain and the innervating spirit. The concept of the inspiration of the Gospels stands in the background. In this combination, the expression "fourfold" (*tetramorph, quadraform*) occurs frequently, and Irenaeus provides it with an inner unity. As one observes the heretical positions, one has often given considerable attention these past two hundred years to the differences between the Gospels. In contrast, Irenaeus stresses their harmony. Demonstrating the harmony of the Gospels and beyond these the Scriptures as a whole, both Old and

New Testaments, becomes one of the central motifs of his biblical interpretation.

After the Gospels, the text of the book of Acts queries witnesses about
the one God (3.12), who are witnesses of the other apostles, among them
Paul! However, since Irenaeus was familiar with the interpretation of the
heretics, he knew that Paul was regarded as the only true apostle among
them. He still attaches passages out of the Pauline letters (Gal 2:8; Rom
10:15; 1 Cor 15:11) in which Paul himself explained that Peter and a
host of other witnesses saw and recognized the same truth as he did. In
addition, Irenaeus points back to the objections of other sects expressed
against Luke or Paul (3.13–15).

The major section of book 3 that has to do with the one Christ begins
with a brief description of the gnostic position (3.16.1). In all their various
distinctions, the gnostics together as a whole "fragment" Christ into two
forms: "Jesus," who more or less belongs to the human world; and "Christ"
or the "Savior," who belongs to the divine Pleroma. The Christ descended
on Jesus at baptism in the form of a dove (see Mark 1:10 par.). Irenaeus
demonstrates that this division into two forms is excluded by apostolic
teaching. This is demonstrated subsequently by a series of scriptural attestations. In addition to John 1:14 and 18, a central text for Irenaeus upon
which he frequently calls, he mentions texts from Matt 1 with its Old Testament citations found there, Paul, Mark, Luke, and John, which, taken
together, show that Jesus was the same human son as well as the Christ
and the Son of God who died for our sins on the cross.

An excursus (3.17) explains what actually transpired at Jesus' baptism:
it was the Spirit who descended like a dove upon the Son of God. Then
follow additional Pauline texts that demonstrate that he continued to
speak of the incarnation and the suffering of this same Christ (3.18.1–3).
The chain of proof is concluded with the words of the Lord in which Jesus
himself explains that he, the Son of Man, will suffer, be crucified, and then
be resurrected on the third day (Matt 16:13–21; also cited are 16:22–25;
10:18, 32–33, 39, among other texts). Finally there follows a theological
explanation (3.18.7) that, taking up the beginning in 3.18.1, explains *why*
God had to become human. It does not suffice that God gave humans
the law through Moses, for the law, since it was spiritual, could point
out sins but not gain victory over them. "It was necessary that he who
would destroy sins and liberate humans who were worthy of death would
himself be a human. He who would become accountable for those sins
through means of servanthood had to die at the hands of humans in order
to allow humanity to escape the power of death." When the gnostics deny

the incarnation of Christ, they have not grasped what is the most decisive feature of the gospel. As one sees from the following citation, this argumentation has grown out of the interpretation of a Pauline text, namely, the statement in Rom 5:19 (augmented by an allusion to Gen 2:5) that speaks of the consequences of the disobedience of the *one* ("still formed out of the uncultivated earth"; thus reads the Greek text) human (Adam) and the consequences of the obedience of the *one* human (Christ). The Adam-Christ typology is in Irenaeus an element that binds and yet at the same time distinguishes the two Testaments. The citation of Paul is still in a secondary place and is expanded through an allusion to Isa 7:14: "*one human being who has been born of a virgin.*" As we shall yet see, Irenaeus is preparing the way for the thoughts of the following section. The mixture and entwining of the Old and New Testament citations in this and many other places should not remain unnoticed. This shows that for Irenaeus the entire Scripture of the Old and New Testaments comprised a single unity. Thus, it would be wrong to maintain that he cites them without distinction, for he recognized the distinguishing aspects of the two Testaments, however also the same authority of the two parts of the Bible.

This becomes clear from another aspect in the following chapters (*Haer.* 3.19.1–21.9). In this section Irenaeus undertakes to oppose the Ebionites, who saw Jesus simply as a human being, the son of Joseph and Mary. Those who supported this position did not know of the Immanuel born of the virgin (Isa 7:14), the incarnation of the Word, or the Son of God becoming the Son of Man (John 8:36). Thus these spurners, who renounce the gift of being adopted as sons of God, are directed to Ps 82:6–7: "For this reason, therefore, the Word has become human and the Son of God the Son of Man so that the human by mixing with the word [a bold image!] acquires adoption and becomes the Son of God." The concept is that we humans may only in this way have the capacity to partake in imperishability and immortality. If we are incorporated with imperishability and immortality, this presupposes that imperishability and immortality are a part of who we first were (i.e., in the same way Christ became human). Therefore the perishable is absorbed by the imperishable. This is a paraphrase of 1 Cor 15:53–54 (see also 2 Cor 5:4), to which is added a citation from Gal 4:5a (3.19.1).

That Christ is both human and God is supported in the following section (3.19.2–3) by copious brief citations and allusions to Old and New Testament texts (e.g., Isa 53:8; Jer 17:9; Matt 16:17; John 1:13). The obviously effortless transition from an allusion to the others demonstrates a complete mastery of the biblical materials. In distinction from many of his predecessors, Irenaeus appears not to have used preexisting collections of prooftexts but rather went directly back to the Bible itself, which he obviously thoroughly knew by heart. In the selection of the biblical passages, especially out of the Old Testament, one may certainly recognize traditional examples. Examples of such common biblical exegeses are the elements of Immanuel (Isa 7:11–12), that is, "Immanu-El," "God with us"; expressions that are interpreted through the elements of ancient church confession formulas, such as "descended into the underworld" (see Eph 4:9) and "ascended into the heights" (see Eph 4:10); and the conviction completed with additional citations that both have taken place for humanity. In addition, there is the "sign of Jonah" (Matt 12:39–40), which brings into play the most important features of the Old Testament story of Jonah.

The following section, which deserves special attention, treats the "first" and "second" Adam (3.21.10–23.8). The concept of "repetition" (*anakephalaiosis, recapitulatio*) possesses central significance for Irenaeus's theology (the term occurs twenty-four times in his writings). In *Haer.* 3.18 he already formulated what is important to him in this correlation. "We have shown … that the Son of God…, when he came in the flesh, became a human who recapitulated [reassumed] within himself the lengthy history of humanity. He afforded for us in this interrelationship the salvation that we had lost in Adam. Jesus Christ won back for us the image and semblance of God" (3.18.1). The significant concept for Christian theology in all the following centuries, the idea of salvation history, is set forth here for the very first time.

Anticipating countless discussions about the appropriateness or inappropriateness of the idea of "salvation history," Irenaeus, through the contrast between Adam and Christ and the thought of "repetition," addressed the problem of redemption history. This problem lies in the fact that, for Irenaeus, the history of humanity, as it is exemplified and reflected by the history of Israel, is to be regarded as the history of calamity. Salvation history can be reclaimed only by the complete return of the original purpose of human history, a change that has been obtained by means of the Christ-event. Irenaeus wishes to express with the concept of "repetition" that Christ, as the second Adam, began to right this history by starting it over, only now it is a history that leads to salvation. Thereby Irenaeus attaches his thinking, as was already clear in *Haer.* 3.18, to the theology of Paul. In Rom 5, this contrast between Adam and Christ as the first man and second man provides the basis for this view of salvation history. In the section beginning with 3.21.10, this manner of treatment is taken up once again. Here Irenaeus cites once more Rom 5:12, 19. In this connection, he renews his rejection of the gnostics, who rejected the full humanity of Jesus and his incarnation and recognized in him only one who appeared to have a body.

The following chapters present a detailed exegesis of the story of paradise and the fall due to sin. Thus, Gen 2–3 is related to the correspondence between the old and the new Adam. In 3.22.3 is added the correspondence between the old and the new Eve (i.e., Mary). In Gen 2–3 there are different places where the Pauline sections about the first and second Adam in Rom 5 and 1 Cor 15:45–46 are cited directly and indirectly. Paul has, of course, a different purpose in 1 Cor 15:45–49. In his comparison between the first and second Adam, he wishes to move beyond to the statement in verse 50: "Flesh and blood cannot inherit the kingdom of God." Correspondingly, the earthly [Adam] and the heavenly man [Christ] stand over against each other. This is spoken to the Christians, who participate in both. In the resurrection they shall be clothed with a heavenly body (1 Cor 15:42–43, 51–52). With these statements, Irenaeus then occupies himself with another passage (15:9–14) in which he stresses his defense against the gnostics and partially against 1 Cor 15, noting that even this earthly body of humans will partake in the resurrection. The gnostics, of course, denied that anything material would have a part in the kingdom of the Spirit.

Because Irenaeus stressed the unity of the one God against Marcion and the gnostics, he found it necessary to demonstrate that the Old Testament belonged with the New. In addition, Irenaeus developed in a lengthy account (4.20–35) the argument that was previously included in the tradition, that Christ's coming already had been promised in the Old Testament. He stresses that the significance of this prophecy could now be recognized, since Christ had arrived. "Since it was set forth through types and parables, which were not understood by humans, the fulfillment of what was prophesied has taken place, namely, the arrival of Christ" (4.26.1). Therefore, while Irenaeus could reach back to Justin and to other apologists who were certainly known to him, he still develops new points of view.

A central argument developed in order to explain the differences between the Old and New Testaments, and not just to point out their correspondences, has to do with the divine economy. Objections to the Old Testament had been noted by its critics, especially Marcion and the gnostics, in the most pressing manner. These were among those who were opposed to the godly nature of Old Testament piety and the all-too-human character of the God of the Old Testament. Irenaeus writes, "There is (only) one and the same God, the Father, and his word endures forever throughout the human generations, if also in different economies" (4.28.2). In taking up the criticism of the gnostics directed toward the pious of the Old Testament, Irenaeus stresses that they were imperfect human beings.

> Should, however, someone ask: "How, then, could God not make humans perfect from the beginning?" he should know that all things are possible to God.... What is created, however, because it had not yet assumed in the beginning what it would become, therefore must be less than the one who had created it.... Because they [humans] are not uncreated, therefore they must lag behind the One who is perfect. Because they came later, they are more childlike; because they are more childlike, they are still unaccustomed and inexperienced in coming to a perfect way of life. (4.38.1)

In the future, humans through experience can eventually learn what is good and become obedient through means of the commandments God has given them (4.39.1; see 3.20.2). Thus emerges the famous idea that appears in the later history of theology, the motif (if not also the expression) of "conformation" (accommodation): "In this way the Word of God, although it was perfect, became a child among humans, not because of itself, but rather on account of the childlike nature of humans, becoming in this way comprehensible, in a way that the human being could grasp it" (4.38.2).

Still another idea for the understanding of the divine "economy" is important in Irenaeus, that of education. "Thus God has formed humans from the beginning on account of his gift. He elected the patriarchs on account of their salvation; however, he formed the nation as he taught the unteachable to give obedience to God. He prepared the prophets after that to acclimate humans to dwell on the earth, to carry his spirit, and to enter into community with God" (4.14.2). The announcement beforehand of the new covenant through the prophets also served to educate humans, "in order that they would believe him, continuing to advance and to mature through the performances of the covenant to come to the perfection of salvation" (4.9.3). In this sense, progress in history is also recognizable: "If God is always the same, thus he makes humans, who reside with him, to continue to make progress toward him. Also, God never ceases to do good things for humans and to elevate them to become those who are from God" (4.11.2).

Certainly Irenaeus knew very well about the many meanings, for example, of prophecy and the riddle-like character of many Old Testament words: "The prophets, therefore, did not see the revealed appearance of God but rather the economies and the secrets [mysteries] through which a human being sees God" (4.20.10; citing as evidence Exod 33:20–22; 1 Kgs 19:11–12; Ezek 1). The example of Ezekiel, who saw only the "semblance" of the glory of God seated on his throne (Ezek 1), "still points more clearly to the fact that the prophets have seen only in part the divine economies of God; however, they did not behold him at all."

The difficult concept "economy" must be translated here perhaps as "partial revelation." The different "economies" build the various sections of the history of revelation, from which the whole then results. Irenaeus first provides a comprehensive overview of the perfection in Christ. He then uses in a modified form the image of a body with many members (see 1 Cor 12:12–13; Rom 12:4) in order to make clear the origin of the common depiction from the different sections of the words of individual prophets (4.33.9). In order to grasp a common depiction, inspiration is necessary for the reader of the Bible. "And what the others all address is the fact, as we have shown in abundance, that the prophets have said that which the truly spiritually endowed [the truly spiritual] will interpret. This spiritually endowed person also has shown the special movement of the economy [= the design of salvation] of God and speaks of the common constitution of the activity of God. He shall always recognize the same God, always the same Word [= Christ] of God, and even if he has not revealed it to us now, he will also discern the same Spirit of God" (4.33.15). Only from the same overall picture, which is made accessible by the perfection in Christ, is it possible to assign each individual prophetic word, partial in itself, to its place.

The unity of the revelation of the Three-in-One (see 1.10.1 with its Trinitarian formula of confession) nature of God in both Testaments is underlined by Irenaeus. He allows the Word (Logos), that is, the Son of God, whose becoming human was the goal of history, to participate throughout the sequences of time in Old Testament events of revelation. This theology of the Word is in the broadest sense the consequence of his interpretation of John 1:4: "The Word has become flesh." Irenaeus already commented on this affirmation in 3.20.3, and he mentions it again in 4.20.2, with other passages that address the belief that Jesus Christ has been given all power in heaven and on the earth. Especially informative for our summary, however, is the statement in 3.18.7 (continuing the already cited sentence): "How could we participate in adoption to become his sons, had we had not experienced community with him by means of the Son? If the Word had not become flesh, would there have been entrance for us into this community? Therefore, he also entered human existence in every generation by which he transmitted to all [humans] community with God."

In spite of the possibility of referring this to the stages of life experienced by individual humans (as in 2.2.4), there is also here arguably the meaning of the different epochs of human history, if one considers here the possible word use of the Latin *aetas* as "age." In any case, there are found in Irenaeus other passages that clearly state that the "Word" already was present in the Old Testament revelations of God. Here one sees once again that Irenaeus developed his thesis in his debate with the gnostics around the interpretation of a biblical term. This may be seen in Matt 11:27. The statement "No one knows the Son save the Father and no one the Father except the Son" was translated by the gnostics in the past tense, who explained it in the sense that the "strange" God," the Father of Jesus Christ, was first known through this one's appearance. The Old Testament God is, therefore, another deity, not the Father of Jesus Christ. Against this theory Irenaeus develops (4.6) the correct exegesis of Matt 11:27. It is correct that the Father can be known only through the Son. The Father, however, is the Creator, and he wills all to know him. He would continue to be unknown, if he had not revealed the Son. In reality, "the Word already reveals through the creation the Creator God and through the world the Lord as the Creator of the World" (4.6.6). The Word was present from the beginning, and "through the Law and the Prophets the Word proclaimed himself and the Father" (4.6.6).

The Word was already present in the Garden of Eden: "Paradise was so beautiful and good that the Word of God walked about, strolled around, and spoke with the humans about future things" (*Epid.* 12). In addition, the word not to eat of the fruit of the tree was given to Adam through the Word (Gen 3:18): "Given is namely the commandment to the humans through the word: Adam, says (the Scripture), heard the voice of the Lord" (*Haer.* 5.17.1). Irenaeus, who understands the meaning of the "Word" (Logos) in the Prologue to John to relate to Christ, thus regards all references to the word of God in the Old Testament to have the same implication. Since the Old Testament speaks often of the word of God, there is then developed a thoroughgoing christological understanding of the Old Testament. He comes to the same conclusion in his understanding of the statement in John 5:46–47: "If you believed Moses, then you would believe in me, for he has written about me. If, however, you do not believe his writings, you will not therefore believe me." For Irenaeus, Christ has "clearly shown that the writings of Moses are his speeches" (4.2.3). He concludes this by saying about John 5:39–40, "that everywhere in his works the Son of God is shown in his writings, once in speaking with Abraham, once with Noah giving him instructions [for the ark], once in inquiring of Adam, once allowing Sodomites to receive their judgment, when he appears at the time Jacob is headed on his way, and once when he speaks with Moses from the bush" (4.10.1).

The different appearances of God to the patriarchs are not appearances of God the Father but rather the Word. "For it was not the Father of all, who cannot be seen from the world, and the Creator of all … who spoke … with Abraham but rather the Word of God, who was always present with humanity" (*Epid.* 45). That which holds true for the words of Moses also holds true for those of the prophets: "If, therefore, Moses, so also without question are the speeches of the remaining prophets" (*Haer.* 4.2.3). The Word appears to the prophets also in their visions:

> Therefore, neither Moses nor Elijah nor Ezekiel has actually seen God…; what, however, was seen by them were the appearances of the radiance of the Lord [Ezek 1:28] and the predictions of future things. Thus, it is obvious that indeed the Father cannot be seen, as the Lord has said: "God has never been seen by anyone" [John 1:18]. However, his Word has shown the brilliance of the Father and revealed his economies. (4.20.21)

In order to understand these interpretations, it is important to keep in mind the double meaning of the translation of *kyrios* as "Lord" for the name of God in the Septuagint. Not only "Word" but also "Lord" can easily be understood as referring to Christ. In the New Testament, one may observe clearly the transition from the Old Testament name of God in the Septuagint. The New Testament regards "Lord" to be a designation of Jesus (see esp. Phil 2:11 and the usage in Paul). Irenaeus has here selected a clear and significant choice in his "literal" exegesis: "Lord" is a word for Christ.

In opposing the view of the heretics who maintained that the law was given by a different God than the Father of Jesus Christ, Irenaeus presents his explanation of Rom 10:4 (Christ the "end of the law"): "How could Christ be the end of the law, if he was not also its beginning? That is to say, whoever brings the end has also produced the beginning" (4.12.4). Also, regarding the law, Irenaeus points to the harmony of the Testaments. He refers to Matt 23:2–4, according to which Jesus commanded his audience to keep the law as it was taught by the scribes and the Pharisees but only forbade that they imitate their deeds (4.12.4). In the entire

section of 4.12–16, Irenaeus undertakes to describe the gospel as the fulfillment of the law. To this belongs the references to Matt 15:3 (4.12.1),
to the "greatest commandment" (Matt 20:37–40, including the citation of
Deut 6:5; Lev 19:18; 12:2–3), and to Matt 5:17 (4.13.1, repeated in 4.13.3).
The concept of education also plays a role here: the law given to the slaves
(i.e., to the people of Israel) in respect to bodily matters should educate
them to be truly obedient to God's commandments. Now, however, those
who are free, liberated by means of the Word, are to follow it unbounded
in order to accomplish even more. The commandments of the Sermon
on the Mount were understood in this sense as a better law for those who
are free (4.13.3); they are not antitheses but rather expansions of the law.
In addition, the commandments that were given to Israel were given for
their well-being: the laws of the cult served to educate them in true worship (4.14.3–15.1) or, for example, the allowance of divorce (Deut 24:1),
as a concession (4.15.2). However, also in this regard Irenaeus sees Paul's
instructions in 1 Cor 7 as a New Testament parallel. Circumcision, the
Sabbath (4.16.1–2), and the Decalogue (4.16.3–4a) were signs and symbols of the "laws of the Gospels" that were to come. Irenaeus appeals,
above all, to Matthew in order to defend the harmony between the law
and the gospel, provoked by the polemic of the gnostics against the law.
Even though he makes use of Paul's understanding of law and gospel, as
may be seen from the reinterpretation of Rom 10:4, this view, at least in
this context, is not taken into consideration. In another passage (4.4.2)
he speaks, by contrast, of the temporal end of the law within the framework of his view of salvation history: "Now, then, since the law began
with Moses, it consequentially ceased with John [the Baptist], for its fulfillment, Christ, had come" (then follows a citation from Luke 16:16). The
same holds good for the dispersion from Jerusalem: "What even has a
temporal beginning consequently also must have a temporal end" (4.4.1).

In addition to the newly formed theory derived from Johannine statements about the presence of the "Word" in the Old Testament events of
revelation, Irenaeus represents also the traditional interpretation of the
working of the Holy Spirit in the Scriptures. He is able to bring both of
them together: "The Scriptures are perfect, since they are spoken by the
Word of God and the Spirit" (2.28.2). It is the Spirit who throughout the
history of revelation "gives the knowledge of the truth, which brings on
the stage the economies of the Father and the Son for every generation of
humans, as the Father wills it" (4.3.7). Therefore, the well-known formula
that the Spirit spoke through Moses, David, and the prophets is found also
in Irenaeus. Obviously, this means verbal inspiration. This is attested even

by what the sentence recently cited seems to say (4.28.2). Yet Irenaeus does not compose a complete doctrine of inspiration. Rather, he points to the evidence of the reliability of the Scriptures in Christian interpretation ("without interpolation," 3.21.3) by the additional reference to the ancient, well-known legend of the origin of the Septuagint (3.21.2–3; see above). This is the inspired text he claims as his source in his arguments against the gnostics, who defended their explanations by reference to other translations. For Irenaeus, the Greek translation of the Old Testament also is the result of "the inspiration of God."

When one places next to each other the aspects of the revelation of the Father through the Son and the Holy Spirit's inspiration of the Scriptures, as Irenaeus would have it, one is able to speak of a Trinitarian understanding of revelation, for these are in fact aspects of the revelation of the God who is Three-in-One. With this, Irenaeus's understanding of the Bible is shown to be deeply theologically constituted. He demonstrates his thesis that there is only one God with the help of his dogmatic-methodological tenet in every individual passage of the Old Testament (which is enlightened by the New Testament). Through their inspiration as spoken by the Word and in the Spirit and the availability of the gift of the Spirit for the righteous reader, there comes a true knowledge of Scripture (in contrast to the "falsely so-called gnosis"), which, for Irenaeus requires nothing more. Here is found a striking two-track argument.

On the one hand, one encounters a large number of expressions in the sense of the sentence cited from 2.28.2, according to which the Scriptures are "perfect." Irenaeus is able to reproach the gnostics by arguing that they do not wish to see the true sense of Scripture, even though it is indeed "clear and obvious" (5.13.2). There is a natural sense of Scripture that the Gnostics twist in an unnatural fashion (1.9.4). When the Scripture also speaks in parables (the word means "likeness" and "not clear" at first; a type of literary conveyance especially and favorably used by the heretics) in many places, such unclear statements must be interpreted with clear and explicit passages, for "the parables conform to that which is said clearly and explicitly" (2.28.3). Irenaeus speaks in this context of "a single harmonious melody" that resonates through the many voices (2.28.3).

The unclear statements are, however, in the minority: "All Scripture, both the prophetic writings and the Gospels, and similarly all that can be included, even if not all are believed, openly proclaim, without any ambiguity, that a single God has created all things through his word" (2.27.2). Also, as for the words of the Lord, one should hark back only to those "that do not teach about the Father in parables but rather simply in clear language" (4.41.4). This should be done in opposing the gnostics. In so doing, Irenaeus deals with the historical facts that may be demonstrated (see above). Luke, the companion of Paul (according to the Acts of the Apostles), is legitimated by his being a student of this apostle. He not only accurately described his common journeys with Paul (3.14.2) but also transmitted reliably in his Gospel many things that we (as in Luke 1–3 and in other statements from his own unique material) learn only from him (3.14.3). Irenaeus stresses this because Marcion and the gnostic Valentinus especially made use of Luke (only the parts they considered authentic) to support their teachings.

However, if one wished to hypothesize that Irenaeus, corresponding to his theory of the perfection and clarity of the Scriptures, must have operated with an interpretation limited to the literal meaning of words, one would be disappointed. One also discovers in his writings a great number of allegorical meanings, as, for example, when he explains the statement in Dan 2:34–35 that "a stone was cut not by human hands" in the following way. "The statement 'without hands,' that is, those belonging to humans, in the careful carving of the stone, signifies that his [Christ's] coming into this world occurred without the assistance of a human hand. This means that without the assistance of Joseph it was Mary alone who cooperated with the 'economy'" (3.21.7). The two daughters of Lot (Gen 19:30–38) are interpreted as "the two synagogues" (Judaism and the church) in *Haer.* 4.31.1–3. Even the parables of Jesus, like the one about the workers in the vineyard (Matt 20:1–6), are interpreted allegorically: this shows, according to Irenaeus, that there is only one Lord who, during different periods since the creation of the world, has sent workers into the vineyard (the world). "There is now only one vineyard, even as there is only one righteousness, and one lord of the house, thus there is only one Spirit of God who rules over all. Equally so, there is only one reward, namely, one denar that each receives, the depiction and the inscription of the king, that is, the knowledge of the Son of God" (4.36.7). As we have seen, this corresponds thoroughly to the contemporary methods of interpretation that Irenaeus also unselfconsciously used with the certain awareness, even in this way, to hit upon the actual concern of the Scriptures.

One needs to consider the fact, however, that allegory in Irenaeus is founded in a completely different way than was the case with Philo. On the one hand, the separation between what is bodily and observable meaning and the spiritual meaning in a Platonic sense would directly contradict Irenaeus's antignostic attitude. On the other hand, one does find in him also the traditional principle for the transmission of the features of a literal meaning to a "spiritual" meaning. A good example of this is his explanation of Lev 11:2 (5.8.3): the commandment to eat only animals that chew the cud and have cloven hooves signifies, according to Irenaeus, Christians, for they chew the cud; that is, they meditate on God's law (the Scriptures) day and night. They have cloven hooves, for they believe in both the Father and the Son. The pagans are represented as animals who neither chew the cud nor have cloven hooves, while the Jews are symbolized as those who chew the cud but do not have cloven hooves. They meditate on the Scriptures but do not believe in Christ. In his polemic against the gnostics, Irenaeus explains that the one God and the one Christ are present in both Testaments. His concern is to provide evidence that serves the variety of his methods. Obviously, he does not consider it necessary to decide between methods, since to him all of them appear possible. This is an error only to the modern observer who seeks to have clear rules as to which method to follow.

Still, even with the use of all these methods, a residue remains. Irenaeus speaks about this when he notes that we are unable to find solutions for everything present in Scripture. "There are things that we must leave to God, who has created us, while we correctly know that indeed the Scriptures are perfect.... We, however, by comparison, are smaller and exceedingly inexperienced vis-à-vis the Word of God and his Spirit and thus lack the knowledge of his mysteries" (2.28.2). Therefore, "we solve some matters by the grace of God; some things, however, we leave to God" (2.28.3). There are questions to which the Scriptures provide no answer, as, for example, what God did prior to the creation of the world (2.28.3) or how the Son emerged from the Father (2.28.6). Finally, God remains also for Irenaeus inscrutable. God has revealed the Word, but "even so he has maintained the invisibility of God" (4.20.7). The heretics are irrationally pompous when they maintain that they know the unfathomable mysteries of God (4.20.7).

This self-enhancement of the "gnosis falsely so-called" is thoroughly brought into judgment in book 2 and is contrasted to the "true gnosis," which Irenaeus is unable to discover anywhere else in church tradition. With this, we come to his second fundamental principle, which modifies the teaching of the perfection of Scripture.

> True knowledge [gnosis] is the teachings of the apostles and the ancient [didactic] system of the church in the entire world and the character of the body of Christ according to the succession of the bishops, who carried forth on behalf of those [apostles] in the present locations of

the church. These acquired for us as an unfalsified preservation of the Scriptures, as a complete treatment, without suffering any addition or shortening, a reading without distortion, a legitimate and understandable interpretation of the Scriptures [the entirety of the Scriptures], without danger and sacrilege. (4.33.8)

Therefore, one must "read the Scriptures carefully with the presbyters of the church, who possess the apostolic teaching" (4.32.1). Alluding to 1 Cor 12:28, Irenaeus speaks of where one needs to learn the truth. One needs to know "where the gifts [charismata] of God are deposited, in whom resides the succession of the apostles in the church.... They even watch over our faith in the one God who has made everything ... and interpret for us the Scriptures without danger" (4.26.5). "Therefore, one must obey the presbyters who are in the church and are the successors of the apostles. With the succession to the office of bishop, they receive the gift of the truth according to the pleasure of the Father" (4.26.2).

Irenaeus emphasizes both here and in other passages that the traditions of the truth derive from the apostles, who are pictorially designated as the twelve pillars on which the church rests (4.21.3). Certainly, even the later ranking of the bishops of Rome is already announced in Irenaeus, when he emphasizes the special dignity of the succession of bishops in the community founded by the apostles Peter and Paul. It is necessary to establish the proclamation of the church, since this "is changeless and continues to remain the same in the witness that derives from the prophets and apostles and all of their students," and lives in the faith of the Christians that has been effectuated by the Spirit. "Wherever the church is found, there is the Spirit of God, and where the Spirit of God is, there is the church and all grace; the Spirit, however, is the truth" (3.24.1; see John 5:6). Whoever is outside the church, as, for example the gnostics, is unable to discover the truth.

It is astonishing that, in addition to the statements concerning the perfection of the Scriptures, which are self-interpreting, there are some expressions about the role of tradition. Lessing, among others, mentioned this in connection with his question as to whether one can be a Christian without the Bible (Axiomata 8). Irenaeus refers to the same issue in his statement: "Had the apostles not left anything at all to us in written form, then one would only have to follow the tradition, which was given over to those with whom the church is entrusted" (3.4.1). In this connection, Irenaeus also points to the pagan nations who believe Christ, who "without paper and ink have received their salvation from the Holy Spirit who has written on their heart and maintains carefully the ancient tradition." They "have accepted these gifts without alphabetic letters" (3.4.2).

Here it appears to be virtually the case that the Bible is unnecessary for faith. Still, one should consider that the sentence in 3.4.1 is purely hypothetical, since the existence of the Scriptures as the basis of faith is central to Irenaeus's thinking. Formally seen, the statements turn on the meaning of the singleness of tradition beside those of the exclusiveness of the Scriptures. In addition to this, however, it should be noted that Irenaeus holds as possible a debate only over negligible questions, which then can be decided by reference to the tradition, while all of the central matters in the Scriptures are clearly enough interpreted. In addition, no contradiction exists between Scripture and tradition, for the content of the Scriptures is nothing other than "the thinking of the apostles, who from the beginning on were eyewitnesses and servants of the Word" (4.preface; see Luke 1:2). Further, the apostolic tradition is identical with the writings of the prophets and the apostles, as is also their correct interpretation (3.21.3). The writing and the oral preaching of the apostles likewise have the same content. One is able to recognize this connection also in the common structure of book 3: the remarks about the Scriptures in the main section are framed by short reflections at the beginning (3.3.1–4.2) and the end (3.24–25), in which comments are made about tradition and the preaching of the church.

Also, as regards content, Irenaeus speaks of a "canon [rule] of truth" that the faithful Christian receives at baptism (1.9.4). In the Trinitarian confession of faith in 1.10, which reflects a symbol of baptism (this idea does not occur, however, in Irenaeus), we find him providing a summary, if also in a loose formula. Indeed, the brief formula of confession as the canon of truth does not suffice. Twice (3.15.1 and especially 4.35.4) Irenaeus designates the Scripture itself as the "rule of truth." However, it is only this when it is interpreted in the correct way. The gnostics, according to Irenaeus, construct through a jumbled composition of mosaic stones that originally formed the "royal picture" of the Scripture an image of an "unsightly fox" (1.8.1; 1.9.4). Indeed, there is a single teaching that is central for Irenaeus: the oneness of God as the Creator. This can be called the "rule of truth" (1.22.1; see also 3.11.1). The idea is therefore more comprehensive than Scripture or a formulated confession of faith. The "rule of truth" designates the entire content of faith. This can "in different languages [dialects] be formulated" (1.10.2) and means the truth that is given to the church as a whole.

Irenaeus is the first church theologian with his theological thinking of Scripture. He is a catholic thinker in the original sense of the word. As one can clearly recognize, this was necessary for him in the battle against the gnostics, with their dualistic and mythical system, the arbitrary explanations of Scripture that sprang from it, and their interventions into the substance of text and canon (see Marcion). Key antignostic statements that he makes concern the oneness of God, who is the Creator and Father of his Son Christ, and the Word, who also serves as the intermediary of divine revelation in the Old Testament. These affirmations were determinant for him in his entire interpretation of Scripture.

This defensive position taken against the heretics certainly contributed to the cohesion of Irenaeus's position regarding Scripture. His basic principles allowed him to emphasize the harmony he saw in almost every sphere: harmony between the Old and New Testaments, which for the first time assumed the same rank as "Scripture," even though the concept was seldom used for the New Testament texts; harmony between law and gospel; harmony even between the four Gospels; and harmony by the same token between Scripture and tradition, with neither placed over the other. In this latter instance, Irenaeus clearly constructed a bridge across the tensions between positions that appear to be mutually exclusive. On the one hand, he affirms the perfection of the Scripture, which is clearly understandable in and of itself, and, on the other hand, the necessity of its combination with the truth located in tradition. He indicates that the concept of the comprehensiveness of truth requires that the two be arranged to exist side by side. In the later periods of the history of the church, Scripture and tradition had to be broken apart, especially when at any one time one or the other was carried to an extreme. As for the later creedal statements, one cannot invoke Irenaeus for any particular point.

Irenaeus was especially important for the history of biblical interpretation, in that he laid the foundation for the concept of harmony for understanding individual passages of Scripture. The sense of a biblical statement is hit upon correctly only when the meaning conforms to the entirety of the Scriptures. We see that this thought is not entirely new, since we encounter it already as a fundamental principle of Jewish biblical interpretation.

Irenaeus was a pioneer biblical theologian of both Testaments, for he was not simply conditioned by his chronological location. He achieved something individually significant for the problem of the relationship of the two Testaments, which continued on in the church. His theory about the presence of the "Word" in all the Old Testament occasions of revelation, which proceeds from his interpretation of John 1:14, may appear today venturesome. However, as we saw in the course of our description of the development of his works, this view corresponded to a prevailing principle of interpretation considered "scientific" at that time. It was used similarly by Hellenists, Jews, and Christians of the period; simply stated, it contends that the wording of a text is to be closely observed and that characteristic sayings are to be developed from it that produce meaning. In this form, it is actually outdated. For a Christian dogmatic, the problem of the presence of the triune God in the different periods of salvation history demands an answer that goes beyond this.

Irenaeus, by contrast, broke new ground in his view of salvation history. Due to the criticism of the gnostics and Marcion directed toward the Old Testament God and Old Testament piety, he was challenged to develop the concepts of the divine "economy," to point to the adjustment of God to humanity in their childlike stages and development and their education throughout the events of the old people of God, and then to make the way open for a view that sees the Bible related to history but that also takes seriously its human side. Granted, these were only in an incipient form, but dogmatics held the upper hand in the final analysis for Irenaeus, for this was conditioned by the defense he had to undertake. Indeed, he allows one necessarily to recognize, as we saw in several places, that even he, in spite of his not giving up on his harmonious system of the whole, was unable to answer every question. Some things remained a divine mystery. On the whole, his works against the heretics offer an impressive reading when one makes the effort to read all five volumes. One encounters in these one of the most significant Christian thinkers.

4.6. The Way of the Soul toward Perfection: Origen

One can justifiably say that Origen was the first Christian theologian whose work moved from within the inner realm of the church outward into the Hellenistic world. Born in approximately 185 c.e., likely in the cosmopolitan city of Alexandria, a number of factors provide certain suppositions about his origins and education. In spite of his Greek-Egyptian name ("born of Horus"), Origen was the son of Christian parents. His father, possibly named Leonidas, died during a persecution of Christians around 201 c.e. At the time, Origen was sixteen years of age. He was so moved by this experience that he also was clearly ready to follow his father in experiencing the death of a martyr. Only his mother's craftiness reputedly hindered him from doing so.

With the execution of his father, the entirety of the family's possessions was confiscated. The mother was left destitute to care for seven children. A wealthy Christian matron took Origen, the eldest of the children, into her home. There lived also a well-known heretic by the name of Paul, who spent considerable time educating the youth. Only later did Origen come to harbor suspicions about him. He was taught by this Paul and was very strongly influenced by his teachings. Along the way, he devoted himself to the study of Greek literature and grammar to the point that he soon began to offer instruction in these fields and to earn his livelihood from this.

From the time of Philo to the end of the second century c.e., Alexandria was the main city of Hellenistic culture. There were to be found various cults, Jews, and Christians, among whom were gnostics and followers of the great church. Present also were the different philosophical schools and their leading thinkers.

While Origen operated his grammar school, he continued to learn through the readings of philosophical texts and sought during his free time to obtain the education of a "master of philosophy." It is debated whether this instructor was the famous Platonist Ammonius Saccas, the teacher of Plotinus. After some years (around 206 c.e.), a new persecution of the Christians broke out. Bishop Demetrius and most of the catechumens receiving instruction fled the city. Confronted with this situation, Origen assumed responsibility for his own catechetical instruction, having assembled a circle of young people interested in Christianity. He taught the Bible to them at regular intervals. Since people opposed to Christianity often could identify him, he concealed himself by moving from place to place. However, some of his fellows were captured and executed. When the persecution ended in 211 c.e., Bishop Demetrius and the clerics returned, and Origen opened immediately once again his grammar school and continued, with the bishop's approval, his instruction in the faith. Soon he gave up his grammar school, sold his secular library, and devoted himself exclusively to his churchly vocation. His enthusiasm drove him to emasculate himself, taking literally the understanding of Matt 19:12 in order to "devote himself entirely to the word of God" (Eusebius, *Hist. eccl.* 6.8.1). He completely occupied himself with the Bible in education, commentary writing, and preaching of biblical texts. This was his life's mission.

In pursuing this goal, he occupied himself with the text of the Bible. The Septuagint manuscripts used in the church and available to him were partially corrupt. The meaning thus was often unclear. Origen wished to compare them with the Hebrew original. A former Palestinian Jew who had converted to Christianity and then immigrated to Alexandria taught him Hebrew and the Rabbinic methods of interpretation. Later he began to produce a work based on his textual criticism. This was a composition designed to produce the primary Hebrew text (in a Greek transcription) in four columns (Tetrapla) with the Septuagint and other Greek translations; he later expanded this to six columns (Hexapla). His objective was, above all, to improve the Septuagint by filling in the gaps and omissions by reference to the primary text.

His travels took him to Rome (ca 215 c.e.), to Bosra to the Roman governor of Arabia, and finally even to the mother of Caesar Septimius Severus, Julia Mamaea, during her sojourn in Antioch (231/2 c.e.). His fame grew, as did the number of people, mostly educated, who visited him in Alexandria. He eventually gave to his student Heracles the task of instructing the catechumens and proceeded then to teach only those who continued in his advanced course in the manner of the philosophical schools. Among others, he succeeded in converting to orthodoxy a wealthy Valentinian, Ambrose, who became his patron and financed the scribes who could write swiftly in order that Origin could dictate his numerous commentaries. However, Ambrose also prompted him to work expeditiously by continuing to ask of him new volumes.

Meanwhile, Origen's conflict with his bishop, Demetrius, increased, since the latter obviously had begun to doubt the orthodoxy of the widely known scholar. This conflict emerged over the philosophical background of his teaching and the content of the early writings produced at that time. One example is that of Origin's text *On Nature*, which, while not surviving, was directed against the gnostic dualism that sought to distinguish between the ultimate good and the ultimate evil of the nature of humans and angels. Origen sought to demonstrate that God's judgment regarding sinners may not be considered final, unless the fallen angels are not given the opportunity to repent and thereby experience salvation. Indeed, the gnostic teaching that souls are forever intrinsically good or evil may not be viewed as compatible with both divine righteousness and the freedom of heavenly and earthly souls to choose their own paths. Theoretically speaking, even the devil finally may experience salvation. He discussed this problem particularly in a public debate with the gnostic Candidus. The consequence of this debate led Origen's adversaries, including for a time even Heracles, to conclude that the scholar of Alexandria had announced positively that even the devil would be saved ("the restoration of all"; see 1 Cor 15:28). Rather, Origen probably understood the statement to be a hypothetical "worse-case scenario."

Above all, Origen continued to amplify his interpretation of the Bible. After an initial commentary on the Psalter (later replaced by a more mature one), he commented on the laments of Jeremiah and above all the book of Genesis. This commentary reveals that he had already established his typical methods that we later will be able to recognize in a more precise manner. He explained that behind the obvious meaning of a word there is a concealed, spiritual connotation that one may ultimately determine. The criticism raised against this understanding is inherent in the question: "Does Origen deny the historical reality of the Scriptures?" This question pressed him to delay for a time his writing of his commentary in order to write a foundational defense that explained his methodology: *First Principles* (*Peri archōn* = *De principiis*). He even was constrained temporarily to leave Alexandria in order to take up residence in Jerusalem (230 C.E.). However, finally Demetrius requested that he return home. Back again in Alexandria, he began to dictate a multivolume commentary on John, interrupted by a journey to Antioch. In 232 he then renewed his travels, this time to go to Athens, another center of Hellenistic philosophy.

In taking the coastal highway, he passed through Caesarea in Palestine, where, surprisingly, he was ordained a presbyter. This occasioned a protest from his current bishop, Demetrius, that was written in a letter sent to Bishop Pontian of Rome. Bishop Demetrius issued a complaint against his colleagues Theoktist of Caesarea and Alexander of Jerusalem. Pontian wrote back that Demetrius was correct in his complaint. However, Demetrius died in 233 C.E., and Heracles became his successor. In the meantime, Origen, disappointed, left Athens before he even was able to situate himself in the city. He remained in Caesarea, where he stayed until 245 C.E., a period of residence interrupted only by a new persecution of Christians between 235 and 238 C.E. This was a productive time for his various projects.

One of these was his comprehensive commentary series, which he continued to write. Ambrose served as his skilled scribe, allowing Origen to dictate to him, first of all, his commentary on John's Gospel, followed by his commentary on Genesis. Later Origen dictated to him the commentaries on the Pauline Epistles and the Prophets. During this period he also continued to preach every morning on Old Testament texts and three times a week on texts from the Gospels and Epistles of the New Testament during eucharistic worship services.

His instruction of new, recently baptized catechumens, who participated in these eucharistic services, is also important for understanding the content of his principles of exegesis. He also tutored a young relative of the governor, serving as an instructor in the aristocrat's house. After concluding a second sojourn in Athens (245–246 C.E.), he returned to Caesarea.

He dictated additional commentaries dealing with the prophetic books, Canticles, and the Psalter. His commentary on Matthew followed that of John. In between these, Origen took care of another request of Ambrose. He had sent him a request to offer a rebuttal to another anti-Christian literary attack, this one from the pagan Celsus ("True Word"). Origen delivered this rebuttal in the form of eight volumes entitled *Against Celsus*. What we know of the writing of Celsus comes from citations in this work by Origen.

Origen almost had come to the end of his life without having achieved his goal of martyrdom, which he had had since his youth. In the persecution that occurred during the reign of Caesar Decius (249–251 C.E.), he was incarcerated and tortured. Even so, he still survived this imprisonment, if only for a few additional years. The exact date of his death is unknown; he is said to have been sixty-nine years of age.

Only a portion of Origen's immense productivity during his life has survived. Most of what exists comes from the Latin translation of Ruffinus (ca. 345–410 C.E.). Already some of Origen's contemporaries regarded him as a heretic, and he was rejected during the so-called Origenistic controversies toward the end of the fourth century. However, in 543 C.E. his rejection was finally officially declared throughout the entire church. Because of this controversy, the suppression of his writings was far-reaching. However, even his later critic Jerome used Origen's commentaries extensively for those he himself wrote. Selected individual exegeses were preserved in the Canten manuscripts of the Greek Church (collections of the interpretations of various church fathers on a particular text). A wealth of source material is available for those seeking to reach a judgment about Origen's methods of interpretation, thanks to the efforts of modern editors of his works.

Adequately describing Origen's principles of interpretation is rendered both easier and more difficult by the fact that he himself articulated these in a section of *De principiis* (4.1–3). One is able to explain correctly his expressions found there, if one compares both the form and manner by which Origen practically pursues his exegesis of texts. They have often been understood in scholarship as conflicting. Origen had already hinted at the theme, "Scripture," in the preface. There he briefly mentioned the idea of the content of apostolic teaching and preaching that may pose certain questions regarding details or reasons that remain open. "These must be investigated vigorously with acuity and explored from Holy Scripture" (1.preface.4). To the teachings of the church belong also those that have to do with Holy Scripture:

The Scriptures are written by the Spirit of God and have not only the meaning that is obvious but also another that is hidden for the most part. The things that are portrayed are namely the images [*formae*] of certain secrets [sacraments] and the depiction of divine things. The entire church is of one accord over these things: the entire law is spiritual [see Rom 7:14], although what in the law is spiritual is not entirely understood, but rather only those things that the grace of the Holy Spirit has given in the words of wisdom and of knowledge. (1.preface.8)

In this passage one can already clearly recognize the manner in which Origen takes up a well-known word of Paul and continues in an entirely defined direction. When Paul contrasts his own sinful nature ("fleshly") with the spiritual nature of the law, Origen delves into the deeper meaning of the Scripture, which can be understood only by means of the gifts of the Spirit, which, taken together, are the means of knowing.

We find ourselves in Alexandria. The Hellenistic intellectual background of this city obviously influenced Origen's understanding of Scripture in a decisive way. The task of the interpreter (here Origen is thinking foremost of the preacher), on one hand, is an intellectual matter. There is a deeper, concealed meaning to detect behind the simple, literal meaning. On the other hand, interpretation is not only an intellectual endeavor; for this understanding the gift of the Spirit is an indispensable presupposition.

In book 4 of *De principiis*, Origen further expands his understanding of Scripture. He seeks in this text the divine nature of the Scriptures of the Old and New Testaments (both are here already definite concepts) to pinpoint the activity of the two persons Moses and Jesus. Moses' activity is apparent in that his teachings and the laws that he proclaimed awakened among many nations the desire to accept them as a body of rules for life. None of the heathen philosophers or lawgivers was able to succeed in doing this. In the same way, the proclamation of Jesus, brought to the "Greeks and Barbarians, wise and unwise," "is associated with the religion announced by him" (4.1.2). In spite of persecutions, the Christian message subsequently has been proclaimed throughout the entire world. For this reason the prophecies of Jesus himself were fulfilled (Matt 24:14; 7:22). "The fact that what was said has entered with such overwhelming power shows that he is truly God who has become a human person in order to give to humans his teachings about life" (4.1.2).

Origen then moves to a traditionally shaped demonstration that Christ was prophesied in the Old Testament (4.1.3–4), discussing in particular the election of the pagan nations and his mission to them. Out of this unfolds the point "that the Scriptures, which have prophesied about him [the Old Testament], are inspired by God, have announced his coming, and have reported his teachings with all power and authority" (4.1.6). This inspiration of the Old Testament is demonstrated with the coming of Jesus (whose appearance was prophesied by the Old Testament prophets). "It was scarcely possible to give clear examples of the inspiration of the ancient Scriptures before the coming of Christ" (4.1.6). Now, however, it is possible to provide "evidence." In addition, in a careful and attentive reading of the prophetic word, there is also the experience of a "trace of enthusiasm" that convinces Origen that the Scriptures are not only human but also divine.

As Origen at the conclusion of this chapter shows (1.7), the divine nature of Scripture is not obvious to the uneducated. There are texts difficult to understand in addition to those that are simple. In order to understand the more difficult ones, humans require the wisdom given by God, not simply human wisdom. It is a groundbreaking insight for Origen's program that he cites in this passage Heb 6:1, "We attempt 'to leave behind what at the beginning was said about Christ,' that is, the basic teachings, 'in order to be led to perfection.'" Origen anticipates this perfection, already present in the form of a wisdom that has been "engrained" in Christians, which grasps the long-concealed mystery now revealed though the prophetic Scriptures and the appearance of Jesus Christ.

In the second chapter that follows, Origen speaks of the correct manner to read and to understand the Scriptures. A purely literal understanding by the Jews and gnostics leads to miscomprehensions and gross errors (4.2.1). All are led astray who are not familiar with the spiritual sense of Scripture (4.2.2). However, those who are so familiar are clear that the Scripture contains a "mystical economy" (see Irenaeus!). Many things that appear to be objectionable or scandalous, as, for example, Gen 19:30–38, are explicable only as a type. Likewise, the prophets as well as the Gospels are full of riddles and dark words and are thus difficult to understand, if not for the grace that is given to one. The same is true of the letters of the apostles, which also contain many difficult passages (4.2.3). In order to discover the right path (4.2.1) in one's journey through the Scriptures, the "key to understanding" is required (4.2.1).

Following this Origen comes to his famous statement that, in spite of appearing unequivocal, in fact is easy to misunderstand. He cites a verse from the book of Proverbs: "Write this down for you three times with admonishment and knowledge in order that you may give a true answer to the questions asked to you!" (Prov 22:20–21). He explains this passage in the following way: "One must write therefore three times the thoughts of Holy Scripture in his heart, so that the more simple is edified by that which is the flesh of Scripture—this we name the direct view, for one who has been strengthened somewhat by its soul, however, the perfect …. by the spiritual law" (with a citation from 1 Cor 2:6–7). This passage has been understood in general to mean that Origen teaches here a threefold sense of Scripture. By contrast, it is conspicuous that nowhere in his later practice of exegesis does he carry out this threefold sense. Only in 4.2.6 are mentioned a few less than enlightening examples for a meaning of the "soul" of the Scriptures. In addition, one could discover three classes of biblical readings that may be distinguished. The classes of readers or hearers consist of those who are satisfied with the literal reading of the Scriptures, those who consider the "soul" of the Scriptures (however, what does he mean by this expression?), and the perfected, who understand the Scriptures in their spiritual meaning. However, the separation of the thoroughly differentiated classes is obviously not intended. The "way" that Origen has in mind should lead each Christian to an increasingly deeper understanding! The purpose imposed on the enlightening Spirit is to lead to the spiritual knowledge of the Scriptures (4.2.7). If one realizes that Origin was familiar with his "Hebrew" (Jewish) manner of interpretation, one will recognize in the number three a connecting element between saying and interpretation that is a typical example of the exegesis of a key concept, which we already have encountered in characteristic examples. Origin has associated with the number three the (Greek) tripartite division of humans, consisting of body, soul, and spirit, which he certainly understands in an ascending order of rank. The purpose of the way of a Christian reading the Scriptures is to understand the spiritual meaning.

Moving forward, similarly to what he did following 4.1, he considers the teachings, especially those that lead to life. Moses and Jesus are placed in a certain sense in a line. In his idea of "economy," we see reflected something of the ideas concerning education that we have already encountered in Irenaeus. It is typical that both theologians were influenced by the Hellenistic environment in which they lived and thought. However, Irenaeus uses this Greek background in a different way. In his thinking, the emphasis is placed entirely on salvation history. Origen has the individual and his or her particular "way" in mind to achieve the "goal," even though it is within the framework of the church. For this we turn to the explication of some of the examples that come from his rich exegetical work.

We begin with his sermons on the book of Jeremiah. This is advisable because a portion of the sermons, which numbered originally more than forty and were delivered by Origen during the daily morning worship in Caesarea, has been preserved in the Greek original, while the others that deal with different Old Testament as well as New Testament books exist only in a Latin translation.

In the first sermon, Origen initially interprets the first three verses of Jer 1. These verses contain nothing more than the indication of the kings of Judah reigning during the period of the prophet's activity and some comments on the historical circumstances of the activity of Jeremiah. After Origen has first read the passage, he provides a concise explanation of its literal meaning ("what was said," *Hom. Jer.* 1.2). Indeed, he has already placed this description under the question: "What, then, does this history mean to me?" In order to direct his audience to the actual meaning (the "purpose"; see 4.1), Origen began his sermon with a programmatic statement: "God is quick to do good but also hesitant to punish those who deserve to be." In an introductory section, before he began to speak about the Jeremianic text, he had already pointed to the examples of Jonah's announcement of judgment against Nineveh that was not carried out (Jonah 3:4) and the salvation of Lot and his family from the destruction of Sodom (Gen 19). Origen now expresses the view that the commission of Jeremiah would have the same consequence:

> God had condemned Jerusalem on account of its sins, and they [its inhabitants] were fated to be delivered into captivity. Even so, when the time had come under the reign of the third ruler, this philanthropic God still sent this prophet before the time of captivity, which he had foreordained in order that they might consider and on the basis of the prophetic word repent. He had commissioned the prophet himself even to prophesy during his own experience of imprisonment under the second and third ruler. There was, to wit, the long and enduringly patient God providing them an extension ... in which he demanded that the audience make confession in order to turn aside the grim fate of captivity. (1.3)

The preacher, therefore, knows to work beyond the meaning of the existing prosaic data to delve into the inner attitude of the prophet's own contemporary audience. This text also has a significant theological aspect for this audience: "We have now something useful from the section, which relates to the time period of the prophet: God in his philanthropy admonishes those who hear him in order that they may not suffer captivity."

This generally valid statement now allows him to make the transition to the next step, which the preacher is always to take: "Something of this kind is also valid for us. If we sin, we also must become prisoners. If 'such a one goes over to Satan' (1 Cor 5:5), there is no difference from what is stated above; that is, the Jerusalemites go over to Nebuchadnezzar" (1.3). The demand to confess grows from this basis, which Origen directs to his audience: "On account of our sins, imprisonment is also threatened, and we become, if we do not change our thoughts, handed over to Nebuchadnezzar and the Babylonians, with the result that the Babylonians torment us in a spiritual sense" (1.4).

Two things are clear here. First, Origen thinks on different levels. There is the plane of the literal meaning, which means the historical event. In addition to this, however, there is a differently construed, spiritual sense. The Greek concept of *noetos* expresses that this is at the same time the rational sense. Behind the literal meaning, the actual, deeper meaning must be pursued. This is the fundamental principle of allegory. We have already encountered this in Alexandria in the thinking of Philo. To a large extent, Origen is also a Platonist. Second, it is certainly the case that there is in actuality no mention of allegory that may be discovered in this section dealing with sermons. It is striking that, instead of this, one finds material of a moralistic and pedagogical character and a direct link to the audience. Origen draws a parallel between the audience of the prophets and his own contemporary audience. The first concern of the preacher is obvious, and therefore this section offers a concrete example: to call the audience to repentance and moral improvement. "The words of the prophets, the law, the apostles, and our Lord and Savior Jesus Christ" (1.4) have this meaning for him. He finds it, therefore, in the entire Bible. He is able to call it also the "uplifted" (analogical) meaning (2.12). The section of the sermon concerning Jeremiah is also an example of this type of use of the text (see Jer 2:21–22). In the first section of this sermon (2.1), Origen deals with the question the prophet directs to Israel: "How have you become transformed into a bitter plant, you degenerate vine?" As the background of the literal meaning, there is for Origen the view that "God planted the souls of humans as a good vine, yet they transformed themselves to become the opposite of what the Creator had willed."

According to the interpretation that Origen provides, the prophet wishes to point out a problem to his audience: From what did evil originate, if God created all things good? The explanation offers a combination of Gen 1:26 and 1 Cor 15:49: if God had originally created humans according to his image, then humans have now, due to sin, become those who bear the "image of the earthly." Thus, it is incumbent on them to recover the "pattern of the heavenly." In addition, this explanation of the literal meaning leads to a higher stage that reaches beyond that of moral exhortation. It is obvious that the renewal of humanity involves not only God's forgiveness of sins but also one's own action: a turning back to God is expected. It is not clear at this point whether or not Origen, in his citation of 1 Cor 15:49, thinks of the matter of Paul's contrast between the humans from the earth (see Gen 2:7) and the heavenly human (Jesus Christ). It is a matter of debate whether Origen, in close proximity to the thinking of the gnostics, distinguished between an earthly, material region and a heavenly, spiritual one. That this interpretation appears to be the case is evident from the handling of this theme in his prologue to the commentary on Canticles. "If someone exists who still bears 'the image of the earthly' according to the outer person, this one is driven by earthly desire and love; but the one who bears 'the image of the heavenly' in the inner person is moved by heavenly desire and love."

This fundamental presupposition also shapes the background for the treatment of the history of Israel, as it is showcased in the twenty-seventh sermon, which concerns the stations of Israel during the wilderness wandering. In this sermon one discovers an interesting prologue in which Origen points to the difficulties that certain biblical writings pose for the audience as they seek to enjoy them as edifying "food." To this may belong also the book of Numbers: "If the book of Numbers is read to this one [the one listening to the preacher] and especially those passages that we now have in our hands, he shall judge that these are not able to provide anything useful nor to assist as a medicine the healing of his soul." However, the purpose of interpretation is even far more pressing. "It would be regarded as an impious and strange judgment to the universal faith that what is written through the Word of God possesses nothing that is useful and contributes nothing to salvation but rather merely narrates events that already are past."

Origen takes this as the point of origin for his interpretation with the indication that the exodus of the children of Israel from Egypt may be compared in a twofold manner by comparing it with the spiritual exodus of every Christian out of "Egypt": "either we forsake the heathen manner of life and succeed to the recognition of the divine law, or our soul exits the dwelling of this body." Origen is reminded of John 14:2, which contains the key word "stations" (comparable in Greek and Latin to "rest house," which was common in the ancient streets of the empire, or "dwelling"). He, however, surprisingly explains these "stations" as "leading to the Father." He then returns to the exodus from Egypt. As the children of Israel were oppressed in Egypt and were led by Moses to God, "so also, when *we* were in Egypt, I mean by this the errors of this world and the darkness of ignorance in which we carried out the works of the devil in the desire and salaciousness of the flesh, he had pity on our oppression and sent his Word, that is, 'his firstborn son' (1 John 4:9), in order that he might free us from the ignorance of error and lead us to the light of the divine law."

These expressions are instructive in two ways. They are, on the one hand, an example of the form of allegorical exegesis that Origen pursued. The history of Israel in its different episodes is a symbol of the transmission of an event in which the hearers of the preacher are both the actors and those who are affected. Historical occurrences of the past *signify* the inner processes of the soul. On the other hand, Origen understands these inner processes as the "way," the direction that the individual Christian must travel in order to go to "the Father." The "exodus" is certainly the first step in this journey. It involves doing away with errors and "fleshly" desires and taking on the "divine law." This is the same that Origen had imposed on his audience in his sermons on Jeremiah. It is significant to note that this occurs not only as a consequence of the activity of humans but also through the sending of the "Word," Jesus Christ, even as Origen formulates it following the Prologue of the Gospel of John. In this passage (*Princ.* 1.2.6), it is clear that Origen understands the "Word" to be the divinity of Christ, who was the "image of the unseen God." Origen's ethical appeal rests, therefore, on a theological basis. He is able to exhort his audience to repent only because God through Christ encounters them with his grace. This is developed to a further extent in what follows.

Following this beginning point, Origen occupies himself in the main section of this sermon with the actual content of its text (Deut 33), which sets forth the stations of Israel's wandering in the wilderness. The initial point he makes concerning these stations is their number, forty-two, which Israel should have covered during the journey. Origen compares these to the forty-two generations between Abraham and Christ (Matt 1:17). These forty-two generations are the forty-two stations of the descent of Christ into the "Egypt of this world." The last station of this descent is the virgin birth. This became, then, the first of the stations, that Origin's audience was to achieve. It was to be attained by

> those who wish to leave Egypt, whereby we abandon the service of idols
> and the worship of demons ... and believe that Christ ... has come into
> this world. Thereafter, we will strive to advance and to ascend the indi-

vidual stages of faith and virtues. And if we pursue them until we arrive
at perfection, it shall be said of us that we have progressed along the
individual stages of virtue until, having arrived at the highest apogee of
our instruction and our progress, the promised inheritance is reached.
(*Hom. Num.* 27.3)

Thus, the stations of Israel's wilderness wandering become a symbol of
the ascent of the soul to its final destination, and this may be compared
to the entrance into the land of promise. It is also conspicuous here that
the characterization of this ascent is compared to a process of education
where "virtues" reside at the center. In another passage (27.4), "the exodus
out of Egypt to the land of promise" is also designated as the "ascent of
the soul to heaven and the sacrament of the resurrection of the dead." The
purpose of this ascent is described as the direct vision of the "true light
that enlightens all humans" (John 1:9). This is also an example of Greek
thought. Origin points to the spiritual meaning with the words that we
have to do with "mystical descriptions." What is meant is the deeper sense,
which is obtained through allegorical interpretation.

Origen's allegorical interpretation of Canticles has continued to be
important for the entire history of biblical interpretation, including the
present. Broken parts of the approximately contemporary, similarly shaped
work of Hippolytus of Rome on Canticles have been preserved. The same
is true of what were originally Origen's ten volumes of complete commentaries on Canticles. All that has survived of his commentaries covers Cant
1:1 to 2:1–14 and is preserved only in Latin translation. His sermons on
Canticles that have been preserved reach approximately the same verse.
No other book of the Bible has continued to be the object of allegorical
interpretation like that of Canticles. This is true especially in Catholic
exegesis. The existence of a collection of secular bridal and love poetry in
the Bible understandably presented special problems of interpretation to
readers in both Judaism and Christianity. In Judaism, the allegorical interpretation already had begun in the first century C.E. Christian exegesis
soon followed with similar methods.

The Canticles commentary is of particular interest because Origen
in a lengthy prologue expresses in precise detail his understanding of the
book. He starts with the differences in the description of the creation of
humanity in Gen 1:26–27, which speaks of God creating humans after
his own image, and Gen 2:7, which speaks of the creation of humanity
from the dust of the earth. Since both statements are attributed to Moses
(only modern source criticism has revised this judgment), Origen must be

speaking of the creation of two separate persons. At this point, a statement from the apostle Paul is helpful. Origen is happy to call upon the authority of this one who knows "the precise answer and offers assurance in these matters," even if he reinterprets him in his typical way. In 2 Cor 4:16 Paul spoke of two human beings that are contained in each person: the "outer" and the "inner" human. This distinction, which Origen understands dualistically from his Hellenistic approach, offers him the appropriate avenue for the interpretation of Canticles: "We wish thereby to show that in the divine Scriptures, homonyms, that is, similar denotations, and the same words designate the same extremities of both the outer person and the inner person. These are compared with each other not only by means of the same words but also according to the matter itself." "From this it is clear that the names of the members are not in any way to be related only to the external body but also must be understood as the parts and virtues of the unseen soul. Although these do have the same words, they also mean often and without any ambiguity designations not of the outer but of the inner person."

We have here before us the theoretical basis for the allegorical method of interpretation. As one can see, Origen does not proceed in an arbitrary manner. His fundamental supposition, that words are capable of an assigned meaning to become metaphors, can also be demonstrated by modern linguistic studies. Now, the rule encompassing an entire biblical book allows one to understand all its words as metaphorical expressions, and the presuppositions of the content residing behind them construct the allegorical system.

A presupposition for Origen's understanding of the content of Canticles is his view that the book is a marriage song performed as a drama. This means that the book is a continuous unity. Four dialogue partners are found in the book: the bride; the bridegroom; the maidens and girlfriends of the bride; and the friends of the groom. However, Canticles may not be interpreted literally. The one who does not yet have the necessary inner maturity will be carried "from spirit to flesh, shall be nurtured by fleshly desire, and shall appear to be moved and enticed away from the provocation of Holy Scripture to the lust of the flesh." In the figurative sense, Canticles concerns the love "that has bound and associated the church as the bride of Christ, which wishes to be united to him through the word." This is the allegorical meaning that Origen has developed, and it continues into the future history of the interpretation of Canticles. In rabbinic literature, it is the relationship between Israel and God that contrasts with the Christian interpretation. This, however, is not the only plane on which

Origen seeks to offer an allegorical explanation. Obviously, he follows a tradition that already has been transmitted to him. For example, Hippolytus of Rome had already interpreted the book according to this tradition in his commentary, while Origen develops his position in another direction.

He prepares his own position through a thorough consideration of the literature that was traced back to Solomon. Three Old Testament writings are attributed to Solomon: Proverbs; the Book of the Preacher (Qoheleth); and Canticles. According to Origen, the content of these three books corresponds to the Greek sciences of ethics, physics, and metaphysics, which the Greeks adopted from Solomon. Josephus had already expressed this feature, which was encountered in Jewish apologetics. Morality teaches virtue, physics the laws of nature, and the instruction of what is "visible," as it is named, beholds something of the divine and heavenly things through the transcendence of the things that are apparent. Solomon wished to teach these three sciences in his three books, so

> he first of all taught morality in Proverbs, summarized secondly natural law in the book of Ecclesiastes, which explains a great deal about natural things, and separated what was useful and necessary from what was useless and senseless in order to leave behind nothingness and to seek the useful and the correct. The topic of "the visible" he transmitted in the small book that we have at hand, namely, the Canticles, in which he instilled the love for the things that are heavenly and the longing for the divine matters of the soul under the images of the Bride and the Bridegroom. In these he taught how one comes to community with God by the path of love.

The series of these three Solomonic books designate, however, at the same time, the way of knowledge that the individual has to travel.

In the canon of the three wisdom books, therefore Origen discovers the reflection of three stages of ascent of the soul, which is his most important theme. Canticles comes to assume the highest stage, which leads from the sphere of the apparent along the path to the unseen, heavenly, and eternal.

The vision of the divine is the highest stage (i.e., the Greek ideal) that humans are capable of achieving. This stage of the Origenic ideal corresponds to pedagogy, since it is reached through teaching and learning. In addition, Origen observes, "these threefold forms of divine philosophy" are incorporated by the three ancestral fathers: Abraham, to whom morality belongs; Isaac, who digs a well (natural science); and Jacob, who saw in his vision a heavenly ladder.

Corresponding to the fundamentals cited in the preface, Origen forms in detail his interpretation of Canticles. He distinguishes between a "historical" interpretation (with the change of persons in the form of a drama) and a spiritual one. "The spiritual understanding corresponds to that which I said in the preface, either the association of the church with Christ under the title of the bride and bridegroom, or by the relationship of the soul with the word of God" (*Comm. Cant.* 1.1).

Origen interprets each individual phrase one after the other. The structure of a paragraph normally is the same. (1) First of all, the respective sentence or part of the sentence is cited literally. This delimitation is pursued according to the respective change in the person of the speaker assumed by Origen. (2) In the second step, Origen identifies the speaker and describes the dramatic situation reflected in the statement. This step is the "historical" interpretation. Here the wording of the sentence is repeated yet again. (3) The third step consists of the explication of the "inner" or "spiritual sense" especially in regard to the church. (4) The fourth step starts anew and explains the intent of the text in regard to the ascent of the soul. (5) In the fifth step, Origen turns to the reader or includes him or her into the "we form" of the dramatic situation. The differentiations between these five steps are not always clear. However, the steps themselves are usually recognizable.

The clearest methodological considerations are found in the beginning of the commentary. At the opening sentence of the book, "Let him kiss me with the kisses of his mouth," the marriage song with a change in persons is interpreted first in order to present the "historical" sense of the text. A bride who has already obtained fitting marriage gifts from her noble bridegroom waits ostensibly on his coming and his kisses. When he delays in coming, "she turns in prayer and entreats God for help, since she knows that he is the father of the bridegroom." Origen continues:

We shall determine, however, whether the inner meaning may be organized adequately and rightly so that this statement refers to the church's desire to be bound to Christ. I understand by the term *church* the entire assembly of the saints. Consequently, the church would be, so to speak, one single person representing all [members], when he speaks and says: …he himself comes and "let him kiss me with the kisses of his mouth"; that is, he [the church] may pour the words of his mouth into my mouth so that I may hear him speak himself, I may see him teach himself.

Origen also formally announces the next step: "in the third place of the interpretation we introduce the soul, whose entire position consists in the fact that it is bound up with the Word and God, becomes associated with him, then enters into the mysteries of his wisdom and his knowledge even as the bride enters into the chambers of the heavenly bridegroom."

Origen then states that as long as the soul was incapable of understanding the Word of God itself, it may receive the "kisses," the meanings of their teachings, which must be accepted. "Where, however, it already has begun to discern the darkness, to untie what is tangled, to resolve the intricate, to explain parables and riddles and the words of the wise with measured principles of explanation, then they are already able to believe the 'kisses' of their bridegroom," that is, to have experienced the Word of God. The implementation for the audience follows in the final step.

> Thus, we often have discovered something by means of our ears, without one having admonished us concerning questions over divine teachings and meanings. Further, we often want to believe that we have received "kisses," which have been given to us by the bridegroom, that is, the Word of God. However, if we can inquire about something relating to divine denotations and are unable to discover them, then we wish to implore God for the visitation of his Word and say: "Let him kiss me with the kisses of his mouth."

As one can see, Origen pursues the allegorical method, which understands certain basic terms metaphorically, in a consistent fashion. The example we treated demonstrates strikingly at the same time the expressed, intellectual understanding of the "way" of the soul, which the allegorical interpretation of the verse of Canticles serves. It concerns progress in the understanding of the teaching, which initially is transmitted through the instructions of morality ("men and doctors") and then by means of the enlightenment of the Word of God (Christ) itself. By means of the determination of the content of the sphere of the implementation of allegory, this is at the same time a regulated, rigorous application and by no means allows an arbitrary imagination to be expressed. However, it certainly appears to be arbitrary to us when any favorite statement of Scripture, when it at first glance appears to be so far removed from its intended meaning, is examined in this manner. However, it is exactly in this manner that the methodological artistry appears to consist!

The interpretation of the church and of the soul can also be brought together in one action, as, for example, in the explication of Cant 1:4b: "The king has led me into his chamber; we want to exalt and rejoice in you." According to the historical meaning of this text, the "chamber" of the king is explained as his treasury. Origen continues: "However, the place that is of concern is the church, which comes to Christ, or the soul, which adheres to the word of God. For what can we take the 'chamber' of Christ and the 'treasury', into which he introduces his church or the soul that adheres to him, if not for the secret and concealed mind of Christ?"

Whether Origen also found, in the sequence of the verses and partial verses of Canticles that are interpreted in succession, a progression of the content in the sense of a further advance of the soul in the knowledge, direction, and the most secret, heavenly teaching of Christ cannot be said with certainty, since his commentary breaks off at Cant 2:15. One could assume this in analogy to his expression in the preface about the sequential arrangement of the three Solomonic books of wisdom as a whole (see above). However, the remaining, much shorter sermons on Canticles do not provide additional help, since they end almost in the same place.

The sermons also offer an allegorical interpretation of Canticles, although in a much briefer form. Having waived the explanation of the historical meaning, the preacher goes immediately to the spiritual meaning. By way of example, at the beginning of the introduction one reads the statement: "Let him kiss me with the kisses of his mouth!": "Its meaning is, 'How long does my bridegroom send me kisses' through Moses and through the prophets?' It already has been a considerable time that I wish to touch his face, that he himself may come to me, that he himself may descend. She therefore implores the father of the bridegroom and says to him: 'Let him kiss me with the kisses of his mouth.'" The external form of the explanation is similar here, for it, in any case, ends with a renewed, literal citation of the Word that is made clear. In the center stands also here the encounter with Christ. However, in this case it is with his person, for there is no mention of his teaching. Also, this no longer has anything to do with the soul but rather exclusively with the church. However, the hearers are also those who are meant. They are still not those who have made progress as readers of the commentary but rather beginners who still have before them the stage of purification: "We, however, if we hear this, stink still from sins and vices" (in opposition to the fragrance of Christ, whom the church encounters, according to Cant 1:3). However, "If the bridegroom has touched me, I also become 'fragrant'… and his 'salve' comes upon me so that I am able to say with the apostles: 'I am a sweet fragrance of Christ in all places.'" Origen's pastoral position thus has influenced his interpretation without causing him to alter his fundamental method.

Origen also wrote commentaries on many New Testament books and presented numerous sermons on New Testament pericopae. From among these commentaries, parts of his comprehensive commentary on John in Greek and books 10–17 (Matt 13:36–22:33) of the original twenty-five books of the comprehensive Matthean commentary have been preserved. From the corpus of New Testament sermons, only thirty-nine on sections of the Gospel of Luke have been preserved by Jerome in his Latin translation.

In his interpretation of the Gospels, Origen follows other methodological principles than in his exegesis of Old Testament writings. In his introduction to his commentary on John, he provides a detailed explanation. He stresses that "the Old [Testament] is not the gospel, since it does not point to 'the one who has come' [see Matt 11:3/Luke 17:19; Heb 10:37] but rather to the one who is anticipated to come." "To this it may be said that the Law and the Prophets, prior to the arrival of Christ, who had not yet come and would make public the mysteries in them, did not contain what belonged to the thought of the gospel" (*Comm. Jo.* 1.6). "The entire New [Testament], however, is the Gospel" (1.3). What is especially valid for the written Gospel is the recognition "that each Gospel is a collection of messages explaining salvation to those who believe. These messages bring salvation, which is not to be accepted in a false understanding.... What is taught is the arrival of the 'firstborn of all creation' [Col 1:15], Christ Jesus, who comes to bring salvation to humans" (1.5). The actual content of the Gospel is, therefore, Christ himself, which proclaims his coming to humanity.

But two planes are to be distinguished in the written Gospels. The letter of the text "will be read by all according to the literal meaning that is audible by means of the spoken voice to each one who opens with his corporal ears." "Those who, however, will correctly comprehend the [word of the Bible] must in truth say: 'We have the mind of Christ in order to understand the gift that has been given us by God'" (a mixed citation from 1 Cor 2:16, 12). Both planes can also be described as audible and as corporal or sensual (the latter Origen compares to the "eternal gospel" of Rev 14:6), corresponding to the bodily and spiritual nature of Christ (1.7, 8). The actual content of the "spiritual" Gospel, however, is Christ himself, leading Origen to point to the "I am" words in the Gospel of God (1 Cor 2:2; 1:30; Col 1:19; 2:19; etc.; *Comm. Jo.* 1.9). The purpose of a "spiritual" understanding is to become one with Christ (a concept for Origen supported by Gal 2:20), "for everyone who is perfect 'no longer lives' any longer, but rather 'Christ lives in him'" (1.4). From this unfolds the purpose of the Gospel: "For also now upon this depends the translation of the sensual perception of the Gospel into the spiritual. For what would be an explanation of the sensual perceptions, if it could not be translated into the spiritual? ... Our entire effort consists of seeking to penetrate into the depth of the Gospel's meaning and to ascertain the truth laid bare by the signs" (1.8).

Since, however, now in the Gospels Christ himself is taught, the course of interpretation is abbreviated a complete step. Once more, in the interpretation Origen offers first an explanation of the historical meaning in which he transmits the circumstances and external processes described in the relevant section. On occasion a teaching is attached. After this, however, follows the explanation of the spiritual sense. The intermediate step is necessary for the Old Testament texts in providing the meaning of the "spiritual" sense for those who lived at that time. The transition to the analogy between the Israel of the Old Testament and the church is the soul. Now the intermediaries are no longer necessary. Christ himself is present in the text of the Gospels. Thus, there is left only the step of transferring the literal sense in which Christ is revealed in his humanness to the spiritual sense in which his divinity is disclosed.

Typical for Origen's interpretation of the Gospels is especially his commentary on Matthew. In spite of all the individual variations, we discover the same basic structure throughout this text: (1) a very short text, often only a clause, is cited literally; (2) there follows a more or less detailed explanation of the literal meaning, occasionally also connected with an attached teaching; (3) the spiritual meaning is explained; and (4) strikingly, the turn to the audience is often lacking until after the meaning of several sections is offered.

As an example, we select the interpretation of Matt 16:28 (*Comm. Matt.* 12.31–35). First Origen cites the text, "Truly I say to you that there are some among you standing here who shall not taste of death," which is only the first half of the verse. In respect to the literal meaning, Origen points to the view of "some" interpreters who related the statement to the transfiguration of Jesus on the mountain. Thus it means "that Peter and the two remaining apostles did not taste death before they saw the Son of Man coming in his dominion and glory." Here the alternative readings of two groups of manuscripts are combined. This could be a form of contextual exegesis, since the corresponding pericope in Matt 17:1–13 directly follows. To this interpretation of the literal meaning, Origen adds:

> This interpretation of the Word, that the three apostles did not taste death until they saw Jesus transformed, conforms to those who (as Peter named them) have become like "newborn children" who "long for pure

milk" (1 Pet 2:2). Paul says concerning this: "I have given you milk to drink, not solid food" etc. (1 Cor 3:2). And each literal interpretation (I hold) that can edify those who cannot grasp the greater matters may probably rightly be named milk, which flows from the holy "land" of the Scriptures, "the land flowing with milk and honey" (Exod 13:5).

Origen wishes, therefore, the literal interpretation to be accepted, although he restricts it specifically to an interpretation for beginners. Regarding the exegesis of the key word "milk," a series of passages come to his mind, of which a modern interpreter would probably recognize as relevant only 1 Cor 3:2.

However, Origen is unsatisfied with the literal meaning, so he proceeds subsequently to the next step. In so doing he expands to a further extent the associations with the key word "milk."

> However, he who is weaned [Greek: "denied milk"] like Isaac is worthy of the pleasures of the meal that Abraham hosts on the occasion of the weaning of his son [Gen 21:8]. The one who is "weaned" may well search after the whole food in these words and in the entire Scriptures [see Heb. 5:14]. In my opinion, this is something different than what is indeed nourishment [a key word from 1 Cor 3:2; even so, Origen does not give adequate consideration to the alternative of milk and whole food that is mentioned there], neither whole food nor all that is figuratively called "vegetable" and serves as nourishment for the one who is indeed weaned but still is not powerful but rather is weak. This corresponds to the statement: "One who is weak eats vegetables" [Rom 14:2]. Even so, it is like that from which Samuel was weaned, namely, his mother's milk, and has become sanctified by God [1 Sam 1:23–28].… And this one is likely the son of grace who like one who is nourished in the temple of God requires flesh. This flesh is the sacred food of the one who is perfect and at the same time is like the priests.

Origen then comes to the spiritual (allegorical) interpretation (12.32). His interpretation first involves (1) the significance of the term "to stand." He explains this in the following manner: "There are some who stood in the place where Jesus himself stood and who were firmly established in their souls by Jesus." This corresponds to the fundamental approach of Origen evident everywhere in his writing. Parallel passages to be mentioned are Deut 10:10 and 5:31. (2) Origen subsequently deals with the part of the verse in 16:28b (not cited up to now). He discusses, first of all, the phrase, "to see the Son of Man coming in his dominion." His first remark concerning this phrase reads:

There are distinctions, namely, also among those who stand by Jesus. Therefore, not every one who shall stand by the Savior shall not taste of death but rather only some of them who have a better position, until they shall see the Word that arrives, by the humans, that is, the one who is called therefore the Son of Man, coming in power. For Jesus does not always come in his sovereignty when he does come. For the beginner, namely, is able to see him coming, not in a lordly and commanding manner, but rather as less important than many words among humans.

Finally, Origen explains the cited word of Isa 53:2–3 (correctly) as a look backward:

And there were some of those who shall say that they behold his grandeur beyond their own earlier times, as the Word at the beginning that they grasped in its advent, which possessed "neither form nor beauty." There is, therefore, a royal worth of the Word that has been made manifest, which has been assumed entirely and openly beyond all other words. This assumption of position is seen to be over all other words that issue forth from some of those who stand by Jesus who are able to follow him when he goes before them and ascends the "high mountain" of his revelation.

The last allusion shows that Origen also in this allegorical explanation reaches back to the literal understanding, that already lay before him obviously in some of his predecessors in reference to Matt 17:1–13. Now, however, the passage no longer has to do with the earthly Jesus but rather with the Word, the Greek notion of Logos. This term is adapted even in its ambiguity (a word in its simple meaning but then also for Christ [John 1:1, 14] and for reason), which brings to expression Origen's specific position. In Christian understanding, it arguably has to do with as close a communion with Jesus Christ as possible in which God himself is bound with humans. However, in a Greek meaning, the term also always has to do with knowledge.

This becomes still clearer in a subsequent subsection (12.35) in which Origen undertakes to explain the wider form of Matt 16:28b (which presumably lays before him in the manuscript he uses): "to come to see the Son of Man in his dominion and glory." He remarks concerning this: "Whoever sees the superiority of the Word and apprehends it and refutes the plausible forms of things that are indeed lies and yet set forth as truth is the one who sees 'the Son of Man coming in his dominion.' When, however such a person sees how the Word not only cancels all the power

of conviction of the contrasted word but also entirely and clearly demonstrates also his own teachings, then he beholds his dominion as well
as the glory that is added to it." In any case, this is not understood as
purely intellectual in nature, if the truth, which is here spoken about, is
in Origen clearly a truth that is given through revelation. Therefore, the
fruit of spiritual enlightenment is effectuated through the Word that has
become man.

In the following section (12.33), Origen offers his explanation of the
idea of "death" in the clause "to taste of death." Origen defines "death" by
placing it in opposition to the concept of "life." The life, however, is Christ.
This comparison issues from John 11:25 and Col 3:4. "The enemy of this
life, however, which also is 'the last of all his enemies to be destroyed'
[1 Cor 15:26], is death, which the sinful soul experiences. However, the
opposite disposition that occurs in the soul that lives uprightly lives as
a consequence of this righteousness." According to Deut 30:15, 19, each
one who exists between life (i.e., Christ) and his enemy (i.e., death) may
choose what he will do. The one who sins actualizes the curse of Deut
28:66–67. A new citation with the key word "life" in John 6:33 refers to the
"Bread of the Word," Jesus, and thus produces a wider association: Christ
is the living bread, while "his enemy, death, is the bread of death. Each
soul, receiving the gift of reason, however, is nourished by either the living
bread or the bread of death and indeed accepts the good or evil teachings."
The ideas of "life" and "death" are explained in the sense of the Platonic
tradition, according to which the soul is nourished through the display of
the good; the literal understanding is thereby pushed aside.

There remains for Origen only the task of explaining the use of the
word "taste." This is not difficult for him.

> It occurs like the eating of common food. Occasionally one only tastes it,
> and occasionally one eats more of it. Thus it is also with these loaves [of
> life and death]: one eats of them only by scarcely tasting, or one partakes
> fully, because he is good or on the way to becoming good with the living
> bread that comes from heaven [John 6:33]. But the wicked eats from the
> bread of death, which is death, and those who seldom or only slightly
> sin taste perhaps only of death. But those who have accepted virtue taste
> not even of death but rather are nourished always by the living bread.

The explanation of the indication of time in Matt 16:28 still remains:
"until they see the Son of Man coming in his dominion." Origen occupies himself with time in a further chain of argumentation (12.34). At
this point he must ward off the obvious, literal understanding of the mes-

sage given to the disciples who are addressed and yet would later taste of death. Over against this, "we shall show that according to a custom of Scripture the word 'until' only sets forth the time in which the indicated result is certain to occur. However, the thing mentioned is not defined so absolutely that the opposite of what is said might in any case occur." One example is when Jesus says to the disciples, "See, I am with you every day until the end of the age" (Matt 28:20).

> When he says this, did he wish then to be with them only "until the end of the age"? He perhaps proclaimed to them that he would be present after the consummation of the period of the world. Did he perhaps proclaim to them that when the (so-called future) following period would occur he would no longer be with them...? However, I think that in all likelihood no one would venture to maintain that after the consummation of the age the Son of God would no longer be with his disciples.... However, if the expression "until the end of the age" had had such a meaning, then are we obviously not forced to accept that those who saw the Son of Man come in his dominion would taste death, after having been judged worthy thus to see him?

In this case Origen was satisfied to point to a single parallel passage in order to take out of consideration the impetus of the literal understanding.

As we learned from Origen's sermons dealing with New Testament texts, the only collection that remains consists of the thirty-nine that deal with the Gospel of Luke, preserved in Latin translation by Jerome (although there are a few Greek fragments). They are considerably different from all other works, including the sermons that deal with the Old Testament. They are relatively short, their structure is simple, and they usually treat only a single theme that is presented in the form of a teaching extracted from a text that is spiritually explained. The sermon sets forth the transition between the different historical planes, since it treats New Testament materials. In addition, it often has a markedly stronger dogmatic content than other statements. Thus the sermons address the theme of the inspiration of the four canonical Gospels, in contradistinction to similar works that should not be recognized (*Hom. Luc.* 1, on Luke 1:1–4), the theme of sinlessness and justice (*Hom. Luc.* 2, on 1:6), the theme of angels (*Hom. Luc.* 12 and 13, on 2:8–12, 13–16), the theme of the war between Satan and Christ for the dominion of the world (*Hom. Luc.* 30 and 31, on 4:5–8, 9–13), or ethical themes such as the commandment to love the one God (in Christ) (*Hom. Luc.* 25, on 3:15), or how the human, who is in the image of God, should actualize his or her commission in creation (*Hom. Luc.* 34, on 20:27–40, 21–26; see also *Hom. Luc.* 8). Since the sermons interpret, first of all, the prologue of Luke, the teaching of Mary also plays a significant role (especially *Hom. Luc.* 6–8, on 1:24–33, 39–45, 46–51). We encounter here repeated statements regarding the theme of the "virgin birth," also well known to us, a theme that later on shall play a role in the Catholic piety focused on Mary, as, for example, the affirmation that Mary remained a virgin after the birth of Jesus. The siblings of Jesus, who are mentioned in the New Testament, are presented as the children of Joseph by an earlier marriage (*Hom. Luc.* 7.4; also in *Comm. Jo.* 1.4 and a fragment concerning John).

By contrast, this technique of interpretation has a great deal of similarity with the method that may be observed in Origen elsewhere. The text that is addressed is divided into many small sections, which then are handled in a series. Occasionally a shorter sermon is devoted to a single passage. Origen's well-known approach confronts us throughout his writings, even when, as is often clear, Jerome has not translated literally the original Greek wording.

An example of a brief sermon dealing with an individual sentence is found in *Hom. Luc.* 3, on Luke 1:11. "The angel of the Lord, who stood at the right side of the altar of incense, appeared to him [Zechariah]." The entire sermon treats a single fundamental thought: "The corporal things, which cannot perceive, add nothing at all themselves to what may be seen by another. Only when the eye of another is directed upon some things does he see them, whether they wish to be seen or not, due to the fact that he directs his attention to them.… By contrast, those things that are higher and more godly, even if they are present, are not seen, even if they themselves do not wish it so" (3.1). The Platonic distinction between the bodily and the spiritual world is thus also here for Origen the starting point of his reflections. The second sentence obtains according to Origen not only for the appearances of God the Father before Abraham and the prophets (3.1) but also for Christ and the Holy Spirit and even for the angels (3.2). In the following clause (3.3), Origen broadens the consequences further when he maintains that this is true not only in the present but also in the future world, "when we shall have left this world." Even more it may be concluded "that not only God or the angels will appear, … but they will be seen only by one who has a pure heart and will thus be described as one who is worthy of seeing God." This also obtains in regard to Christ, "when he was seen in bodily form. Not all who saw him could see. They saw, to wit, only his body. However, in regard to his being the Christ, they could not see him. His disciples, by contrast, saw him and beheld the grandeur of his divinity." Thus, "those alone saw Jesus whom he held to be worthy to do so."

In the concluding section, the demand then follows that is directed to the audience: "Also we will, therefore, endeavor [to work toward this] to this end that God already even now appears to us … and in the future age will not conceal himself from us. Rather, we shall see him face to face" (1 Cor 13:12). The sermon then concludes with a hymn of praise of the Three-in-One God (3.4). If one read the sermon isolated from other texts, one could easily conclude that Origen was a pure moralist who saw salvation exclusively dependent on human striving. This is certainly not the case, for implicit here and in other texts Origen knowingly declares that humans themselves cannot come to faith in God and to the spiritual knowledge that he imparts as the highest of purposes. From his pastoral intention, however, he can formulate his interpretation of the text in a completely one-sided manner. Certainly, a considerable weight already is placed on human action in his description of the "way" (see above).

The sermons on Luke also reflect the same views found in the other works of Origen. However, they are much simpler and conform to the views his hearers are able to comprehend. That Origen was a popular preacher who functioned from his pastoral position is something that one is always able to trace. Like all of his expressions, they are an example of that typical spirituality developed in the Christian Hellenistic circles of Alexandria. In Asia Minor, other spiritual presuppositions prevailed, as we already have seen, for example, in Irenaeus.

SUMMARY

This journey through the early history of the interpretation of the Bible brought into view an abundance of perspectives and a wealth of foci and methods with which the interpreters of the Bible explained the sacred Scriptures according to their assumptions of thought and in light of their confession and intellectual history.

We began with the Old Testament witnesses to the continuing interpretive endeavors of explaining the texts of the Hebrew Bible, pointing to a progressive adaptation of a fixed, written, and authoritative tradition to the circumstances and needs of successive periods. Thus, the words of threat of the preexilic prophets, when the calamity they announced had taken place and Judah reached in the Babylonian exile the lowest point in the history of the nation, were supplemented by words of salvation announcing a new beginning. It was characteristic of these later prophetic words that they did not supersede the older ones but rather simply were attached to them as an explanation that transformed the meaning of the older prophecies. Normally they were anonymous, so that it remained for later scholarship to learn to separate them from the older traditions. This shows that the words of the preexilic prophets already had acquired a unique authority in exilic times so that each new message had to refer to them in order to participate in this unique authority. Here we are on the way that led to the origin of the sacred Scriptures and their final canonization. Deuteronomy played this role for the forms of expression and ideology in an entire domain of Old Testament literature. Something different occurred with the details of the Chronicles. Here we have an example of how a sphere of tradition, the history of the monarchic period, was newly explained according to a fixed ideology. The authors of the books of Chronicles augmented the established sections of an older source, the Deuteronomistic Books of Kings, without hesitation, self-composed descriptions that are far removed from historical reality. As we saw, however, they did not intend a photographically precise picture of the past. They wished to make the circumstances of their own present time intelligible to their readers from the historical past, something that the writers of the Deuteronomistic History already had wished to do in regard to their audience. In their idealization of the figure of David, they provided their own contemporaries a pattern. From David's exemplary service for the temple, they were to take hope for a better future in view of their own dismal reality.

If we wish to utilize the Old Testament according to our point of view as a source for reconstructing historical developments, we must keep in mind the entirely different purposes of the biblical writers. Their procedure was seen by us to be legitimate from their situation. All of them as a whole were led by the definite conviction that history is not only determined by means of human actions but also that its events were led decisively by God, who makes known his will in the commandments, speaks through the prophets, and stands behind the deeds of all political actors.

With the Septuagint, which set forth the Holy Scriptures of the Old Testament as already fixed even though the extent of the canon was debated, we were led to the second section of the history of interpretation. The Septuagint offered an example of how each translation is already an interpretation, because another language points to other forms of thought and expression. In contrast to the life circumstances of the original, those of the translators and their publics required an adaptation to another sphere, if the text was to reach beyond to address its new readers. The earliest example of the direct application of a biblical text to an actual situation according to pesher methods is found in the Qumran texts, which are especially enlightening because we possess in them direct witnesses of an earlier period of Judaism. They are also enlightening because they show how a particular community discovered its own special situation in the individual features of the wording of the earlier biblical texts.

With his allegorical interpretation of the Bible, Philo is a solitary figure within Judaism, because he explained the Holy Scriptures as a book of instruction, the truth of which is understood in the sense of Greek philosophy. It is easier to understand his thought if one correlates it to similar endeavors in Greek and Hellenistic philosophy to interpret the classical epics of the early period of Greek history as witnesses to the different systems of the philosophy. The fundamental conviction that Philo learned from the pagan philosophers was that there was only *one* undeniable truth and that the witness of the tradition could not contradict the knowledge of reason. Therefore, it was not only the superficial literal meaning of Homer or the Bible, which appeared to stand in opposition to reason, that could be true. Rather, one must penetrate to the deeper meaning residing behind the literal reading of the text. To our historical and philologically sharpened powers of discernment, the allegorical methods that were adopted appear absurd and nonsensical. However, this approach corresponded to accepted hermeneutical presuppositions operative at the time.

Beyond this, however, one should ask whether the acceptance of a deeper sense that lies concealed behind the surface of a text is not the presupposition of every form of exegesis. Modern textual theories have taught us once again to hold in higher regard these perspectives of depth that are connected with the symbolic content of language itself and are the presupposition of poetic art. Indeed, there remains to consider the issue of how a type of deeper meaning can be found and how far removed it may be from the surface sense. These issues are always open to methodological analysis. The excessive use of allegory and its transformation of meaning in ancient philosophy, however, cannot resist such an examination, because it imputed to the authors of the texts intentions in absolute contrast to the character of their works.

In contrast to Philo and the ancient philosophers, it is remarkable how reserved Christian interpretation of the Bible was, considering the methods available to them. The clearest indication of this is the reticence to engage in allegory, outside of Origen, who was the Christian interpreter most influenced by the Hellenistic environment, which played a minimal role. Christianity is, like its mother religion Judaism, a form of belief grounded in the events of history. Instead of eternal truths, it appeals to the events of the past that possess a function of grounding ideas and beliefs that are understood as vital for the present. Beside the narration of history, myth (e.g., the biblical primeval history) can also play a role in early Christian interpretation as a form of speech that shapes in narrative form ideas that are considered to be valid for humanity in general. Typological thought, which finds significance in events of the past that are considered to have correspondences with the present and brings together the periods of salvation history, appears to be far stronger in Christian biblical interpretation.

A longer chapter in our description of early biblical interpretation was devoted to the topic of the Old Testament in the New. From this it became clear how extensive the place given to the Old Testament citations was in almost all parts of the New Testament. Since the Christ-event and its significance for the Christian community provided the central content of the entire New Testament, the abundant citation of the Old Testament in the New shows how widely it was accepted by early Christianity and how much the entire Bible was given consideration in the grounding of the salvific significance of the Christ-event. This included the Testament that was common to Jews and Christians.

Jesus Christ himself, as far as we may determine in our historical reconstruction, was firmly rooted in the soil of the Old Testament in both his proclamation and his understanding of his commission. With his appearance, his proclamation continued the message of John the Baptist that the kingdom of God, which was an eschatological expectation of the end time in the Old Testament, had drawn near, indeed in reality had broken into history. He associated this in-breaking of the kingdom of God with his own person, in contrast to the Torah. He claimed an unlimited authority that he asserted presumably in regard to his being the Old Testament Messiah and possibly the expectations of the Son of Man. In contrast to the traditional hope concerning the Messiah, the new understanding was that Jesus had understood his affliction in the image of the Suffering Servant of God in Second Isaiah. Jesus added this to his understanding of his commission. Even if he had not spoken of himself in these terms, his disciples quickly opened the door to this understanding in terms of Isa 53. In the formulation of the early Christian confession transmitted by Paul, there is the following feature: Christ died for the sins of humanity, an affirmation that became a central expression of the Christian faith.

In spite of his borrowing of many techniques of contemporary exegesis, we found in Paul a very free manner of dealing with the Scriptures. His frequent lack of concern with the original contexts of the Old Testament citations that he collected served his specific teaching about the sinfulness of all humans and the doctrine of justification through faith alone. Thus, he drew on the Hebrew Bible to demonstrate the basis for these beliefs. His gospel, succinctly stated as the message of redemption through Christ, provided him the key for understanding Scripture. Thus, in contrast to Philo, he permitted the Scriptures to have a thoroughly historical location, for he was familiar with an ongoing history of God with humanity. However, he, like many others, could presuppose it as a common Christian tradition that existed among his readers.

The remaining New Testament writings, which here could be examined only in part in regard to their dealings with the Old Testament, are united in their common view that the Scriptures could be read only through the lens of faith in Christ. They explain the relationship in what were on occasion different ways. While Matthew speaks of the Scriptures fulfilled in Christ, he understands the Old Testament as essentially the promise of Christ and the concomitant Torah that continues to be valid for Christians; the emphasis of the speeches contained in the Acts of the

Apostles is placed more on the idea that this Testament is a prophecy of Christ. The author of the Letter to the Hebrews brings to the attention of his readers, who are in the midst of internal difficulties, the view that Christ surpasses the Old Testament institutions. This is seen especially in the office of the high priest. In the Apocalypse of John we encounter a Christian visionary who richly illustrates his view of final things with Old Testament images. However, these are not mere external trappings but rather contain authentic features of vision. John stands as a living apocalyptic seer in the midst of a living tradition. He is distinguished from other seers in the fact that the Lordship of the Lamb, Jesus Christ, stands in the middle of his expectations. For him, the Christian community is the eschatological people of God passing through the oppressions of the end time.

Methodologically speaking, the New Testament interpretation of the Old Testament has much in common with Jewish exegesis. This is not unexpected, if one recognizes the Jewish origins of the apostles and the earliest Christian community in Jerusalem. The uniqueness of the Christian understanding of the Bible as contrasted to the Jewish view, which was increasingly limited to the rabbinic interpretation of the Torah, especially following the failures of the political expectations of the Zealots and the apocalyptic seers, resided in the exclusivity of relating the entire Old Testament to Jesus Christ.

Such an exegesis is not without presuppositions. That must be stressed over against the theories that wish to speak of an exegetical ideal unconstricted by presuppositions. The one who shares this ideal—although recent hermeneutics has long since exposed it as an erroneous conclusion—will disapprove of this Christian preunderstanding by considering it tendentious and logically alien to our own methodology of New Testament exegesis. If one wishes, however, at least to respect the integrity of the views of those first Christians who brought their faith into the interpretative process, then they will be allowed to discover their own situation in these earlier understandings by means of their own questions, which they addressed to the Holy Scriptures held in common with the Jews. This understanding of faith expressed in their confession is that for them Jesus Christ signified salvation and that they therefore had to read Scripture in view of him. That these early Christians made use of methods of interpretation that were commonly found in their own historical period is not a matter of wonder. Still, in their view they held more strongly to the historical aspect of this reality than did rabbinic Judaism and especially the pagan philosophy of their own time.

The early Christian writings that followed could not fully maintain the theological high point of the New Testament. The Epistle of Barnabas deviates significantly from the more customary Christian interpretation of the Old Testament. This writing regards the Old Testament only as prophecy and as a spiritual foreshadowing of Christ, even as it contests this Testament's validity from the very beginning. The Old Testament is completely and entirely ripped away from the Jews. The church in general did not follow this position, and Barnabas was not assumed into the New Testament canon. The Letter of 1 Clement represents the opposite position. It refers ever again to the Old Testament in connecting its ethical admonitions to Christian virtues and in relating Old Testament figures to the paradigms of pious and God-fearing behavior. The gospel in a Pauline sense scarcely even plays a role. Even the Old Testament cultic proscriptions were converted into Christian worship practices. This writing does not see a break in the history of salvation. The church stands in direct succession to Israel. In addition to this, 1 Clement calls attention to the words of Jesus, which were available to its author in an oral tradition probably independent of the Gospels. Also here the author prefers admonitions, as they appear, for example, in the Sermon on the Mount. Although Clement was familiar with several New Testament writings, some of the Pauline letters, and probably also Hebrews, it is not possible as of yet to trace a canonical legitimacy given to these texts.

Around the middle of the second century c.e., we see the early Catholic theologians engage in the defense of the teachings of the church against the authority of the state and also against Judaism. However, they also enter into conflict with the streams of influence within the church that were gnostic or extremely close to gnosis. In these conflicts, the great church not only maintained its position but also gained an increasing influence. In the periods addressed in this volume, the persecution of the church certainly did not come to an end, since the power of the state continued to reside in pagan hands. Until well into the fourth century c.e., paganism was a thoroughly vital spiritual power. As regards Judaism, the relation during that period grew increasingly hostile.

In respect to the understanding of the Bible, the most important result of this period is the church's continued retention of the Hebrew Bible as an integral part of its Bible. The effort of Marcion to restrict the Christian Bible to several New Testament, especially Pauline, writings failed. Irenaeus of Lyons fended off the attack of gnosis on Christianity in a large-scale theological project. He for the first time submitted that the Old Testament and the New Testament, which was not finalized, were to be regarded as equal and spoke of a harmony between the two Testaments. This was due to the fact that for Irenaeus there was only one God who speaks in both Testaments. He is the Creator and Lord of history (the concept of salvation history is important for Irenaeus), however also the Father of Jesus Christ. Subsequently, the dualism and world-denying proposal represented by Marcion and the gnostics was successfully rejected by the church's apologists. In this way, Christianity was kept from degenerating into one of the ancient mystery religions. Christian faith continued to be bound to the world and to history, both of which were fields of divine action of the one God. Being active in the world, not fleeing from it, became the basis of Christian ethics.

Origen assumes a special place. His acceptance of a deeper, spiritual meaning of Scripture, which must be sought and brought forth from behind the literal understanding, betrays the influence that Hellenistic philosophy had on his thinking. The Greek understanding is also the real viewpoint practiced in both his interpretation and especially his biblical preaching. He sought to instruct readers and hearers of the Bible to lead their souls up the stages of virtue to their heavenly goal. The extensive use of the allegorical method corresponds to the hermeneutical principle that the meaning of the Bible, which can be opened up only in this way, is the "spiritual understanding" that can lead to perfection. This perfection, an authentic Greek ideal, resides for Origen in spiritual knowledge. It may be reached only in stages and is a goal that may not even be attained by the average Christian.

Although the church later condemned Origen on dogmatic grounds, his method, which proceeds from a manifold understanding of Scripture, and his spiritualism had a great deal of influence on the later church. One could regard the thought of Origen to be that of an elitist, if one was not aware of the fact that he had delved vigorously into the needs of the community in his preaching. He wished to guide all Christians on their spiritual journeys.

This volume could set forth from the fullness of the extensive materials only a selection. The one who is intimately familiar with earlier church history will miss many exegetes, such as Hippolytus of Rome, Tertullian of Carthage, or Clement of Alexandria, the predecessor of Origen. Even among the New Testament writings and their use of the Old Testament, only a selection could be examined. From the analysis of the previous examples, however, a history of biblical interpretation may be pieced together in spite of individual differences in details. Later exegetes reach back to the works of their ancient predecessors, both to those known to us only by name and others who are not familiar. There were many older works written out in ample fashion that only recently have been compiled from surviving materials, as well as others that were handed down only in oral tradition that pointed to a common set of themes and tenets. The traditional Old Testament passages that deal with Jesus as the Messiah are a case in point, as we encountered, for instance, in Justin. Originality was not an ideal in antiquity, but rather one was situated in the common tradition of the church, also relating the understanding of the Bible.

Also, there was a great deal in common in the interpretive methods used by both Jews and Christians. Together they were indebted to Greek philology for most of this methodology. In spite of the fact that they had widely divergent canons, a common basis for Jewish and Christian interpretation existed in the fact that both religions considered the Old Testament to be binding. Certainly the objectives of Jewish and Christian interpretation developed in different directions. The Hellenistic culture played a role that was the self-evident general horizon for Jewish and Christian interpreters, even when each community occupied a separate existence in the Roman Empire. One may observe a direct influence of Greek philosophy on a proportionately small number of exegetes. Of the thinkers who were examined in this volume, only two were strongly influenced by this source: Philo and Origen. The opposition between the historical message of the Bible and the eternal truth that philosophy strived to obtain was too great. Where there existed a strong ideological binding to the Greek worldview, one usually discovers that the heretics, Marcion and the gnostics, could not accommodate this to the Old Testament but rather ascribed this text to a lower deity.

With the death of Origen, we come approximately to the middle of the third century c.e. This time point is a suitable one to conclude our description in the first volume. The original plan to deal with the entire history of interpretation of the Bible in a single volume soon had to be given up. This would have led only to a very cursory outline that would have lacked concreteness. Instead, I have decided to offer the possibility of setting forth a survey of individual examples with a wealth of citations from sources that were composed in ancient languages and are difficult for modern readers to access. This allows the comprehension of the development of the steps of interpretation, which enables the reader to have a legitimate understanding of the interpreters' positions and methods. One will encounter with new esteem these exegetes and their works. Their zeal for the faith, their enormous knowledge of the Bible when compared with modern standards, and their philosophical education will be held in deep respect. Nevertheless, the impression that their methods of interpretation and points of view leaves is one of their strangeness and demonstrates the break that separates them from us, for we are the products of the Enlightenment and subsequent periods. Now we are finally learning the value of some of their fundamental principles, which causes us again to reflect on our own approaches. This is true, for example, of the rule that the Bible as a whole must be the standard for judging individual phrases. However, this revising of our opinion about the value of the insights from the history of interpretation is still in it infancy.

Selected Resources and Readings

Suggestions for additional readings are arranged by chapters. Commentaries on individual biblical books are not listed.

General

Dobschütz, Ernst von. "Vom vierfachen Schriftsinn: Die Geschichte einer Theorie." Pages 1–13 in *Harnack-Ehrung: Beiträge zur Kirchengeschichte*. Leipzig: Hinrichs, 1921.

Kraus, Hans-Joachim. *Geschichte der historisch-kristischen Erforschung des Alten Testament*. 4th ed. Neukirchen-Vluyn: Neukirchener, 1988.

Mulder, Martin Jan, and Harry Sysling, eds. *Mikra: Text, Translation, Reading and Interpretation of the Hebrew Bible in Ancient Judaism and Early Christianity*. CRINT 2/1. Assen: Van Gorcum; Philadelphia: Fortress, 1988.

1. Biblical Interpretation within the Bible

Barth, Hermann. *Die Jesaja-Worte in der Josiazeit*. WMANT 48. Neukirchen-Vluyn: Neukirchener, 1977.

Becker, Joachim. *Israel deutet seine Psalmen: Urform und Neuinterpretation in den Psalmen*. SBS 18. Stuttgart: Verlag Katholisches Bibelwerk, 1976.

Fishbane, Michael. *Biblical Interpretation in Ancient Israel*. Oxford: Oxford University Press, 1985.

Hertzberg, Hans-Wilhelm. "Die Nachgeschichte alttestamentlicher Texte innerhalb des Alten Testaments." BZAW 66 (1936): 110–21. Repr. as pages 69–80 in idem, *Beitrage zur Traditionsgeschichte und Theologie des Alten Testaments*. Göttingen: Vandenhoeck & Ruprecht, 1962.

Mosis, Rudolf. *Untersuchungen zur Theologie des chronistischen Geschichtswerkes*. FthSt 92. Freiburg: Herder, 1973.

Springer, Simone. *Neuinterpretation im Alten Testament: Untersucht an den Themenkreisen des Herbstfestes und der Königspsalmen in Israel.* SBB 9. Stuttgart: Verlag Katholisches Bibelwerk, 1977.

Welten, Peter. *Geschichte und Geschichtsdarstellung in den Chronikbüchern.* WMANT 42. Neukirchen-Vluyn: Neukirchener, 1973.

Willi, Thomas. *Die Chronik als Auslegung: Untersuchungen zur literarischen Gestalt der historischen Überlieferung Israels.* FRLANT 106. Göttingen: Vandenhoeck & Ruprecht, 1972.

Willi-Plein, Ina. *Vorformen der Schriftexegese innerhalb des Alten Testaments.* BZAW 123. Berlin: de Gruyter, 1971.

2. Between the Testaments

Hengel, Martin. *Judaism and Hellenism: Studies in Their Encounter in Palestine during the Early Hellenistic Period.* Translated by John Bowden. 2 vols. Philadelphia: Fortress, 1974.

2.1. Translation as Interpretation: The Septuagint

Jellicoe, Sidney. *The Septuagint and Modern Study.* Oxford: Oxford University Press, 1968.

Schreiner, Josef. "Hermeneutische Leitlinien in der LXX." Pages 356–94 in *Die hermeneutische Frage in der Theologie.* Edited by Oswald Loretz and Walter Strolz. Schriften zum Weltgespräch 3. Freiburg: Herder, 1968.

Ziegler, Joseph. *Untersuchungen zur Septuaginta des Buches Isaias.* Alttestamentliche Abhandlungen 12.3. Münster: Aschendorff, 1934.

2.2. Early Jewish Interpretation: The Qumran Scrolls

Betz, Otto. *Offenbarung und Schriftforschung in der Qumransekte.* WUNT 6. Tübingen: Mohr Siebeck, 1960.

Braun, Herbert. *Qumran und das Neue Testament: Ein Bericht über 10 Jahre Forschung (1950–1959).* 2 vols. Tübingen: Mohr Siebeck, 1962–1964.

Bruce, F. F. *Biblical Exegesis in the Qumran Texts.* Grand Rapids: Eerdmans, 1959.

Elliger, Karl. *Studien zum Habakuk-Kommentar vom Toten Meer.* BHT 15. Tubingen: Mohr Siebeck, 1953.

Lohse, Eduard, ed. *Die Text aus Qumran: Hebräisch und Deutsch: Mit masoretischer Punktation, Übersetzung, Einführung und Anmerkungen.* Darmstadt: Wissenschaftliche Buchgesellschaft, 1986.

Vermes, Geza. "Die Schriftauslegung in Qumran in ihrem historischen Rahmen." Pages 185–200 in *Qumran.* Edited by Karl E. Grözinger et al. WdF 160. Darmstadt: Wissenschaftliche Buchgesellschaft, 1981.

2.3. The Philosophers' Interpretation of Homer and Hesiod

Buffière, Félix. *Les Mythes d'Homere et la pensée grecque.* Paris: Belles Lettres, 1956.

Hesiod. *Sämtliche Werke.* Translated by Thassilo von Scheffer. Vienna: Schünemann, 1936.

Homer. *Iliad.* Translated by A. T. Murray and William F. Wyatt. 2 vols. LCL 170–171. Cambridge: Harvard University Press, 1999.

———. *The Odyssey.* Translated by A. T. Murray. LCL 105. Cambridge: Harvard University Press, 1975.

Homers Odyssee, griechisch und deutsch. Translated by Johann Heinrich Voß. Edited by E. R. Weiß. 2 vols. Berlin: Tempel, 1914.

Pépin, M. Jean: *Mythe et allégorie: Les origines grecques et les contestations judéo-chrétiennes.* Paris: Études augustiniennes, 1976.

2.4. Allegorical Interpretation of Scripture: Philo of Alexandria

Amir, Yehoshua. *Die hellenistische Gestalt des Judentums bei Philon von Alexandrien.* Neukirchen-Vluyn: Neukirchener, 1983.

Christiansen, Irmgard. *Die Technik der allegorischen Auslegungswissenschaft bei Philon von Alexandrien.* Tübingen: Mohr Siebeck, 1969.

Goodenough, Erwin R. *An Introduction to Philo Judaeus.* London: University Press of America, 1986.

Heinemann, Isaak. *Philos griechische und jüdische Bildung.* Reprint from several publications of sections. Hildesheim: Olms, 1962.

Sandmel, Samuel. *Philo of Alexandria: An Introduction.* New York: Oxford University Press, 1979.

Siegfried, Carl. *Philo von Alexandrien als Ausleger des Alten Testaments.* Repr., Aalen: Scientia-Verlag, 1970.

Stein, Edmund. *Die allegorische Exegese des Philo von Alexandreia.* BZAW 51. Gießen: Töpelmann, 1929.

3. The Old Testament in the New

Campenhausen, Hans von. *The Formation of the Christian Bible*. Translated by J. A. Baker. Philadelphia: Fortress, 1972.

Dodd, C. H. *According to the Scriptures. The Sub-structure of New Testament Theology*. London: Nisbet, 1952.

Ernst, Josef, ed. *Schriftauslegung-Beiträge zur Hermeneutik des Neuen Testaments und im Neuen Testament*. Munich: Schöningh, 1972.

Goppelt, Leonhard. *Typos: The Typological Interpretation of the Old Testament in the New*. Translated by Donald H. Madvig. Grand Rapids: Eerdmans, 1982.

Hanson, Antony T. *The Living Utterances of God: The New Testament Exegesis of the Old*. London: Darton, Longman & Todd, 1983.

Lindars, Barnabas. *New Testament Apologetic: The Doctrinal Significance of the Old Testament Quotations*. London: SCM, 1961.

Smith, D. Moody, Jr. "The Use of the Old Testament in the New." Pages 20–65 in *The Use of the Old Testament in the New and Other Essays: Studies in Honor of William Franklin Stinespring*. Edited by James M. Efird. Durham, N.C.: Duke University Press, 1972.

3.1. The Kingdom of God Has Drawn Near: Jesus Christ

Albertz, Rainer. "Die 'Antrittspredigt' Jesu im Lukasevangelium auf ihrem alttestamentlichen Hintergrund." *ZNW* 74 (1983): 182–206.

Berger, Klaus. *Markus und Parallelen*. Part 1 of *Die Gesetzesauslegung Jesu: Ihr historischer Hintergrund im Judentum und im Alten Testament*. WMANT 40. Neukirchen-Vluyn: Neukirchener, 1972.

Feneberg, Rupert, and Wolfgang Feneberg. *Das Leben Jesu im Evangelium* (QD 88). Freiburg: Herder, 1980.

Flender, Helmut. *Die Botschaft Jesu von der Herrschaft Gottes*. Munich: Furche, 1968.

France, R. T. *Jesus and the Old Testament: His Application of Old Testament Passages to Himself and His Mission*. Downers Grove, Ill.: InterVarsity, 1971.

Grimm, Werner. *Weil ich dich liebe: Die Verkündigung Jesus und Deuterojesaja*. Arbeiten zum Neuen Testament und Judentum 1. Frankfurt am Main: Herbert Lang, 1976.

Higgins, A. J. B. *The Son of Man in the Teaching of Jesus*. SNTSMS 39. Cambridge: Cambridge University Press, 1980.

Perrin, Norman. *Rediscovering the Teaching of Jesus.* New York: Harper & Row, 1967.

Riches, John. *Jesus and the Transformation of Judaism.* New York: Seabury, 1980.

Riesner, Rainer. *Jesus als Lehrer: Eine Untersuchung zum Ursprung der Evangelien-Überlieferung.* WUNT 27. Tübingen: Mohr Siebeck, 1981.

Ruppert, Lothar. *Jesus als der leidende Gerchte? Der Weg Jesu im Lichte eines alt-und zwichentestamentlichen Motivs.* SBS 59. Stuttgart: Verlag Katholisches Bibelwerk, 1972.

Sanders, E. P. *Jesus and Judaism.* Philadelphia: Fortress, 1985.

Stein, Robert H. *The Method and Message of Jesus' Teachings.* Philadelphia: Westminster, 1982.

Strobel, August. *Die Stunde der Wahrheit.* WUNT 21. Tübingen: Mohr Siebeck, 1980.

3.2. PRIMITIVE CHRISTIAN EXPLANATIONS OF THE CHRIST-EVENT

Gubler, Marie-Louise. *Die frühesten Deutungen des Todes Jesu: Eine motivgeschichtliche Darstellung aufgrund der neueren exegetischen Forschung.* OBO 15. Fribourg: Universitätsverlag; Göttingen: Vandenhoeck & Ruprecht, 1977.

Koch, Dietrich Alexander. "Beobachtungen zum christologischen Schriftgebrauch in den vorpaulinischen Gemeinden." *ZNW* 71 (1980): 174–91.

Lohse, Eduard. "Die alttestamentlichen Bezüge im neutestamentlichen Zeugnis vom Tode Jesu Christi." Pages 112–24 in idem, *Die Einheit des Neuen Testaments: Exegetische Studien zur Theologie des Neuen Testaments.* Göttingen: Vandenhoeck & Ruprecht, 1973.

Ruppert, Lothar. *Der leidende Gerechte: Eine motivgeschichtliche Untersuchung zum Alten Testament und zwischentestamentlichen Judentum.* Würzburg: Verlag Katholisches Bibelwerk, 1972.

Tödt, Heinz-Eduard. *The Son of Man in the Synoptic Tradition.* Translated by Dorothea M. Barton. NTL. Philadelphia: Westminster, 1965.

Wolff, Hans Walter. *Jesaja 53 im Urchristentum.* 4th ed. Gießen: Brunnen, 1984.

3.3. THE SCRIPTURE IS WRITTEN "FOR OUR SAKE": PAUL

Bonsirven, Joseph. *Exégèse rabbinique et exégèse pauline.* Paris: Beauchesne, 1939.

Dugandzic, Ivan. *Das "Ja" Gottes in Christus: Eine Studie zur Bedeutung des Alten Testaments für das Christusverständnis des Paulus.* Würzburg: Echter, 1977.

Ellis, E. Earle. *Paul's Use of the Old Testament.* Edinburgh: Oliver & Boyd, 1957.

Kleinknecht, Karl Theodor. *Der Leidende Gerechtfertigte: Die alttestamentlich-jüdische Tradition vom "leidenden Gerechten" und ihre Rezeption bei Paulus.* Tübingen: Mohr Siebeck, 1987.

Koch, Dietrich Alexander. *Die Schrift als Zeuge des Evangeliums: Untersuchungen zur Verwendung und zum Verständnis der Schrift bei Paulus.* BHT 69. Tübingen: Mohr Siebeck, 1986.

Lindermann, Andreas. *Paulus im ältesten Christentum: Das Bild des Apostels und die Rezeption der paulinischen Theologie in der frühchristlichen Literatur bis Marcion.* BHT 58. Tübingen: Mohr Siebeck, 1979.

Michel, Otto. *Paulus und seine Bibel:* Gütersloh: Bertelsmann, 1929. Repr., Darmstadt: Wissenschaftliche Buchgesellschaft, 1972.

Vielhauer, Philipp. Paulus und das Alte Testament. Pages 33–62 in *Studien zur Geschichte und Theologie der Reformation.* Edited by Luise Abramowski and J. F. Gerhard Goeters. Neukirchen-Vluyn: Neukirchener, 1969.

3.4. The Promise Is Fulfilled: Matthew

Gundry, Robert H. *The Use of the Old Testament in St. Matthew's Gospel.* NovTSup 18. Leiden: Brill, 1967.

Künzel, Georg. *Studien zum Gemeindeverständnis des Matthäus-Evangeliums.* CThM.A 10. Stuttgart: Calwer, 1978.

Rothfuchs, Wilheim. *Die Erfüllungszitate des Matthäus-Evangeliums.* BWANT 88. Stuttgart: Kohlhammer, 1969.

Stendahl, Krister. *The School of St. Matthew and Its Use of the Old Testament.* Philadelphia: Fortress, 1968.

3.5. The Old Testament Is Prophecy about Christ: The Sermons of the Book of Acts

Ellis, E. Earle. "Midraschartige Züge in den Reden der Apostelgeschichte." *ZNW* 62 (1971): 94–104.

Kränkl, Emmeran. *Jesus der Knecht Gottes: Die heilsgeschichtliche Stellung Jesu in den Reden der Apostelgeschichte.* BU 8. Regensburg: Pustet, 1972.

Stemberger, Günter. "Die Stephanusrede (Apg 7) und die jüdische Tradi-
tion." Pages 154–74 in *Jesus in der Verkündigung der Kirche*. Edited by
Albert Fuchs. SNTU.A 1. Linz: Fuchs, 1976.
Wilckens, Ulrich. *Die Missionsreden der Apostelgeschichte*. WMANT 5.
Neukirchen-Vluyn: Neukirchener, 1974.

3.6. Christ Surpasses the Old Testament Institutions: The Epistle to the Hebrews

Schröger, Friedrich. "Das hermeneutische Instrumentarium des Hebräer-
briefverfassers." Pages 313–29 in *Schriftauslegung: Beiträge zur
Hermeneutik des Neuen Testamentes und im Neuen Testament*. Edited
by Josef Ernst. Munich: Schöningh, 1972.
Williamson, Ronald. *Philo and the Epistle to the Hebrews*. ALGHJ 4.
Leiden: Brill, 1970. See especially 313–29.

3.7. A Christian Visionary in the Succession of the Prophets: The Apocalypse of John

Boxall, Ian. *The Revelation of Saint John*. Peabody, Mass.: Hendrickson,
2006.
Lupieri, Edmondo. *A Commentary on the Apocalypse of John*. Grand
Rapids: Eerdmans, 2006.

3.8. A Refutation in the New Testament: The Letter of 2 Thessalonians

Lindemann, Andreas. "Zum Abfassungszweck des Zweiten Thessa-
lonicherbriefes." *ZNW* 68 (1977): 35–47.

4. The Early Centuries of the Common Era

Aleith, Ava. *Das Paulusverständnis in der Alten Kirche*. BZNW 18. Berlin:
Töpelmann, 1937.
Grant, Robert M. *A Short History of the Interpretation of the Bible*. 2nd ed.
Philadelphia: Fortress, 1984.
Margerie, Bertrand de. *The Greek Fathers*. Vol. 1 of *An Introduction to the
History of Exegesis*. Translated by Leonard Maluf. Petersham, Mass.:
Saint Bede's, 1991.

Sundberg, Albert C. *The Old Testament of the Early Church*. Cambridge: Cambridge University Press, 1964.

Tröger, Karl-Wolfgang. *Altes Testament, Frühjudentum, Gnosis*. Gütersloh: Gütersloher Verlagshaus Gerd Mohn, 1980.

Vielhauer, Philipp. *Geschichte der urchristlichen Literatur: Einleitung in das Neue Testament, die Apokryphen und die Apostolischen Väter*. Berlin: de Gruyter, 1975.

4.1. FURTHER DEVELOPMENT OF THE TORAH: THE EARLY RABBINIC INTERPRETATION OF SCRIPTURE

Bacher, Wilheim. *Die Agada der Tannaiten*. Strassburg: Trübner, 1903. Repr., Berlin: de Gruyter, 1965.

———. *Die exegetische Terminologie der judischen Traditionsliteratur*. 2 vols. Leipzig: Hinrichs, 1905. Repr., Darmstadt: Wissenschaftliche Buchgesellschaft, 1965.

Kadushin, Max. *A Contextual Approach to the Mekilta*. New York: Jewish Theological Seminary of America, 1969.

Maass, Fritz. "Von den Ursprüngen der rabbinischen Schriftauslegung." *ZTK* 52 (1955): 129–61.

Neusner, Jacob. *The Rabbinic Traditions about the Pharisees before 70*. 3 vols. Leiden: Brill, 1971.

Patte, Daniel. *Early Jewish Hermeneutic in Palestine*. SBLDS 22. Missoula, Mont.: Scholars Press, 1975.

Safrai, Shmuel, ed. *Oral Tora, Halaka, Mishna, Tosefta, Talmud, External Tractates*. Part 1 of *The Literature of the Sages*. CRINT 2/3. Assen: Van Gorcum; Philadelphia: Fortress, 1987.

Seligman, Isaac Leo. "Voraussetzungen der Midraschexegese." Pages 150–81 in *Congress Volume: Copenhagen, 1953*. VTSup 1. Leiden: Brill, 1953.

Strack, Hermann L. and Günter Stemberger. *Introduction to the Talmud and Midrash*. Translated by Markus Bockmuehl. Edinburgh: T&T Clark, 1991.

Urbach, Ephraim E. *The Sages, Their Concepts and Beliefs*. Translated by Israel Abrahams. Cambridge: Harvard University Press, Jerusalem, 1979.

4.2.1. The Old Testament Is Only for Christians: The Letter of Barnabas

Bihlmeyer, Karl, and Wilhelm Schneemelcher, eds. *Die Apostolischen Väter.* Tübingen: Mohr Siebeck, 1956.

Dassmann, Ernst. *Der Stachel im Fleisch: Paulus in der frühchristlichen Literatur bis Irenäus.* Münster: Aschendorff, 1979.

Klevinghaus, Johannes. *Die theologie Stellung der apostolischen Väter zur alttestamentlichen Offenbarung.* BFCT 44.1. Gütersloh: Bertelsmann, 1948.

Koester, Helmut. *Synoptische Überlieferung bei den apostolischen Vätern.* TUGAL 65. Berlin: Akademie-Verlag, 1971.

Wengst, Klaus. *Tradition und Theologie des Barnabasbriefes.* AKG 42. Berlin: de Gruyter, 1971.

4.2.2. A Letter of Exhortation Based on the Old Testament: The Letter of 1 Clement

Breytenbach, Cilliers, ed., *Encounters with Hellenism: Studies on the First Letter of Clement.* Arbeiten zur Geschichte des antiken Judentums und des Urchristentums 53. Leiden: Brill 2004.

Wengst, Klaus. *Didache, Barnabasbrief, Zweiter Klemensbrief, Schrift an Diognet.* SUC 2. Munich: Wissenschaftliche Buchgesellschaft, 1984.

Ziegler, Adolf Wilhelm. *Neue Studien zum ersten Klemensbrief.* Munich: Manz, 1958.

4.3. Early Apologetics: Justin Martyr

Barnard, Leslie William. *Justin Martyr: His Life and Thought.* Cambridge: Cambridge University Press, 1967.

Osborn, Eric Francis. *Justin Martyr.* BHT 47. Tübingen, Mohr Siebeck, 1973.

Prigent, Pierre. *Justin et l'Ancien Testament: L'argumentation scripturaire du traité de Justin contre toutes les hérésies comme source principale du Dialogue avec Tryphon et de la première Apologie.* Études bibliques. Paris: Librairie Lecoffre, 1964.

Shotwell, Willis A. *The Biblical Exegesis of Justin Martyr.* London: SPCK, 1965.

Skarsaune, Oskar. *The Proof from Prophecy: A Study in Justin Martyr's Proof-text Tradition: Text-Type, Provenance, Theological Profile.* NovTSup 56. Leiden: Brill, 1987.

4.4. The Abrogation of the Old Testament? Marcion and His Program

Aland, Barbara. "Marcion: Versuch einer neuen Interpretation." *ZTK* 70 (1973) 420–44.

Harnack, Adolf von. *Marcion: The Gospel of the Alien God.* Translated by John E. Steely and Lyle D. Bierma. Durham: Labyrinth, 1989.

Hoffmann, R. Joseph. *Marcion, On the Restitution of Christianity: An Essay on the Development of Radical Paulinist Theology in the Second Century.* American Academy of Religion Academy Series 46. Chico, Calif.: Scholars Press, 1980.

Ory, Georges. *Marcion.* Cahier hors-série. Paris: Cercle Ernest-Renan, 1980.

4.5. Harmony of the Testaments: Irenaeus von Lyon

Bacq, Philippe, *De l'ancienne à la nouvelle alliance selon S. Irénée: Unité du livre IV de l'Adversus haereses.* Paris: Lethielleux, 1978.

Brox, Norbert. "Irenäus." In *Von Irenäus bis Martin Luther.* Volume 1 of *Klassiker der Theologie.* Edited by Heinrich Fries and Georg Kretschmar. Munich: Beck, 1981.

MacKenzie, Iain M. *Irenaeus's Demonstration of the Apostolic Preaching: A Theological Commentary and Translation.* Aldershot, Hants : Ashgate, 2002.

Osborn, Eric. "Irenaeus of Lyons (2nd Century)." Pages 121–28 in *The Blackwell Companion to the Theologians.* Edited by Ian S. Markham. Blackwell Companions to Religion. Chichester, U.K.: Wiley-Blackwell, 2009.

Rousseau, Adelin, and Louis Doutreleau, eds. *Irénée de Lyon: Contre les hérésies.* SC 263–264. Paris: Cerf, 1979–1982.

4.6. The Way of the Soul toward Perfection: Origen

Logan, Alastair H. B. "Origen (c.185–254)." Pages 170–86 in *The Blackwell Companion to the Theologians.* Edited by Ian S. Markham. Blackwell Companions to Religion. Chichester, U.K.: Wiley-Blackwell, 2009.

Lubac, Henri De. *Histoire et esprit: L'intelligence de l'Ecriture d'après Origène.* Paris: Cerf, 1930. English: *History and Spirit: The Understanding of Scripture according to Origen.* Translated by Anne Englund Nash. San Francisco: Ignatius, 2007.

Origen. *Commentaire sur l'evangile selon Matthieu.* Introduction, translation, and notes by Robert Girod. SC 162. Paris: Cerf, 1970.

———. *Homilien zu Genesis, Exodus, Leviticus.* Part 1 of *Homilien zum Hexateuch in Rufins Übersetzung.* Edited by W. A. Baehrens. GCS 29. Leipzig: Hinrichs, 1920.

———. *Homilien zu Numeri, Josua, Judices.* Part 1 of *Homilien zum Hexateuch in Rufins Übersetzung.* Edited by W. A. Baehrens. GCS 30. Leipzig: Hinrichs, 1921.

———. *Homilien zu Samuel I, Hohelied und propheten Kommentar zum Holelied in Rufins und Hieronymus' Übersetzung.* Edited by W. A. Baehrens. GCS 33. Leipzig: Hinrichs, 1925.

———. *Homilies on Genesis and Exodus.* Translated by Ronald E. Heine. FC 71. Washington, D.C.: Catholic University of America, 1982.

———. *Homilies on Joshua.* Translated by Barbara J. Bruce. Edited by Cynthia White. FC 105. Washington, D.C.: Catholic University of America, 2002.

———. *Homilies on Luke; Fragments on Luke.* Translated by Joseph T. Lienhard. FC 84. Washington, D.C.: Catholic University of America, 1996.

———. *Homilies sur Jérémie.* Edited by Pierre Nautin. 2 vols. SC 232, 238. Paris: Cerf, 1976–1977.

———. *Jeremiahomilien, Klageliederkommentar, Erklärung der Samuel-und Konigsbucher.* Edited by Erich Klostermann. GCS 6. Leipzig: Hinrichs, 1901.

———. *Johanneskommentar.* Edited by Erwin Preuschen. GCS 10. Leipzig: Hinrichs, 1903.

———. *Philocalie 1–20.* Edited by Marguerite Harl. SC 302. Paris: Cerf, 1983.

———. *Philocalie 21–27.* Edited by Éric Junod. SC 226. Paris: Cerf, 1976.

———. *De Principiis.* Edited by Erich Klostermann. GCS 22. Leipzig: Hinrichs, 1913.

———. *Vier Bücher von den Prinzipien.* Edited and translated with notes by Herwig Görgemanns and Heinrich Harpp. Texte zur Forschung 24. Darmstadt: Wissenschaftliche Buchgesellschaft, 1976.

Index of Names and Places

INDEX OF SUBJECTS

Index of Biblical References

9 781589 832022